Rural
Communities

Rural Communities

Legacy & Change

Cornelia Butler Flora,
Jan L. Flora,
Jacqueline D. Spears,
and Louis E. Swanson,

with Mark B. Lapping
and Mark L. Weinberg

Westview Press

BOULDER • SAN FRANCISCO • OXFORD

Rural Communities: Legacy and Change was developed to accompany the PBS college-level social science television course of the same name. The thirteen-unit course consists of thirteen one-hour television/video programs, this text, a study guide, and faculty manual. The series and course were developed by Ohio University and the Rural Clearinghouse for Lifelong Education and Development at Kansas State University. Funding is provided by the Annenberg/CPB Project, and the course is part of the Annenberg/CPB Collection of educational video materials.

For information about using *Rural Communities: Legacy and Change* as a telecourse or off-air taping, contact:

PBS Adult Learning Service
1320 Braddock Place
Alexandria, Virginia 22314-1698
1-800-257-2578

For information about purchasing videocassettes of *Rural Communities: Legacy and Change*, contact:

The Annenberg/CPB Collection
P.O. Box 2345
South Burlington, Vermont 05407-2345
1-800-LEARNER

Copyright © 1992 by Ohio University/Corporation for Public Broadcasting

Published in 1992 in the United States of America by Westview Press, Inc., 5500 Central Avenue, Boulder, Colorado 80301-2847, and in the United Kingdom by Westview Press, 36 Lonsdale Road, Summertown, Oxford OX2 7EW

Library of Congress Cataloging-in-Publication Data
Rural communities : legacy and change / Cornelia Butler Flora . . . [et al.].
    p. cm.
Includes bibliographical references and index.
ISBN 0-8133-1476-3. — ISBN 0-8133-1477-1 (paper)
    1. United States—Rural conditions. 2. Sociology, Rural.
I. Flora, Cornelia Butler, 1943–
HN65.R85   1992
307.72—dc20

92-9875
CIP

Printed and bound in the United States of America

The paper used in this publication meets the requirements of the American National Standard for Permanence of Paper for Printed Library Materials Z39.48-1984.

10   9   8   7   6

Contents

v

PART TWO
ECONOMY AND SOCIETY

Tables and Illustrations

Tables

Figures

Boxes

Photographs

Preface and Acknowledgments

Our society today is faced with many problems. Sometimes it seems that forces on the national and global levels create problems and limit solutions. It is also difficult to see what one individual can do to solve these problems.

This book is designed to help identify, analyze, and address problems that are found in rural parts of the United States. It focuses on the community as the place where individuals come together in order to act to solve those problems.

We use sociological theory and research to understand communities and the people who live in them. We see how communities and their residents are products of historical processes and complex relationships. As different kinds of community problems are explored and analyzed, we hope you will have an increased appreciation and respect for your own community and neighbors as well as communities of people very different from your own.

Finally, we hope you will finish this book with a sense of empowerment. By understanding the factors that contribute to community problems and by analyzing the local resource base (people, culture, institutions, and social organization), you can act to make things better in your community. We introduce you to a variety of social problems faced by rural communities, and we give examples of how people have solved them. We hope you will be similarly empowered.

The book begins with a discussion of differences among communities— differences in economic base, differences in culture, and differences in social class. We explore how communities reproduce these differences and develop identities over time.

We then look closely at the interactions between the economy and society. A chapter on capital explores how communities access the financial capital needed to support local businesses and community services. A chapter on the global economy examines how changing economic trends affect local communities and the people who live there. Finally, we examine the impact increased consumption is having on rural people.

The third section identifies the resources rural communities have available—their social infrastructure, their physical infrastructure, and their governmental bodies. By looking at the different kinds of resources available in each community, we can address the basic components of rural communities.

Finally, we deal directly with social change. Power is key for change, so we explore how it can be analyzed. Then we present different ways communities have brought about change, either through addressing special needs of some of their citizens or through general community development.

Rural communities face many problems. Yet these communities provide important resources that can be used to create better lives for all. We hope this course will provide the knowledge and tools needed to do just that.

This book is intended for both classroom and community use. The book can support a course at the introductory level, offering college students an introduction to both basic sociological concepts and rural issues. It is also appropriate for courses that focus on communities or social problems.

The book is unique in its efforts to introduce basic sociological concepts, to apply them to current problems faced by rural communities, and then to explore how communities can organize to solve those problems. The notion of empowerment—that understanding and analysis can result in action taken to resolve problems—is also unique.

This emphasis on empowerment makes the book appropriate for community groups. Examples drawn from rural communities offer both the context from which the problems were chosen and the world to which the concepts can be applied. Community groups will see themselves and their communities throughout because many of the problems addressed are common ones.

This book was written as part of a project to develop a telecourse on rural communities. Consequently, a rich array of resources is available to support it. Thirteen hour-long videotapes were produced in conjunction with the book and can be obtained by calling 1-800-LEARNER. A student guide links the book to these community studies and includes a series of activities designed to apply the concepts and research techniques of sociology to a community. Students and community groups will find these activities especially valuable because they enable the content to take on local meaning. Finally, an instructor's guide is available to assist those who use the materials as part of a telecourse.

This book was developed with support provided by the Annenberg/ CPB Project. First and foremost, we owe special thanks to this organization and its staff, principally Lin Foa. A course of this magnitude could never have been undertaken without their financial support. More important, the book could not have woven sociological context so tightly with community problems had we not had the support to film in rural communities as we were writing the chapters. The rich experience and deep respect for adult learners shared by Lin Foa proved especially valuable.

An advisory committee oversaw all stages of the project and reviewed drafts of the textbook materials. Thanks go to Walter J. Armbruster, D. Stanley Eitzen, Richard Jonsen, Brent Sargent, and Janet Whitaker. Other consulting scholars included Fred Schmidt, Eric Hoiberg, Don Stull, Michael Hibbard, Richard Krannick, Richard W. Stoffle, Stephen F. Steele, and Gary Green. Pat Dewees, codirector of the project, also offered invaluable advice. Susan Adamchak lent both her expertise and editorial support to a number of chapters. Sharon Rice did background research on many of the sites and was instrumental in pulling together several of the figures. All the contributing authors enjoyed considerable support from their home institutions and colleagues.

This set of acknowledgments would not be complete without paying special tribute to the rural people and communities who shared their stories and perspectives with us. Many, many people opened their communities and their hearts, offering us a unique opportunity to explore the wonderful diversity and deep commitment of those who live in rural communities. We earnestly hope that this book captures that diversity and passes their commitment along to others concerned about making their own communities better places in which to live.

The Authors

Part 1

The Evolution of
Community Identity

1

The Rural Landscape

C hristine Walden grew up in paradise. The daughter of schoolteachers in
Mammoth Lakes, California, Christine spent her childhood surrounded
by the majestic peaks, lush forests, and crystal-clear lakes of the Sierra
Nevada range, nurtured by the closeness possible in a town of 2,000. In
1954, all-weather roads and a double chair lift opened, beckoning
skiers to the north face of Mammoth Mountain. By 1986, the town's
population had quadrupled. Christine had also grown up, and she took
a position as a teacher in the same school district for which her parents
had worked. But Christine no longer lives in Mammoth Lakes. Land
development and speculation have driven housing costs beyond what
the salaries paid by the local school district can support. So Christine
lives in Bishop and commutes forty miles each way to work. Paradise
has grown too expensive!

Wade Skidmore grew up working in the mines. One of the fifth
generation of Skidmores to live in McDowell County, West Virginia,
Wade in his childhood was shaped by what was inside rather than what
could be enjoyed on the slopes of the rugged Appalachian Mountains.
He attended school only through the eighth grade. Working in the
mines didn't require much education and offered him a chance to work
at his own pace. For a time, the work was steady and the pay was good.
But as the price per ton of coal dropped, Wade found that he had to
work harder to make ends meet. Then coal-loading machines came
along—machines that could do the work of fifty men. Then some veins
started giving out. Wade's children are now growing up in poverty—
substandard housing, water pollution from mine runoff, raw sewage in
the streams, poor schools, and high illiteracy rates. McDowell County
and Wade Skidmore as representative of many individuals have
become statistics—a region and a people trapped in persistent poverty.

Maurice and Mae Campbell face a decision. The hardware store they inherited from Mae's parents is failing. Their business is one of the few stores left on Main Street, the central business district in Irwin, Iowa. Irwin is a farming community that was settled as the railroads pushed westward across the Great Plains during the middle of the last century. Some of the homesteads settled are still owned by the descendants of the early settlers. Irwin now boasts a population larger than in 1940, but population in the surrounding countryside has been declining for decades. It is a matter of time before Irwin's population declines as well. Meanwhile, the Campbells struggle to finance a business that serves fewer and fewer people.

Billie Jo Williams and her husband are moving to Atlanta. Raised in Eatonton, Georgia, they grew up enjoying the gentle hills and dense stands of loblolly pine in Putnam County. Eatonton is home—both the Williams and Davis families go back to plantation days. But Billie can't find a job. She just finished a degree in business administration at Fort Valley State College. But there are few jobs for African American women in Eatonton other than in the textile factory or as domestics for the rich families who built retirement homes on the lake. Her husband settled into a factory job right out of high school, but figures he can get something in Atlanta. It seems strange. Eatonton has done better than most communities in adapting to change—shifting from cotton to dairying to manufacturing and now to recreation/retirement economies. But most blacks have a hard time finding more than minimum-wage jobs.

Which matches your image of rural America—ski slopes of California, mines of West Virginia, farms in Iowa, or retirement communities in Georgia? If you are like most people, the small farming community of Irwin, Iowa, most closely matches the images conjured up by the word *rural*. Family farms and small farming communities dominate our images, in part because they are a slice of our recent past. In fact, rural areas embrace ski slopes, mines, farms, retirement communities, Native American reservations, bedroom communities next to large cities, and much, much more. Today, rural communities probably differ more among themselves than they do, on average, from urban areas.

The diversity found among rural communities extends to the problems felt as each responds to the social and economic change under way. Some communities share the concerns of Irwin, wondering at what point their population will become too small to support a community. Other farming communities have grown, as they take on the role of regional retail and service centers for surrounding small towns. The recreation-based community of Mammoth Lakes, California, faces rapid growth. Its citizens are

Town and country—a farm with the skyline of Richmond, Virginia, in the background (photo courtesy of the U.S. Department of Agriculture).

grappling with how to protect both the environment and the small-town character they value. Growth in Eatonton, Georgia, has been more gradual, but its black citizens have not shared equally in its success. Those living in McDowell County face poverty, notwithstanding the richness of the land surrounding them.

Despite the stereotype that life in the country is simpler, rural people face many of the same issues and concerns urban residents do. In fact, rural and urban areas are linked. The garbage produced in New York City may find its way into landfills in West Virginia. Food served in Chicago could be made from Kansas wheat grown with fertilizers that increase productivity but that may endanger rural water supplies. A housing boom in San Francisco creates jobs in the lumber industry in Oregon. Unless replanting is widely practiced, however, the jobs last only as long as the forests. Air-quality concerns in Boston could shut down coal mines in Pennsylvania.

Given the close link that now exists between urban and rural areas, we must develop a clearer image of just what *rural* means in today's world. Are rural communities the "Green Acres," "Mayberry," and "Cabot Cove" of television? Or are they the nostalgic images of the pristine farm and lumber mill operated by the family on "The Waltons"? In reality, they are neither. This book examines rural America—its communities, the social problems they face as the twentieth century draws to a close, and the histories that explain those problems.

Defining Rural

Normally, we characterize rural communities by their population size as well as distance from urban centers. Size and isolation then combine to produce other images—relatively homogeneous cultures, an economy based on natural resources, and a strong sense of local identity. These images are only partially true. Rural communities have changed enormously in recent decades. Efforts to define rural communities, then, depend on examining some of these images, both past and present.

SIZE

The most obvious and undeniable difference between rural and urban areas is population size. Efforts to use population levels to define rural regions date back to 1874, when the U.S. Bureau of the Census identified rural counties as those with towns no larger than 8,000 inhabitants. This definition has changed over the years. By 1980, the Census Bureau had introduced the concept of nonmetropolitan counties, counties that could include cities of up to 50,000 people. The definition of who is truly rural

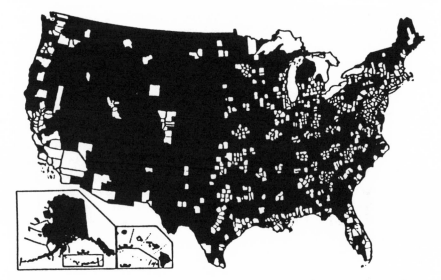

FIGURE 1.1 Nonmetropolitan Counties, 1983. Nonmetropolitan counties are shown in black, metropolitan areas in white. *Source:* Economic Research Service, USDA.

remained more restricted, however: those living in the open countryside or in towns of less than 2,500 inhabitants that lay outside urbanized areas.

Definitions vary across branches of the federal government as well as over time. The Census Bureau in the Department of Commerce defines *standard metropolitan areas* (SMAs) as a county or group of counties having at least one central city of 50,000 or more inhabitants. Rural regions become everything else, collectively referred to as *nonmetropolitan counties*. Figure 1.1 uses this definition to describe the rural character of the United States. The Farmers Home Administration (FmHA) defines rural areas as open country, communities of up to 20,000 residents in nonmetropolitan areas, and towns of up to 10,000 having a rural character but located within metropolitan counties. Agencies that deal with transportation issues define rural communities as those with populations of less than 5,000. So the list continues.

Why are there so many definitions? Governments and organizations create definitions for a variety of purposes—to define those who should be served by a particular program, to identify those who should be exempt from a specific policy, to make their job more manageable, or to target resources. Definitions change because the needs of governments and organizations change. Definitions based on number of residents change because our population constantly grows and moves about. There simply is no single definition of what makes a community rural.

For the purposes of this book, we use *nonmetropolitan counties* to define rural regions of the country. Nonmetropolitan counties, however, can include communities of considerable size. A second factor, isolation, helps distinguish between rural areas adjacent to or removed from population centers.

ISOLATION

Part of the rural image is isolation—a sense that rural people live out their entire lives in the very town in which they were born. In fact, this was never true for all rural people. Loggers, miners, and a host of others routinely moved to wherever they could find work. Other rural people were, in fact, isolated. Canals, railroads, highways, and airways have completely altered that isolation. Improved road systems have also changed the occupations and spending patterns of rural people. Those living near urban areas often commute to work, living in one town and working in another. They buy many of their products in suburban malls. In regions where no metropolitan center exists, small towns have grown to become regional trade centers as people travel to the next-largest city to purchase products and obtain services.

Communication technologies have had an even greater impact on reducing isolation. Rural adults now watch opera from New York, football games from San Francisco, the ballet from Houston, and congressional deliberations from Washington, D.C. On any given night, millions of U.S. viewers—rural and urban alike—tune in to the evening news. Rural people have become as literate, informed, and enriched as their urban counterparts.

Decreased isolation, then, has created the need to move beyond simple urban-rural or metropolitan-nonmetropolitan distinctions. As pointed out earlier, definitions of rural have always been *residual;* they embrace what is left once urban areas are described. Residual definitions ignore differences among what is left, which leads to a diffuse image of just what it is we mean by rural areas. Those living in the middle of Wyoming would describe a different set of problems from those identified by people living a short distance from Atlanta, for example.

In 1986, the Economic Research Service in the U.S. Department of Agriculture (McGranahan et al. 1986) introduced a classification system that distinguishes nonmetropolitan counties on the basis of both size and location relative to urban centers. As summarized in Table 1.1, the term *nonmetropolitan* has now been broken down into six categories based on size (urbanized, less urbanized, and rural) and location (adjacent or nonadjacent to urban areas). The categories based on size help characterize the extent to which a county's population is located in larger cities or

TABLE 1.1 Classification of Nonmetropolitan Counties

Urban Character	Location (percent)	Definition
Urbanized	Adjacent (7)	Counties with an urban population of at least 20,000 that are adjacent to a metropolitan county, with *adjacent* defined as both touching an SMA at more than a single point and having at least 1 percent of the labor force commute to the central county of the SMA for work.
	Nonadjacent (6)	Counties with an urban population of at least 20,000 that are not adjacent by the above definition.
Less urbanized	Adjacent (23)	Counties with an urban population of 2,555 to 19,999 and adjacent by the definition given for urbanized adjacent.
	Nonadjacent (29)	Counties with an urban population of 2,500 to 19,999 and not adjacent by the definition given for urbanized adjacent.
Rural	Adjacent (10)	Counties with no places of 2,500 or more population and adjacent by the definition given for urbanized adjacent.
	Nonadjacent (25)	Counties with no places of 2,500 or more population and not adjacent by the definition given for urbanized adjacent.

Source: D. A. McGranahan, J. C. Hession, F. K. Hines, and M. F. Jordon. 1986. *Social and Economic Characteristics of the Population in Metro and Nonmetropolitan Counties, 1970-1980.* Rural Development Research Report No. 58. Washington, DC: Department of Agriculture, Economic Research Service.

remains dispersed in towns of fewer than 2,500 residents each. Location describes the extent to which county residents have access to urban services. Although this classification system has its limitations, it offers a better description of the different circumstances in which rural communities must function.

HOMOGENEOUS CULTURES?

In its time, Irwin, Iowa, was an ethnically diverse community. A Danish Adventist settled about twenty miles southwest of Irwin and recruited other Danes living in Iowa to join him. Families from Denmark then began immigrating, eventually establishing the town of Elkhorn. In 1872, Emil Flushe began selling railroad land west of Irwin, recruiting friends and relatives from Germany. They formed a town known as Westphalia. So the pattern continued. Towns were created to support the distinct cultures of recent immigrants. Irwin was actually the exception. Founded in 1880, Irwin drew its populations from all these cultures—blending English, Irish, Danish, German, and Norwegian immigrants into a single community.

What is not found in Irwin, of course, are the Asian, black, and Latino cultures that now make substantial contributions to U.S. society. Other rural areas do include these populations. Spanish and Native American cultures occupied much of the West long before U.S. expansion. The abolition of slavery left African families scattered throughout a rural South extending from the Atlantic Ocean to central Texas and as far north as southern Kansas and Missouri. Migrant workers from Mexico followed the harvest as far north as Maine in the east and Washington State in the west.

This history explains a rural America in which counties can be ethnically very different from one another. When counties are ranked by the extent of ethnic diversity, rural counties are among both the most and least diverse. Fourteen of the thirty most diverse counties are rural (Table 1.2). Five of these lie in rural New Mexico, where the San Juan, Sangre de Cristo, Jemez, and Nacimento mountain ranges are home to Latino, Native American, and white cultures. The other rural counties among the most ethnically diverse lie in Alaska, Arizona, Georgia, North Carolina, and Texas.

In contrast, half of the fifty counties that are the least diverse are located in just two states, Nebraska and Iowa. Gosper County, in southern Nebraska, reported only one nonwhite resident in the 1990 census. Harlan County, where Irwin is located, is predominantly white. Parts of the rural South or Southwest are also homogeneous, especially on reservation lands or in counties where either black or white populations are the majority. Although some rural areas have a homogeneous culture, others are as diverse as urban centers.

ECONOMIC AND SOCIAL CHARACTER

Stereotypes of rural areas are agricultural—farmland dotted by occasional villages made up of feed stores, farm-implement dealerships, grain-storage companies, and a general store. Although rural regions have never been solely agricultural, their economic activity was once focused on the extraction of natural resources. Coastal communities looked to the sea,

TABLE 1.2 Thirty Most Ethnically Diverse Counties

Rank	County, State
1	San Francisco, CA
2	Manhattan Borough (NYC), NY
3	Bronx Borough (NYC), NY
4	Los Angeles, CA
5	Brooklyn Borough (NYC), NY
6[a]	Robeson, NC
7[a]	Rio Arriba, NM
8	Queens Borough (NYC), NY
9	Alameda (Oakland), CA
10	Essex (Newark), NJ
11[a]	Aleutian Islands, AK
12	Philadelphia, PA
13	Dade (Miami), FL
14[a]	Caldwell, TX
15	Monterey, CA
16[a]	Hoke, NC
17	Suffolk (Boston), MA
18[a]	Pinal, AZ
19[a]	Fort Bend, TX
20[a]	Valencia, NM
21	District of Columbia
22[a]	Sandoval, NM
23	Hudson (Jersey City), NJ
24[a]	Taos, NM
25	Cook (Chicago), IL
26	Harris (Houston), TX
27[a]	Graham, AZ
28[a]	Socorro, NM
29[a]	Coconino, AZ
30[a]	Chattahoochee, GA

[a] Nonmetropolitan counties.

Source: J. P. Allen and E. Turner. 1990. "Where Diversity Reigns." *American Demographics* 12 (8): 38. Reprinted with permission © *American Demographics* (1990, p. 38).

McDowell County, West Virginia (photo courtesy of the Ohio University Telecommunications Center).

harvesting the seafood native to their waters. Logging companies settled much of the Great Lakes and the Pacific Northwest. Mining communities, such as those in McDowell County, were created once railroads opened up the heart of the Appalachian Mountains. Gold, silver, and iron mining hastened migration westward.

Today, economic activity in rural communities has broadened even further. In 1985, researchers at the Economic Research Service (Bender et al. 1985) proposed a set of seven categories to describe the current economic and social character of rural counties. Those categories and the percentage of nonmetropolitan counties that fall into each are listed in Table 1.3. (The percentages do not add to 100 because counties can fall into more than one category.)

Four of these categories describe a primary economic activity on which counties depend—farming, manufacturing, mining, and specialized government operations. Two categories reflect social issues—counties that have remained persistently poor and counties experiencing the in-migration of people aged sixty and older, called destination-retirement counties. Finally, a separate category describes counties in which one-third or more of the land is owned by the federal government. For some of these counties,

TABLE 1.3 Economic/Social Character of Nonmetropolitan Counties

Type of Community	Percent of Nonmetropolitan Counties	Definition
Farming	29	Farming contributed a weighted annual average of 20 percent or more of total labor and proprietor income over the five years 1975–1979.
Manufacturing	28	Manufacturing contributed 30 percent or more of total labor and proprietor income in 1979.
Mining	8	Mining contributed 20 percent or more to total labor and proprietor income in 1979.
Specialized government	13	Government activities contributed 25 percent or more to total labor and proprietor income in 1979.
Persistent poverty	10	Per capita family income in the county was in the lowest quintile in each of the years 1950, 1959, 1969, and 1979.
Federal lands	10	Federal land was 33 percent or more of the land area in a county in 1977.
Destination–retirement	21	For the 1970–1980 period, net in-migration rates of people aged 60 and over were 15 percent or more of the expected 1980 population aged 60 and over.

Source: L. D. Bender, B. L. Green, T. F. Hady, J. A. Kuehn, M. K. Nelson, L. B. Perkinson, and P. J. Ross. 1985. *The Diverse Social and Economic Structure of Nonmetropolitan America*. Rural Development Research Report No. 49. Washington, DC: Department of Agriculture, Economic Research Service.

tourism and recreational use of the land are the base of economic activity. For others, the land is restricted to military use.

These categories may not yet capture all that is occurring in rural communities, but it is clear that the economic character of rural communities has become more complex. Some rural communities are diversifying, building a broad base of economic activity in much the same fashion as urban centers. Many are shifting away from economies that depend on the extraction of natural resources, finding niches within the broader spectrum of economic activity—offering services to retirees, profiting from tourism, or building a manufacturing base. Although many rural communities continue to focus on a single economic activity, these communities differ more substantially from one another today than in the past. Rural regions are no longer synonymous with extractive industries, let alone agriculture.

Defining Community

Thus far, all our definitions and descriptions of rural areas have focused on counties. Yet people typically act through communities. As of the 1990 census, more than 6 million rural people lived in 9,837 communities of fewer than 2,500 residents. Demographers can count communities, but sociologists have a much harder time defining just what a community is. In this section, we look at the concept of community, the definition used in this book, and the extent to which our study of rural communities has relevance to urban communities.

THE CONCEPT OF COMMUNITY

Sociologists use the term *community* in several different ways, all of which focus on groups of people. In one use of the term, community refers to a place, a location in which a group of people interact with one another. A second use of the term looks at the social system itself, the organization or set of organizations through which a group of people meet their needs. Finally, sociologists use *community* to describe a shared sense of identity held by a group of people.

In rural areas, the concept of community was initially based on a shared sense of place. This sense of place had a social as well as geographical meaning. Stereotypes of rural communities conjure up images of isolated, relatively self-sufficient, sometimes backward or unsophisticated cultures. The stereotype may never have been entirely accurate, but there was a time when rural people turned to their communities for nearly everything. People lived, worked, worshiped, shopped, banked, sent their children to school, and socialized all in the same place. When the community's economy rested on a single resource, such as mining, people even had a shared sense of what it took to make a living. In mining communities, men worked in the mines and women managed the family, both of which were demanding tasks.

Traditionally, then, sociologists thought these three elements—location, social system, and common identity—went together. A community offered a place, a set of social institutions (schools, churches, governments, businesses) through which people's needs could be met, and a shared sense of identity. However, improved transportation has made us more mobile, and telecommunications now puts us in touch with a wider circle of acquaintances. For some people, a sense of community comes from those who do similar things or share common values, not from those living in the same town. We now speak of a community of physicists, for example. These people share a common identity—they interact through meetings, journals, electronic mail, or by telephone—yet they are dispersed throughout the world.

The rural landscape may not have changed much over the past century, but rural communities have been affected by these same changes. Cars enable people to live in one town, work in another, and shop in yet a third. Better roads have allowed schools to consolidate, which has led to social institutions that may be less attached to their communities, both physically and socially. As rural communities broaden their economic activity, people's work roles become very different from one another. Where distances and topography permit, self-sufficient communities have given way to connected, interrelated regions. Despite these changes, a sense of place still figures prominently in a definition of community. Many rural residents maintain an emotional and symbolic attachment to the community in which they live.

In this book, we use *community* to mean place or location. A community may or may not provide the social system through which its members' needs are met. It may or may not provide a sense of identity for its members. What a community does provide is what some sociologists now call *locality*, a geographically defined place where people interact. How people interact shapes the structures and institutions of the locality. Those structures and institutions in turn shape the activities of the people who interact (Lobao 1990).

COMMUNITY IN AN URBAN SETTING

Early research on cities suggested an urban way of life that stood in stark contrast to that in a rural community. Ferdinand Tönnies ([1887] 1963), a German sociologist who wrote during the latter part of the nineteenth century, introduced the terms *gemeinschaft* and *gesellschaft* to distinguish between the two environments. *Gemeinschaft* referred to a society based on personal relationships and face-to-face interactions in which social relations are valued as an end in themselves. *Gesellschaft* described a society based on impersonal, formal, and contractual relationships for which social relations were simply a means to an end. These two terms characterized a rural-urban continuum in which the small, isolated community was at one end and the city at the other.

Such a model may have been appropriate during the early part of the century, but certainly seems less relevant today. Just as transportation has altered the character of rural areas, continued growth has led to cities too large for nearly anyone to comprehend. Modern sociologists argue that those who live in a city arrange and rearrange themselves in a variety of smaller communities, experiencing the city through a series of different social groups. By the same token, improved transportation has enabled rural people to participate in a wider number of social groups, lessening their dependence on the single community. Fischer (1981) concludes that urban dwellers have as close ties with family and friends as do residents of smaller towns.

Our definition of community, then, applies to both rural and urban areas. Communities may have political boundaries, or they may simply have social ones. Communities may be recognized politically and thus endowed with local governments and the power to tax their members. They may also be informal groupings of households, neighborhoods within the larger city. Issues can cause neighborhoods to band together to demand better services from the city just as they inspire rural communities to take control over their economic future. Although the focus in this book is on rural communities, many of the topics are immediately relevant to communities within urban settings as well.

Rural Communities and Change

Rural communities have never been insulated from the social and economic change under way in the broader society. Trends toward an urbanized society have depopulated many rural areas. When national attention focused on transportation after World War II, the result was the interstate highway system, a development that has had a profound effect on rural communities. Telecommunications has broken the isolation experienced in remote regions. Increased competition with foreign products led manufacturers to abandon urban labor markets for rural ones during the 1970s, only to abandon those for even cheaper labor overseas a decade later. The increased mobility of people worldwide has altered the social and ethnic character of rural as well as urban communities. The list of changes could continue.

Given the diversity among rural communities, it is hardly surprising that these and other societal changes have affected individual communities differently. The rural profiles that opened this chapter illustrate some of these differences. The problems Christine Walden describes arise from the rapid growth occurring in Mammoth Lakes, California. Growth in Eatonton, Georgia, has been less dramatic, but African American citizens such as Billie Jo Williams have not really benefited from that growth. Wade Skidmore, the miner from McDowell County, West Virginia, finds his family trapped in poverty. Maurice and Mae Campbell worry that one day Irwin will become just another ghost town. Three patterns—rapid

A shoe-manufacturing plant in southern Ohio (photo courtesy of the Ohio University Telecommunications Center).

growth, low income, and population decline—provide a useful structure with which to examine rural social problems.

RAPID GROWTH

Once visited only on a seasonal basis by the Paiute Indians, the eastern slope of the Sierra Nevada attracted attention when Lt. Tredwell Moore picked up some gold specimens near Mono Lake, California, in 1852. Entrepreneurs opened gold and silver mines along the high ridges, generating profits for mine owners in San Francisco and New York during the latter part of the nineteenth century.

When the mines gave out or became too expensive to work, most miners moved on. Those who had established ranches, farming operations, or small sawmills in support of the mining companies stayed, however. Federal lands could be logged under permit from the U.S. Forest Service; sawmill owners thus had a source of raw timber. When irrigated by mountain streams, the meadows and bottomland offered dependable summer feed for cattle and sheep as well as stocks of hay, wheat, and barley for the winter. By the 1930s, the Mammoth Lakes region supported small-scale mining, ranching, farming, logging, and some tourism. Mammoth Lakes itself was a community of fourteen people.

As the workweek shortened, better roads offered quicker access to the mountains, automobiles became more dependable, and the populations in Los Angeles and San Francisco grew, Mammoth Lakes became an important recreational site. A ski enthusiast from Switzerland moved into the area and began building a ski resort. In the beginning, people had to hike in several miles or travel by all-terrain vehicles to reach Mammoth Mountain.

An all-weather road completed in 1954 opened the region up to larger numbers of skiers. By 1960, the population of Mammoth Lakes had grown to more than 2,000. In 1977, prime ranch land in the Old Mammoth meadows was sold to developers, and the real estate boom began. Developers built condominiums, selling them to people in Los Angeles for use on weekends. People who had grown up in Mammoth Lakes, such as Christine Walden, could no longer afford to live there.

Mammoth Lakes, California, has always been a resource-based community, though its population varied as the economic activity of the region shifted from mining to timber to hiking and fishing and finally to skiing. Today, Mammoth Lakes is one of many rural communities struggling with the problems of rapid growth—high in-migration, high housing costs, increasing taxes that force long-term residents out of the community, and a growing migrant population attracted by jobs in the service economy.

Rapid development impacts the environment as well. Water used for commercial development lowers lakes and decreases the flow of area streams, threatening the very wildlife that beckons hunters and fishers each summer. Forests and meadows are disappearing, and sewage has become a serious problem. Increased use of the land also contributes to soil erosion and a general degradation of nearby wilderness areas.

The term *rapid growth* describes rural counties having growth rates that have exceeded the national average. As shown in Figure 1.2, high growth counties lie chiefly in two bands, one along the eastern seaboard from Maine to Florida and the second in the Southwest. Although the number of jobs is increasing and average incomes per person are relatively good, these communities face a real challenge in managing growth and ensuring that their rural residents benefit from that growth.

PERSISTENT POVERTY

Named after the twenty-fifth governor of Virginia, McDowell County was formed in 1858 and became a part of West Virginia in 1866. Hardy adventurers from Virginia followed Cherokee trails deep into the mountains, eventually establishing homesteads. Later derisively known as hillbillies, these mountain people were fiercely independent. They developed strong kinship and extended-family relationships as well as a lifestyle

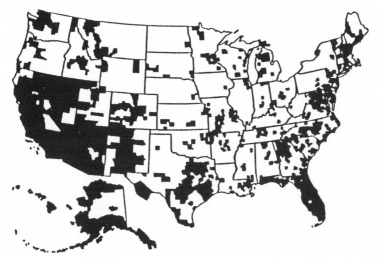

FIGURE 1.2 Rapid-Growth Counties. *Source:* Economic Research Service, USDA.

deeply integrated with the rhythms and resources offered by the land. By 1858, they numbered 1,535 in McDowell County.

McDowell County was opened to outside investment in 1888, when the Norfolk and Western Railroad steamed through the 3,015-foot Elkhorn tunnel and offered access to the Pocahontas coal vein. The railroads owned the land, but leased it to mine operators in 1,000-acre lots. The size of these lots essentially determined the size of and distance between mining towns.

The leases were typically bought by Pennsylvanians, who moved to West Virginia to open the mines. Because the mountain dwellers were both too few and too independent to provide the labor needed in the mines, the mine operators recruited Eastern Europeans from the Balkans and African Americans from the cotton and tobacco fields in the South. Hospital records reveal that by 1912 Hungarians, Italians, Poles, Russians, Slavs, and African Americans had settled in the region. Housing was segregated, but racial distinctions vanished in the mines. African Americans were elected to office as early as the 1890s.

The early mining towns were company towns that provided housing and subsistence to the workers. A miner's purchases in the company store were deducted from his pay. Other wages were paid in scrip, which could then be spent only in the company store. In contrast to the fiercely independent mountaineers, most of the miners had to rely on the company. The mixture of cultures, the creation of artificial communities to support the extraction of coal, and the absolute authority exerted by the operators made collective action within communities difficult.

The population of McDowell County grew steadily, reaching nearly 100,000 in the 1950s. At this point, some 18,000 miners produced 21 million tons of coal each year, roughly 1,200 tons per miner. In 1955, the first mining machines were introduced, which resulted in massive layoffs of handloaders. By 1960, 7,661 miners produced 15 million tons of coal, about 2,000 tons per miner. Companies started selling off the towns, closing the company stores, and allowing miners to buy the homes they had lived in. The oil embargo of the 1970s caused a brief resurgence in the mining camps, but the coal recession of the 1980s resulted in further cutbacks. The population in McDowell County is now just over 35,000.

McDowell County is one of many rural counties struggling with low incomes and the problems of persistent poverty. As the mining companies pulled out, they left families who had known nothing but mining for generations. Illiteracy is high, as is infant mortality. Doctors, dentists, and other professionals are hard to find. Young people see little reason to invest effort in school, because there are no jobs to prepare for. Communities find it hard to attract businesses; there is no tax base with which to build the needed roads, bridges, and industrial parks. Those who can, leave. Those who can't leave simply make do.

McDowell County is among the 242 nonmetropolitan counties classified as *persistently poor* counties. The per-capita income in these counties has placed them in the bottom 20 percent of all U.S. counties since 1950. Ninety percent of these counties are found in the sixteen states shown in Figure 1.3. Nearly 17 percent of rural people in these counties had income levels below the 1987 poverty level, established then as $9,056 for a family of three. Many of these counties have been successful in attracting and creating jobs. In some cases, they have experienced population increases. Unfortunately, the growth in jobs and population has not produced higher incomes for people such as Wade Skidmore.

POPULATION DECLINE

Founded in 1880, Irwin, Iowa, lies along the Nishnabotna River. It is strategically placed on the Chicago and Northwestern Railroad's southwestern branch, which links the town of Canal with Harlan, and on the main line of the Chicago and Great Western Railroad, which runs from Minneapolis to Omaha. In the early days of railroading, communities tended to appear where railroad lines were planned. A land survey released in 1879 showed the Chicago and Northwestern line to the east and south of the Nishnabotna River. In anticipation, merchants built a post office, mill, and general store. When a survey released a year later showed the route moved to the other side of the river, the town moved as well.

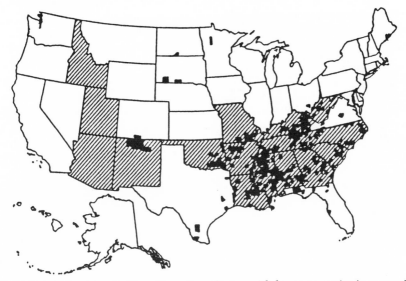

FIGURE 1.3 Persistently Poor Counties. States with low per capita incomes in 1986 are indicated by cross-hatching. Persistently poor counties are marked in black. *Source*: Economic Research Service, USDA.

Unlike the early settlers in Mammoth Lakes and McDowell County, those drawn to Iowa came to stay. They were farmers and ranchers, many from Europe, for whom owning land was important. Profits, when they existed, were used to purchase land. Farmers helped their sons get a start in farming, often by giving them pieces of land that the family had acquired. Because the early settlers all shared the same problems, there was an unusual homogeneity of experience and understanding of life.

Towns such as Irwin existed to serve the needs of these farmers. By 1940, Irwin had a population of 345, but served more than a thousand farm families surrounding it. Farmers bought in Irwin, sold in Irwin, sent their children to school in Irwin, and spent Saturday nights in Irwin. The town (especially the school) served as the social center for the entire region.

Communities such as Irwin are neat, well-kept towns that enjoy a high degree of citizen participation. The schools are excellent, and the broader population is well educated. Outsiders sometimes have a hard time gaining acceptance at first, but social-class distinctions are generally ignored. A "just plain folks" atmosphere prevails.

Irwin's population is actually larger than it was in 1940. Yet the Campbells' hardware store is among the few businesses left. There is no grocery store, just a small convenience store for emergency items. The high school is gone, a result of the latest round of school consolidation.

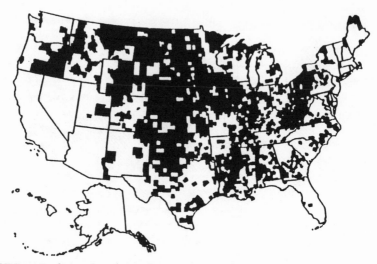

FIGURE 1.4 Declining-Population Counties. *Source:* Economic Research Service, USDA.

The nearest medical services are in Harlan, the county seat located a little more than fifteen miles away. As the farm population dwindles, Irwin struggles to survive.

For towns such as Irwin, the issues are complex. Although the new consolidated school meets the state's standards, it seems less a part of the community. Parents feel that their children have no future in Irwin, yet wonder whether the cities are really better. The county hospital in Harlan may not be able to function much longer under current Medicare policies. The town knows that it needs to maintain roads and other facilities, but a declining population has eroded its tax base.

The term *declining population* applies to counties that lost population over the last decade. As shown in Figure 1.4, most of these counties are located in the upper Great Plains. They are home to a little more than one-fourth of the nation's nonmetropolitan population. For the most part, these populations are well educated and have enjoyed relatively high average incomes in the past. Jobs have not grown fast enough, however, to replace those lost. Some ask whether the residents of this region will become the new poor.

About This Book

The three patterns just described give rise to many of the social problems felt by people living in rural communities. Rapid growth characterizes counties in seventeen states and affects about 25 percent of the nation's nonmetropolitan population. Persistently poor counties are commonly found in sixteen states and involve 41 percent of rural people. Counties in thirteen states see population decline as a serious problem in their rural communities; these states include 27 percent of the U.S. nonmetropolitan population.

Social problems have both objective and subjective features. Although the three patterns describe an objective portrait of some rural conditions, many people could argue that these conditions are not a social problem. What the people of Irwin see as a problem, people in Chicago may regard as inevitable. What the environmentalists in Mammoth Lakes see as a danger, outside investors and local developers see as the price of growth. What the white population in Eatonton sees as acceptable, the African American population may find to be intolerable. Some see the poverty in McDowell County as the responsibility of society, while others see it as the responsibility of the individuals living there. Thus, definitions of social problems depend on what people feel they can control, what they think is fair, and what they value.

ASSUMPTIONS

Perhaps the most basic assumption made here is that the rural perspective is worth exploring. Our society has become so deeply urbanized that we almost assume urbanization to be a natural law. Urbanization was important to industrialization, but many people now argue that the economic reasons for urbanization are no longer as compelling. Others point to economies of scale, arguing that the social costs of overcrowding have now exceeded whatever economies of scale made urbanization preferable. Still others point to the contributions rural areas make to the nation: (1) food security, (2) a sense of land stewardship that protects natural resources, (3) a value system connected to both the land and human relationships, and (4) protection of diversity.

The reality is that more than one-fourth of the nation's people have chosen to live in rural areas. As we make the transition to the information age, it seems appropriate to reexamine rural areas—asking why people have stayed, how federal and state policies have contributed to current conditions in rural areas, and what role individual choice can play in dealing with current social problems.

Given the choice to focus on rural communities, the assumptions summarized in Table 1.4 governed both the selection of topics and organization used for this book. First, we have assumed that change should not be taken for granted. Unlike the objective scientist who observes and then describes nature, we are participants in what it is we are observing. The explanations we build become part of the reality in which we live, affecting the choices we make as individuals and as a society.

TABLE 1.4 Assumptions Used in This Book

1. Change in rural America should be explained, not merely taken for granted or vaguely attributed to industrialization, population growth, or heterogeneity.

2. The analysis of change in rural America must take into account the history of the region and the shifting relationship between urban and rural society.

3. The analysis of change in rural America must take into account the economy— the changing practices of production and shifting values of market exchange.

4. The analysis of change in rural America must take into account political action at the state and federal level.

5. The experiences felt in rural America depend in part on the community responses to both political constraints and individual choice.

Second, we have assumed that what occurs in rural areas is the result of history, more especially the changing relationship between urban and rural society. Although it is simpler to think about rural and urban communities as separate worlds, in reality they are connected. Georgia was established as a colony because of London's problems with debtors. Much of the rural West was settled to provide the resources needed to fuel industrial growth in the East. Timber in Washington was cleared to build the houses in Los Angeles. McDowell County was populated because industry needed coal to operate its factories. Irwin was settled because the railroads needed grain to haul and eastern cities needed a dependable food supply. The connections continue today. In order to understand what is occurring in rural areas, we must continually look to both past and present rural-urban linkages.

Social problems involve human relationships, but much of what leads to these problems can be traced to the economy. A 4-H leader in the Florida Panhandle points out that he cannot separate the problems of child abuse from the problems of persistent poverty. Efforts to build an economy capable of alleviating poverty are as important to him as programs on effective parenting. This third assumption simply points out that the economy—the changing practices of production and shifting exchange values of goods and services—determines much of what works and does not work in a rural community. To understand the changes that have taken place in rural communities, we must understand the changes that have occurred in the economy.

The fourth and fifth assumptions simply describe the tension between public policy and individual choice. The fourth assumption states that political decisions at the state and national level act to influence where and how economic and social change takes place. Problems of rural poverty, ethnic conflicts, or natural-resource extraction can be understood partly in terms of public policy, in terms of the political choices made at the state and federal level.

The fifth assumption adds that the rural experience is the sum of group responses to both political constraints and individual choice. People can make a difference, either through influencing the broader policy agenda that constrains them or through making choices within the policy framework. We are not just victims of society or passive consumers of broader national change. The choices rural people make affect the direction change takes in their communities.

Simply stated, these assumptions argue that rural social problems can be examined in terms of change. Change can be explained in terms of history, rural-urban linkages, the economy, policy choices made at the state and federal level, and individual choices made by communities. We use this framework to examine how current social problems came to be and how those problems might be addressed.

ORGANIZATION OF THIS BOOK

The book has been organized into four parts, each consisting of several chapters. Each chapter opens with one or more rural profiles. These profiles are fictional in the sense that they are not descriptions of real people. The circumstances are real, however. Historical documents, site visits, research journals, telephone interviews, newspaper articles, and a variety of other sources were used to collect information about real rural communities. The problems identified are also real, expressed by people living in rural communities throughout the country.

Problems experienced by individuals often have causes embedded in the institutions and conventions of society. Understanding how this happens is a part of what sociologists undertake as they study human society and social behavior. Each chapter is structured to help the reader move from the social problem voiced by rural people to the sociological problem suggested by the concepts and theories of the social sciences. Seen from this broader perspective, social problems experienced by rural people become societal problems capable of being solved through collective action.

Part 1 offers an overview of rural communities. This first chapter has described the diversity found among rural communities and the patterns that characterize rural responses to economic change. Chapter 2 considers the economic base of a rural community and its relation to the broader society as well as to the local labor force. The culture of small communities is explored in Chapter 3, a process that allows us to examine both the good and bad features of places where everyone knows everyone else. Chapter 4 explores the way in which individuals are shaped intergenerationally by their families and their communities. Social problems can arise when those aspirations cannot be fulfilled.

Part 2 examines the economic environment in which rural communities now function. In Chapter 5 we examine capital, exploring the problems rural communities experience in gaining access to funds and other resources with which to invest in community development. Chapter 6 describes the shift to a global economy and the impact this transition has had on rural communities. Changing consumption patterns and their impact on rural communities are the subject of Chapter 7.

The political and social organizations created to maintain a community and link it to the broader society are the focus of Part 3. Chapter 8 describes the dilemmas faced by state and local government. Chapter 9 describes the economic infrastructure, the physical and social structures that must be in place to support community development. Finally, Chapter 10 examines the social infrastructure, the organizations created to meet the needs of a community's citizens.

Part 4 uses the framework of community change to explore strategies for solving social problems. Chapter 11 describes typical power structures in rural communities and the role those structures play in blocking or facilitating change. Techniques for organizing to meet special needs or responding to specific rural population groups are explored in Chapter 12. Finally, Chapter 13 describes models for effective community change.

Chapter Summary

Many people imagine a rural America characterized by farming, homogeneous cultures, and close-knit communities. In reality, rural communities differ more among themselves than they do, on average, from urban areas.

What is defined to be a rural community has changed over time. In general, definitions of rural include descriptions of both size and location. Current definitions use the distinction between nonmetropolitan and metropolitan counties, equating nonmetropolitan with rural. Definitions of community have also changed. This text defines community as a place or location in which people interact. The community need not provide all the services individuals require and may not necessarily offer community members a common sense of identity.

Rural communities differ in terms of ethnicity and economic activity. Rural communities are among the most ethnically diverse as well as the most ethnically homogeneous, depending on the region of the country in which they are located. Rural counties can be characterized by seven categories that describe their economic or social character: Counties are identified as farming-dependent, manufacturing-dependent, mining-dependent, specialized government, destination-retirement, federal lands, or persistently poor.

In responding to social and economic change, rural communities show three broad patterns of response: rapid growth, persistently poor, or population decline. The character of the social problems experienced is different within each pattern. This book assumes that these social problems can be explained in terms of a community's history, its link to urban areas, the economy, policy choices made at the state and federal level, and individual choices made by the communities themselves.

Key Terms

Community describes a place or location where groups of people interact.

Gemeinschaft describes a community based on personal relationships and face-to-face interactions.

Gesellschaft describes a community in which relationships are impersonal, formal, and frequently guided by contractual arrangements.

Nonmetropolitan counties are those counties that lie outside a standard metropolitan area and do not include a city of 50,000 or more inhabitants.

Persistently poor refers to those rural counties whose per-capita family income was in the lowest 20 percent in 1950, 1959, 1969, 1979, and 1986.

Population decline refers to rural counties that lost population during the last decade.

Rapid growth applies to rural counties that experienced population increases greater than the national average.

Standard metropolitan areas consist of one or more adjacent counties containing at least one city of 50,000 inhabitants or more.

References

Bender, L. D., B. L. Green, T. F. Hady, J. A. Kuehn, M. K. Nelson, L. B. Perkinson, and P. J. Ross. 1985. *The Diverse Social and Economic Structure of Nonmetropolitan America*. Rural Development Research Report No. 49. Washington, DC: Department of Agriculture, Economic Research Service.

Chudacoff, Howard P. 1975. *The Evolution of American Urban Society*. Englewood Cliffs, NJ: Prentice-Hall.

Effrat, Marcia Pelly (ed.). 1985. *The Community: Approaches and Applications*. New York: Free Press.

Fischer, Claude S. 1981. *To Dwell Among Friends: Personal Networks in Town and City*. Chicago: University of Chicago Press.

Lobao, Linda M. 1990. *Locality and Inequality: Farm and Industry Structure and Socioeconomic Conditions*. Albany: State University of New York Press.

Logan, John R., and Harvey L. Molotch. 1989. *Urban Fortunes: The Political Economy of Place*. Berkeley: University of California Press.

McGranahan, D. A., J. C. Hession, F. K. Hines, and M. F. Jordon. 1986. *Social and Economic Characteristics of the Population in Metro and Nonmetropolitan Counties, 1970–1980.* Rural Development Research Report No. 58. Washington, DC: Department of Agriculture, Economic Research Service.

Tönnies, Ferdinand. [1887] 1963. *Community and Society.* Trans. and ed. by C. P. Loomis. New York: Harper & Row.

Warren, Roland L. 1978. *The Community in America.* 3rd ed. Lanham, MD: University Press of America.

2

Economy and Community

J

udy Albrecht glanced through the want ads (Figure 2.1). With wheat prices so low, the farm isn't doing too well. A bit of extra cash would help.

There don't seem to be many jobs. Sal's Grocery is hiring. Sal might even help work out hours so she could be home with the kids after school. He probably can't pay much though, because business has been slow. The hospital is hiring, and it pays better than what Sal could. Besides, the health insurance would be nice. She and Mel had to drop the family's insurance two years ago and haven't been able to pick it back up. Still, it's twenty miles each way and the car might not hold up.

There is an ad for assembling devices in your own home. The area code 813 is in Florida. Wonder if it is a legitimate business? A job like that would still allow her to be around home for Mel and the kids.

Judy wishes a teaching job would open up. Now that the kids are in school, she could finally use the college degree she finished. Still, those jobs don't open up very often. Mrs. Gaudin should retire in another three to four years. The farm needs money now, though!

A quick glance at the want ads gives us a snapshot of a community's economy. It tells us the kind of industries and businesses located there, the types of jobs available, the skills needed for employment, the prevailing wage levels, even the extent to which jobs are available elsewhere in the county, state, or region.

Judy lives near Atwood, a farming community in the Midwest. There are not many jobs in Atwood. Those that are available are part-time or pay minimum wage, enough to supplement income from another source but not enough to support a family. The business district has fewer locally

Help Wanted & Business Opportunity

Employment Opportunities

Part-Time Night Aide In LTC $4.60 Minimum

Full-Time Evening Aide in LTC $4.47 Minimum

Part-Time Day Aide In LTC $4.25 Minimum

Part-Time Hospital Aide - $4.25 Minimum

Excellent Benefits:

- Paid Vacation
- Sick leave
- Holidays
- Pension
- Health Insurance
- Shift differential pay
- Excellent starting wage
- Will train for certification

Apply in person

Minnow County Hospital & Long-Term Care Unit

ASSEMBLE our devices, learn this trade, we send instructions, parts, and check for assembly. Call 813-532-5560.

NOW TAKING applications for help at Sal's Grocery.

OWN YOUR own apparel or shoe store, choose, from: jean/sportswear, ladies' men's, children/maternity, large sizes, petite, dancewear/aerobic, bridal, lingerie or accessories store. Add color analysis. Brand names: Liz Claiborne, Healthtex, Chaus, Lee, St. Michele, Forenza, Bugle Boy, Levi, Camp Beverly Hills, Organically Grown, Lucie, over 2,000 others. Or $13.99 one price designer, multi-tier pricing discount or family shoe store. Retail prices unbelievable for top quality shoes normally priced from $19 to $60. Over 250 brands, 2,600 styles, $18,900 to $29,900: inventory, training, fixtures, airfare, grandopening, etc. Can open 15 days. Mr. Smith, 407-539-4547.

HELP WANTED: Counter person needed at Corner Diner. Apply in person.

HELP WANTED: Part-time demonstrator of toys, gifts, home decor and fashion. Now and until Christmas. No investment, free training. Details without obligation. Call 308-537-1822.

INSURANCE SALES: Looking for a career-minded individual interested in pleasant and dignified sales work with a long-established life insurance group. Excellent training, unlimited earnings potential. Send resume to: Insurance Position, Rt. 1, Macalasty, 89734.

Wanted

WANTED: Part time babysitter in my home for three evenings per week. Hours are 3-10p.m. Two children ages 3½ and 1½. Can offer more hours if desired. Call 532-6718.

WANTED: Good quality alfalfa hay, any form. 532-6878.

WANTED: Piano tuning. Will be in town June 5-19. $40 a piano. Call Tom or John Davis at 568-4131.

FIGURE 2.1 Want Ads from Midwestern Community Newspaper.

TABLE 2.1 Employment Change in Rural Areas (1981–1986)

Type of Employment	Number of Jobs	Percent Change
Jobs gained:		
Eating/drinking places	+155,484	+20.1
Grocery stores	+ 74,995	+16.2
Nursing/personal care	+ 53,717	+19.2
Department stores	+ 47,097	+29.5
Offices/medical clinics	+ 28,647	+22.2
Jobs lost:		
Coal mining	– 41,645	–23.1
Oil-gas field services	– 38,661	–33.9
Telephone communications	– 33,297	–25.7
Crude petroleum/natural gas	– 29,296	–61.8
Machinery & equipment	– 25,311	–16.4

Source: S. Porterfield. 1990. "Service Sector Offers More Jobs, Lower Pay." *Rural Development Perspectives* 6 (3): 4.

owned businesses. Home-based work is becoming more common, especially because women can integrate work with family responsibilities.

Want ads clipped from newspapers in other rural communities would show differences as well as similarities. In contrast to the few job opportunities in Atwood are the hundreds of new jobs created by the ski industry in Mammoth Lakes, California. Most new jobs are in the service sector—answering telephones, cleaning hotel rooms, waiting tables, or shoveling snow. Despite the fact that these jobs offer minimum wage and few benefits, Mexican immigrants see them as opportunities. Local residents such as Christine Walden see the problems: adapting the school to meet the needs of increased numbers of Spanish-speaking children, for example. Mammoth Lakes will not disappear, but it is not the same community Christine knew as a child.

Since the 1940s, the United States has gradually moved away from manufacturing goods to offering services. The trend accelerated during the 1980s, when 1.2 million manufacturing jobs were lost and 12 million service jobs created. Rural areas have been a part of this trend. Jobs in natural-resource–based industries such as mining, agriculture, and oil production have disappeared, while the number of jobs in the service sector has increased (Table 2.1). This chapter examines the economic bases found in rural communities, the types of employment these bases offer, and the problems rural communities face as they experience the shift to a service-based economy.

Economic Base of a Community

Having been born into a community, we rarely stop to ask "Why is this community in this place?" If we think to ask, it is because the community seems out of place. It is isolated or has limited job opportunities, like Atwood. One way of understanding why some communities exist is to look at the economic function the community plays—in the individual lives of its members as well as in the broader society.

DEFINING ECONOMIC BASE

We often characterize rural communities by their primary economic activity, referring to mining towns, farming communities, regional service centers, or railroad towns. What we have actually described is the *economic base* of a community, the core economic activity on which much of the community's local economy depends. Historically, most rural communities had a single economic base. Some still do. Mammoth Lakes, California, has become a recreational town, for example. Communities in McDowell County, West Virginia, still depend heavily on mining.

Following the lead of large cities, most rural communities are now diversifying their economic base. Irwin, Iowa, is trying to add retirement functions to its dominant agricultural base, for example. The development of Lake Oconee means that Eatonton, Georgia, will add recreation to its manufacturing base.

Even if a community has a single dominant economic base, it is still involved in a broader set of economic activities. Because people need a variety of products and services on a day-to-day basis, a community must organize for their production, distribution, and consumption. Most of the jobs Judy saw in the want ads related to products or services needed in the immediate community—grocery-store clerk, counter worker at the local restaurant, aides for the local hospital, manager for an apparel store, and the like.

Rural communities are not self-sufficient, but they generally are active in all four phases of the nation's economy: (1) extracting resources, (2) producing, (3) distributing, and (4) servicing. Extracting resources refers to the collection of natural resources, such as mining, fishing, harvesting crops, or clearing timber. Production includes any process that converts a resource into a usable good or service—what we sometimes refer to today as a *value-added process*. Distribution includes the business and transportation networks needed to move natural resources, products, and services to where each can be consumed. Finally, services include activities needed to support the other three functions and provide for quality of life. Examples include banks, insurance companies, tax preparers, recreation, or tourism.

Manufacturing has become the economic base in many rural communities (photo courtesy of the Ohio University Telecommunications Center).

WHAT DETERMINES ECONOMIC BASE?

"Why is this community in this place?" The answer to this question lies, in part, with history and circumstance. It is impossible to explain the economic base of rural communities without looking back at the economic environment in which the nation was settled.

Whereas Native American tribes used the land to develop a subsistence economy, most Europeans colonized the land primarily for profit. Explorations of the New World were often financed by European governments expecting new wealth in return. A number of English companies actually sold stock to finance early settlements. Once established, these settlements were expected to become self-sufficient and then begin exporting products to pay off their debts.

Land-settlement policies also played an important role in the economic character of early rural communities. In New England, the English Crown gave land to trading companies that, in turn, gave land to groups of settlers. These groups established central villages surrounded by farmland. Farmers worked their fields by day but returned to the village at night. A village-style settlement created an environment capable of eventually supporting other economic functions, such as manufacturing and domestic crafts.

In the South, however, the English Crown gave land directly to individuals. The landowners then settled large, relatively self-sufficient plantations that depended upon slave labor. Few villages or towns were created. Consequently, other economic functions were slower to emerge.

Although a few hardy adventurers were always willing to push westward, efforts to settle land west of the Appalachian Mountains were slow to develop. The discovery of gold and silver brought waves of prospectors westward. Logging companies pushed into the Great Lakes region in search of new timber, once forests in the Northeast had been exhausted.

Despite these early migrations, it was not until Abraham Lincoln signed the Homestead Act in 1862 that substantial settlement of the West began. The Homestead Act gave settlers 160 acres of land each if they would establish a home on the land and work to increase its productivity for at least five years. Railroads also received land grants. They then sold tracts of land to raise funds for the construction of the rail lines. Because the Homestead Act required settlers to live on the land, people remained dispersed across the countryside. Towns were typically founded along transportation links—along rivers, railroads, or highways.

Historically, then, the economic base of rural communities has been tied closely to natural resources. New England was blessed with timber, abundant wildlife, and a coastline, all of which explain its early economic base. The land and climate in Virginia, Maryland, and the Carolinas were well suited to tobacco. Georgia, Alabama, and other parts of the Deep South grew cotton. Both cotton and tobacco were very profitable export crops. The vast prairies of the Midwest offered grassland for livestock and soils capable of supporting cereal-grain production. The Appalachian Mountains were home to rich veins of high-quality coal. The lush forests of the Pacific Northwest drew timber companies westward once timber stands in the Great Lakes region were depleted. In each region, rural communities grew up around the economic base created by available resources.

Transportation networks needed to distribute raw materials and products offer a second reason for rural settlement. When barges and ships moved materials to market, communities were founded along rivers and coastlines. An extensive canal system in Ohio, Pennsylvania, and New York opened up access to the Great Lakes, leading to the settlement of canal villages. Railroads opened up much of the West. More recently, roads and turnpike systems have influenced where rural communities flourished. Many of these communities depend on a natural resource, such as coal or grain, but their role is to distribute rather than extract the resource.

Regardless of whether their economies were based on natural resources or proximity to transportation networks, most rural communities grew in response to urban markets. Increased urbanization created a demand for the Midwest's farm products and the Northwest's timber. Industrialization created a need for McDowell County's coal. The oil crisis of the 1970s revived oil towns from Texas to Montana. When railroads flourished, towns such as Irwin were important links in a network moving farm products to the cities and manufactured products to the country. If some rural communities seem out of place, it is because we have forgotten the important role they once played.

Impact of Change

Natural resources and transportation networks explain why many rural communities were settled, but they do not necessarily explain why some communities flourished and others did not. In 1940, Irwin had a population of several hundred; Mammoth Lakes could count fewer than a dozen year-round residents. By 1990, Mammoth Lakes boasted a population approaching 5,000, but Irwin's had increased only slightly. The same winds of change blew on both communities, yet each was affected differently. A number of factors—technology, changes in transportation, and economic restructuring—help explain rural responses to change.

INCREASED USE OF TECHNOLOGY

The linkage between technology and change is complex (see Box 2.1). The introduction of machines and computers has increased productivity but decreased the number of people needed in several economies. Farmers who plowed with horses typically handled about eighty acres a season. Tractors alone allowed them to expand to 240 acres. In 1950, the average miner produced 1,100 tons of coal per year. Coal loaders and other equipment introduced into the mines boosted the output per miner to 3,500 tons per year by 1970. Manufacturing plants have seen the same trend. Modern sawmills are far more accurate and require fewer line workers than mills of only a few decades ago. Although natural-resource and manufacturing industries remain an important part of the economy, they actually contribute fewer jobs through direct employment.

Jobs are not necessarily lost to the nation's economy. The increased use of technology actually shifts jobs in several ways. In becoming more mechanized, business enterprises substitute capital (money) for labor. Farmers borrow money to buy tractors, substituting borrowed capital for the farm laborers they might otherwise have hired. Substituting capital for labor thus decreases the demand for unskilled labor, but increases the need for banks and other financial services. As more tractors are purchased, employment associated with manufacturing tractors also in-

---

BOX 2.1   TECHNOLOGICAL DETERMINISM?

Rapid social change is often attributed to technology. For example, we commonly point out that the mechanization of farming caused the loss of the family farm. Technology certainly played an important role, but it is not at all clear that technology caused the loss of family farms. Rather than causing social change, technology facilitates social change.

In looking at the development of cultures, anthropologists assume that all forms of technology, from the steel ax to the supercomputer, are tools. To understand their development and impact on society, we must ask why these tools were developed and how they were used. To say that a tool (mechanization of agriculture) caused the loss of the family farm is to ignore the fact that the tool was developed in response to society. Why was mechanization necessary to farming after World War II? Which technologies were adopted and which were ignored?

In the case of farming, it was not technology that caused the dramatic decline in family farms. Market forces and federal policies rewarded increased production, increases that could be accomplished only by introducing labor-saving technologies. Farmers did not adopt those new technologies in order to maximize profits. They did so because they needed technology in order to remain competitive—indeed, even to be able to stay in farming.

Technology is a social product. We create it and use it in response to conditions over which we have some control. To blame technology for our problems is to blame the hammer when we hit our thumb with it. To blame the loss of the family farm on the emergence of new technologies is to ignore the social conditions created by world markets and federal policies.

---

creases. However, if tractors are not made locally, this shifts jobs outside the community.

CHANGES IN TRANSPORTATION

A second factor affecting rural communities has been changes in the transportation industry. Steamboat traffic along the Missouri River settled dozens of towns between Kansas City and the Nebraska state line. By 1855, a town named Doniphan was one of the largest along the upper Missouri, boasting the first grain elevator in Kansas. It was the neighboring town, Atchison, that eventually flourished, however. Atchison was successful in attracting the first rail link to the region.

Continued developments in transportation have affected other rural communities as well. Caliente, a town in southern Nevada, provided water to steam locomotives making the long journey from Salt Lake City to Los Angeles. When diesel locomotives replaced steam ones after World War II, Caliente found its economic base weakened. More recently, interstate highways replaced some of the functions served by railroads. This strengthened the economic base of towns along the highway, but weakened that of towns along abandoned railroad lines. Highways opened access to the Mammoth Lakes ski slopes, making long weekends possible for those living in Los Angeles.

Although rural communities along transportation routes are often the most directly affected, almost all rural communities are affected by the automobile. Once established, communities develop retail activities, such as dry goods stores, hardware stores, or implement dealers. Services are next, starting with barber shops or hotels and then moving to community services including schools, police, or hospitals.

When transportation is difficult, businesses and services must be located near where people live. As roads are improved, business and service activities are consolidated. Children ride buses to school, and parents drive to the next-largest town to shop. Some rural communities have grown into retail trade centers for their region; others have a Main Street that is gradually closing.

ECONOMIC RESTRUCTURING

A third change affecting rural communities has been economic restructuring. The term *economic restructuring* acts as an umbrella for a number of changes in business and industry. The reasons for this change are complex, but can be linked generally to the shift to a global economy and the introduction of information technologies. Both changes will be explored in more depth in later chapters, but here we present a brief description that helps explain how change affects rural communities differently.

In the 1960s and early 1970s, some sociologists and economists found it useful to think of the nation's economy as a dual economy. Business firms could be categorized as either core or peripheral. An economy's core consisted of those relatively few corporations that controlled most of the market. Firms were large, well established, accustomed to using technology, capable of influencing markets and prices, and able to rely upon union labor. Competition was limited. Peripheral firms were smaller and less profitable, used less technology, adopted existing price levels, sold to smaller markets, and were less unionized (Parcel and Sickmeier 1988). Peripheral firms operated in a highly competitive environment.

The shift to a global economy upset the stability of this system. Core firms found themselves drawn into competition worldwide. In order to be more competitive in this expanded market, core firms began taking on characteristics of peripheral firms. Many moved labor-intensive activities to other countries in order to avoid unionized labor. Others began subcontracting activities to peripheral firms.

The impact on rural communities has been mixed. The meat-packing industry, for example, used to locate its plants in urban areas and employ unionized labor. Old-line meat-packing companies are being replaced by new companies that have moved many of their plants to rural areas, in part to avoid unionized labor. The industry retains some characteristics of a core industry, but low wages and higher worker turnover have become more common (Stull and Broadway 1990). Rural communities in which these plants have relocated see enormous growth, but primarily in low-wage jobs.

Large retail merchandising firms, such as Wal-Mart and K-Mart, are replacing peripheral Main Street businesses. Large merchandising firms have both core and periphery characteristics. They have large sales and employment, are price setters, and use advanced centralized inventory and management practices; however, they pay low wages to most of their employees and aggressively keep unions out. Rural communities gain businesses that offer more competitive prices, but lose the self-employed small-business owner.

Features of this economic restructuring also include expanded use of information technologies. The extensive use of computers and introduction of fiber-optic cables capable of transferring huge quantities of data are making the location of a business less important. Stockbrokers find, for example, that they no longer need to live in New York City. A Fax machine, computer, and modem will connect them with market information no matter where they live. Transactions are now accomplished electronically.

Other businesses are finding it less expensive to operate in rural areas. L.L. Bean operates its catalog sales out of Freeport, Maine, a town of 5,000. A bank in the small town of Holton, Kansas, processes most of the student loans made nationwide. For the first time in decades, distances do not present a barrier in many business operations. Where digital switches and fiber-optic cable are in place, rural communities may find themselves attractive to small businesses specializing in information technology.

RURAL RESPONSES TO CHANGE

Conducted in 1790, the first U.S. census listed 95 percent of the population as rural, with most people employed as farmers. Today, fewer than one-third of U.S. inhabitants live in rural areas, and less than 2 percent are farmers. Increased use of technology, new forms of transportation, and changes in the nation's economy have contributed to this transformation. Rural communities have changed—some in terms of population, others in terms of character, and still others in terms of economic base.

The dramatic shift from rural to urban populations means that a number of rural communities have become urban. In its early days, San Jose, California, was an agricultural community founded to serve the Spanish

---

BOX 2.2 FROM THE VALLEY OF HEART'S DELIGHT TO SILICON VALLEY

The Spanish colonized the Santa Clara Valley and established a mission at San Jose in 1777. The Native American population of the valley was brought to the mission to be "civilized" and to provide labor—and most perished in this subdued state. The good soil and abundant water made the area ideal for agriculture, and cattle, sheep, and corn were raised to supply the Spanish missions and military bases. When Mexico gained independence from Spain, the valley, like the rest of California, became part of Mexico.

Settlers from the United States began to arrive around 1825 and gradually established a commercial center in San Jose. Under the leadership of such settlers, California became independent of Mexico in 1846 and a state of the United States in 1850. The discovery of gold in California fueled the growth of San Jose as a commercial center, because it lay along one of the three main routes to the gold fields. Some of those who made money from that gold invested it in San Jose.

As the city grew into a commercial center, the agriculture in the valley shifted from livestock and grains to fruits and vegetables. Industry developed to process the produce, including fruit drying and canning. Infrastructure was necessary to facilitate access to the commercial center (which required street and public transportation) and to serve the new industry (which required public utilities, especially sewage to handle the large amount of waste from the canneries).

After World War II, the booming defense industry located many companies there. An aggressive real estate sector expanded the boundaries of San Jose, providing homes for the working people who staffed the new industries. San Jose offered a good climate, low taxes, plenty of land for low-rise, low-cost buildings, and an absence of unions. A key to its development was its location near Stanford University, a major resource in the development of the electronics industry. With the infusion of massive federal spending in defense, companies such as Hewlett-Packard, Lockheed, IBM, National Semiconductors, and many others were established or relocated to the area. Defense contracts drastically changed San Jose's economic base again.

Source: Adapted from Philip J. Trounstine and Terry Christensen. 1982. *Movers and Shakers*. New York: St. Martin's.

Crown (see Box 2.2). The gold rush of the 1850s transformed it into a commercial center. Then the defense and electronics industries completed San Jose's transition to a metropolitan area. Little of its agrarian past is left.

Other rural communities have remained small but become dependent on neighboring urban areas. Port Jefferson, New York, is a town of about 10,000 along the north shore of Long Island. Part of the New York City metropolitan area, Port Jefferson bears little resemblance to the isolated fishing village it once was. Candor, in south-central New York, still seems like a small town of 1,000. Its economic base has changed greatly over time—from livestock and grains to dairy products to small manufacturing based on local products (tanneries and leather goods). Today, it is a bedroom community for nearby industries and larger cities. Both Candor and Port Jefferson find the economic base of neighboring urban areas of more importance than their own. Their residents no longer rely on the community for jobs.

Circumstance or ingenuity has enabled some communities to adapt. At the turn of the century, Eatonton, Georgia, was a cotton town. When the boll weevil wiped out cotton fields in the 1920s, dairy farming became the economic base of the region. Putnam County, the county in which Eatonton is located, still boasts the largest milk yields in the state. Manufacturing was gradually added beginning in the 1950s, when textile and aluminum-cookware factories opened. Although these companies have left, others have replaced them. Manufacturing continues to employ a greater proportion of the work force than any other sector of the local economy. More recently, recreation has emerged as an economic contributor to the region. Development along a nearby lake, Lake Oconee, is bringing weekenders from Atlanta and enticing retirees to the region. Eatonton's economic base has clearly become more diverse than it was during the cotton days.

Communities dependent on a single economic base have been the most vulnerable. Declining populations are common across the rural Midwest where most communities have relied on farming for their economic base. Timber and mining communities face some of the same problems. Other single-industry communities are growing. Gillette, Wyoming, an energy-based community, is a classic boomtown. Mammoth Lakes, California, is growing because of expanding interest in recreation. Rapid growth and declining populations are both relatively common in communities dependent on a single economic base.

Labor Force of a Community

So far, our discussion of the economic base of a community has focused on the economic activity itself—on the firm or the industry that forms the economic base. The people of a community are also extremely important, because they hold the jobs created by local economic activity. A job meets several human needs. It provides income, regulates daily activity, establishes a sense of identity, and offers opportunities for social interactions and meaningful life experiences. Thus, the kinds of jobs available and the opportunities for creating jobs within communities have enormous implications for the individuals who live there or come to work.

CHARACTER OF THE LOCAL LABOR FORCE

One way of understanding how the local population relates to a community's economic base is to think of people as a pool of labor. To some extent, this pool needs to match the community's economic base or its plans to expand that base. A series of descriptors, such as educational level, age, and gender, help characterize the labor force of a region.

The education and skill level of a labor force refers to either the skills and training acquired or the level of schooling completed by people in a community. Despite the lower status often accorded to natural-resource–based industries, most required workers to develop skills for which they were then relatively well paid. Mining companies in McDowell County recruited experienced miners from Eastern Europe. Manufacturing plants sometimes look for a labor force with previous assembly-line experience before relocating.

Despite the importance of acquired skills, level of schooling is becoming an important asset to a community. Industries that are currently growing, such as computer and information-processing activities, require more highly educated workers. Manufacturing plants planning to convert to new technology look carefully at the educational level of current workers. If current workers cannot be trained to handle the new equipment, companies will simply relocate. Historically, rural areas have lagged urban areas in terms of educational level of the labor force.

The age structure of the community is another important aspect of the labor market. Is there an abundant labor force at the entry level? In many urban areas, a lack of young people willing to work for minimum wage and no benefits has driven up wages for jobs such as fast-food counter worker. In the Midwest, declining populations often result from the exodus of young people. The average age of rural farming communities is increasing, which leaves few workers at the entry level. Consequently, these communities are at a relative disadvantage in attracting manufacturing plants. In addition to being descriptive of the local labor force, the age structure of a community may influence the types of jobs available.

One of the most significant changes in the nature of rural labor forces is the increasing participation of women. Rural women have traditionally participated less in the formal labor market than have urban women. This has been in part because of the importance of women's unpaid economic activities, including caring for livestock, helping with crops, or maintaining the financial records. Changes in the economy have made these traditional activities less effective. Financial pressures have also increased the need for women to seek cash income. Many of the industries that have located in rural areas, including the textile, electronics, and pharmaceutical industries, now employ women. The combination of need and increased opportunity has increased significantly the number of rural women now in the labor force.

Finally, increased mobility makes the description of a rural labor force somewhat complex. Improved transportation has increased the likelihood

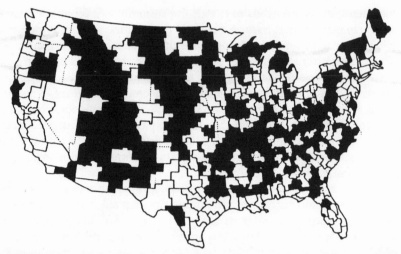

FIGURE 2.2 Rural Labor Market Areas. *Source:* Economic Research Service, USDA.

that someone can live in one town yet commute to work in another. Any description of a labor force often has to be regional rather than local. To capture this activity, economists have introduced the concept of *labor market areas* (LMAs), which include both the residence and work destinations of local people. These areas are multicounty regions that encompass those places where relatively large numbers of people routinely move back and forth from home to work. Approximately half the nation's LMAs are rural (Figure 2.2). Most are quite large, particularly those in the West. Rural people are quite mobile in their pursuit of work.

THE DUAL LABOR MARKET

The labor force consists of all employed persons plus all persons seeking employment. The concept of a labor market, however, assumes that certain jobs are accessible to some individuals and not to others. The labor market can be divided into two segments—the primary and secondary labor markets. Peripheral firms hire mostly from the secondary labor market. As discussed earlier, core industries increasingly hire from both segments of the labor market (Parcel and Sickmeier 1988).

The primary labor market recruits people based on educational and skill level. Jobs have good wages, safe working conditions, opportunities for advancement within the firm, stability of employment, and due process in the enforcement of work rules. Jobs in the primary labor market can be either managerial/professional or craft/skilled worker.

Jobs in the secondary labor market generally have low status, low pay, poor benefits, and little or no chance for advancement. Working conditions can sometimes be less clean and safe. Job security is often low. There is little movement from the secondary to the primary labor market, but much movement by an individual from one secondary labor market job to another. In addition, there is little correlation between education and income (Parcel and Sickmeier 1988). For example, people with certain characteristics may be hired preferentially for the secondary labor market. Thus, in certain firms or industries, women may be hired in low-wage positions with less opportunity for advancement than occurs with men, regardless of formal qualifications such as education.

Most firms generate jobs that are regulated by laws specifying limits on number of hours worked, safety regulations, dismissal procedures, and so on. Records are kept that can document the exchange of work for wages and, thus, the number of individuals employed in a given industry. This is what we refer to as the *formal economy*. The *informal economy* is unregulated by societal institutions (Castells and Portes, 1989). A handshake rather than a contractual relation between employer and employee is the basis for hiring. Individuals hired to do informal activities generally represent the lower part of the secondary labor force. They lack social benefits, are often paid less than minimum wage, are subject to arbitrary dismissal, and often work under unapproved safety and health conditions.

The informal sector has existed for a long time. As Castells and Portes point out, what is new is that it is growing at the expense of previously formalized positions, particularly in urban areas. In rural areas, one kind of informal activity is substituted for another. Informal relations are shifting from the agriculture and natural-resource sectors to the manufacturing and service sectors.

How a community's labor force is divided between the primary and secondary labor markets or between formal and informal activities affects the stability and well-being of a community. For the most part, employment in rural areas is more likely to be in the secondary labor market. Falk and Lyson (1988) show that nearly half of all manufacturing jobs in the rural South are in firms that employ mostly low-wage workers. By contrast, urban centers report only 20 percent of their manufacturing jobs in such peripheral industries. Hanes Textiles is the second-largest employer in Eatonton, Georgia, but nearly all its local employees are in the secondary labor market. Those working at Hanes are paid minimum wage and see limited opportunities for advancement. Most are women; African American women are overrepresented.

Ultimately, a dual labor market benefits firms more than the local community. Labor costs are kept low. Those employed are working at jobs that may not fully use their skills, however, let alone their potential talents. Incomes are limited, which makes it difficult for the local economy to flourish. The community suffers because much of its human capital is underutilized. No one disputes that some jobs are better than no jobs, but companies that rely heavily on the secondary labor market often make a relatively small contribution to the community.

OPPORTUNITY STRUCTURE

Just as the educational and skill level of a community helps determine the types of industries that locate in an area or the businesses that can be initiated, the types of jobs available in turn influence the educational level of the community. When coal mining and logging were profitable, young men often dropped out of high school to go to work in the mines or forests, assuming that within a relatively short time, they would be making more money than their teachers. Thus, any further investment in education seemed foolish and unnecessary. Regions such as McDowell County characteristically developed low commitments to schools.

Towns such as Irwin and Eatonton face a different dilemma. Much of the agricultural Midwest has historically had a strong commitment to education, and well-supported local schools enable most young people to pursue some type of postsecondary education. Once they finish college, however, Irwin's young people go elsewhere. Few local jobs require the skills or knowledge they have developed. In Eatonton, African American women work either for the textile factory or as domestics. When Billie Jo Williams finished her degree in business administration, she found she could not use her education in Eatonton (see profile in Chapter 1).

The interaction between educational level and type of jobs available has become a vicious cycle for many rural communities. The *opportunity structure* of the community—the types of jobs and investment opportunities available—affects the character of the local labor force. The local labor force in turn affects the success of the community in attracting or supporting new business enterprises. Communities that invest heavily in education see the more educated young people leave because of the lack of opportunity. Those who do not invest in education rely on assembly plants for jobs—industries that depend upon the less educated workers willing to accept lower wages. These jobs offer young people little motivation to invest in education. Communities in their efforts to promote local economic development need to focus on more than simply creating jobs; they need to encourage and support a strong educational system.

Economic Portrait of Rural Communities

From the first U.S. census forward, rural communities have grown steadily diverse in terms of economic base. Just as communities change their economic base over time, so too have they continued to differ

At the turn of this century, Eatonton, Georgia, was a cotton town (photo courtesy of the U.S. Department of Agriculture).

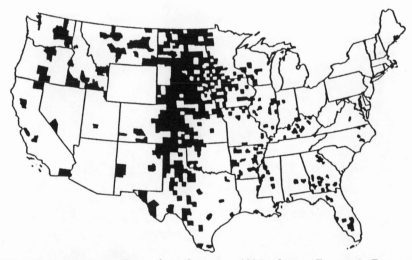

FIGURE 2.3   Farming-Dependent Counties, 1986. *Source:* Economic Research Service, USDA.

dramatically from one another at any point in time. This section examines the many different types of rural economies and the issues communities face as a result of economic change.

NATURAL-RESOURCE–BASED COMMUNITIES

Although a number of factors have reduced the relative importance of natural resources, these endowments are still an important part of rural communities. Traditionally, natural-resource–based economies are grouped into five categories: agriculture, forestry, energy, nonenergy mining, and fishing. All have experienced declines over the past decade, but some have been more resilient than others.

Figure 2.3 shows the distribution of rural counties still dependent on agriculture for 20 percent or more of their total labor and business income as of 1986. Most farming-dependent counties are located in the Midwest, particularly in the Great Plains, where there are few other economic activities. The Northeast reports no agricultural counties, and parts of the arid Southwest also have relatively little agricultural activity. Although people do farm in these regions, farming is a minor contributor to the general economy.

A combination of factors must exist in order for forestry to persist as a source of economic activity. Commercial-quality timber must be present, as must sawmills and pulp/paper mills capable of processing the cut timber. This combination of factors exists in the Pacific Northwest, northern New England, the Great Lakes region, and the Southeast. The counties

FIGURE 2.4 Forestry/Wood Products-Dependent Counties, 1984. *Source:* Economic Research Service, USDA.

shaded in Figure 2.4 show those regions where 15 percent or more of the total of labor and business income comes from forestry and wood-products activity. Although the number of counties involved in forestry activities is small, the industry employs almost twice as many workers as mining, fishing, and energy-related activities combined.

The Rocky Mountain states, Nevada, and parts of the Southwest are substantially dependent upon mining; their economic activity derives from sources of iron, copper, gold, silver, and molybdenum as well as stone, sand gravel, phosphate rocks, and sulfur. Energy-extraction counties include those where reservoirs of coal, oil, and natural gas lie. These are scattered throughout the country: in the Rocky Mountain region, Texas, Oklahoma, Alaska, the Gulf states, North Dakota, Montana, the Appalachian states, and southern Illinois. Figures 2.5 and 2.6 show the distribution of counties that depend on energy and nonenergy mining respectively.

These regions are especially susceptible to boom-and-bust cycles, in which rapid growth can be followed by rapid population decline in response to the price of these commodities in international markets. Although most analysts agree that prices will never again be as high as during the 1970s, many energy and mining communities are beginning to recover some of what they lost during the early 1980s.

Fishing remains an extremely small contributor to the national economy, though it is important to the local economies of some rural communities. The United States currently imports a large fraction of the seafood

Mining continues to be the primary economic activity in some rural communities (photo courtesy of the Ohio University Telecommunications Center).

it consumes. Thus, it seems hardly surprising that the 1980 census reported less than 0.2 percent of the rural labor force as engaged in fishing. Although fishing may not uniquely identify rural counties, it continues to serve as the primary economic activity for some coastal communities. Other agricultural areas are also beginning to explore fish farming as an alternative to conventional crops. Fish are grown commercially rather than harvested from the sea.

Nearly half of all nonmetropolitan counties rely upon a natural-resource–based economy: Roughly 30 percent specialize in agriculture, and another

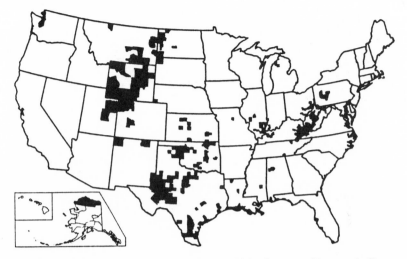

FIGURE 2.5 Energy-Dependent Counties, 1984. *Source:* Economic Research Service, USDA.

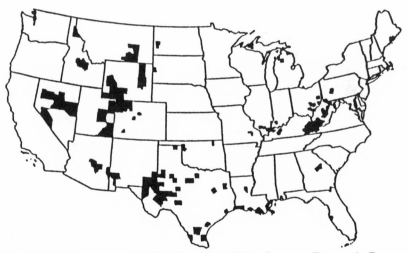

FIGURE 2.6 Nonenergy Mining Counties, 1984. *Source:* Economic Research Service, USDA.

14 percent are involved in forestry, energy, or nonenergy mining activities. Increased mechanization in these industries will continue to reduce the number of workers needed and increase the skills required of those who remain. Agricultural and forestry-dependent counties face continued population decline. Energy and mining communities will continue to move through boom-and-bust cycles in response to international markets.

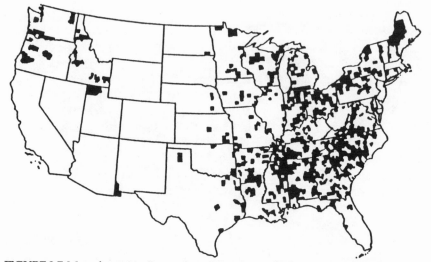

FIGURE 2.7 Manufacturing-Dependent Counties, 1986. *Source:* Economic Research Service, USDA.

For all these counties, efforts to diversify their economic base further are important. Agricultural regions are beginning to look to value-added processes that enable a local labor force to process foods or agricultural products for shipment to urban markets. Where the landscape is scenic, counties dependent on forestry and mining are trying to build tourism and recreational opportunities. They, too, are exploring strategies that enable the local community to add more value to the wood and minerals before shipping them elsewhere. However you look at it, natural resources will continue to provide an important economic base around which rural communities function.

MANUFACTURING COMMUNITIES

About 1950, manufacturing industries began moving from metropolitan to nonmetropolitan areas. By 1979, manufacturing had become the largest single employer in rural areas, providing jobs for 40 percent of the rural work force. Figure 2.7 shows the nonmetropolitan counties where manufacturing accounted for at least 30 percent of the wage and business income in 1986. Most are in the East and Southeast. These counties are often adjacent to metropolitan counties and are home to nearly half of the rural population.

During the 1960s, rural counties profited as manufacturing firms searched for cheaper land, cheaper labor, and lower taxes. Much of the growth in manufacturing occurred in the South, but other areas benefited as well. By the 1980s, however, some firms were moving overseas in search of still cheaper labor. Others were struggling to maintain their operations in an environment of increased competition. Rural counties dependent on manufacturing were hit especially hard because they had very limited alternatives on which to fall back.

Economists report that rural manufacturing is rebounding and argue that manufacturing will continue to be important to rural areas. Efforts to recruit manufacturing firms can have an impact on a community's economy that is broader than the immediate jobs created. Manufacturing also generates jobs in other economic sectors, such as supplies and services, and some of these jobs can be captured within the region. Communities that attract or establish manufacturing operations and then use those activities to stimulate the development of other economic activities can build a network that is mutually supportive and diversified. As discussed in the previous section, efforts to increase the educational level of young people as well as of the current labor force will be helpful in developing or attracting higher-wage manufacturing firms.

SPECIALIZED GOVERNMENT COMMUNITIES

Communities largely dependent on government are usually the locations of such public institutions as military bases, prisons, universities, public lands, and administration centers. About 23 percent of all nonmetropolitan counties depend on government employment for their economic base. Research on these counties reveals both advantages and disadvantages to this dependence.

Government counties experienced substantial growth during the late 1970s and early 1980s. Although wages are typically lower, job stability is significantly higher than in counties dependent on manufacturing or natural resources. In exchange for growth and stability, however, these communities appear to lose tax revenue. Most government activities use local services but return less in tax dollars than do private businesses. For the most part, government counties seem insulated from the economic changes that affect natural-resource–based counties, but remain vulnerable to political changes. Despite this vulnerability, most government-dependent counties have remained relatively stable.

DESTINATION-RETIREMENT COMMUNITIES

A number of retirement communities are emerging in rural areas. Retirement counties (Figure 2.8) are defined as those that experienced a net in-migration of people aged 60 or over from 1970 to 1980 equal to 15 percent or more of their residents in that age group. Located in areas of scenic beauty and recreational opportunities, these counties are most heavily concentrated in the Sunbelt extending from California and parts

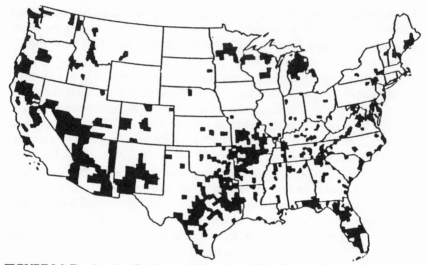

FIGURE 2.8 Destination-Retirement Counties, 1979. *Source:* Economic Research Service, USDA.

of the Pacific Northwest through the Southwest and along the Gulf Coast to Florida. Another set of retirement counties is clustered in the upper Great Lakes states. Retirement counties are notably absent in the Great Plains and the Cornbelt.

Of all age groups, senior citizens are the least likely to move. Yet migration rates of the elderly continue to increase. Research suggests that some of these migrants move in search of care or support from family members living elsewhere. Others are looking for a milder climate, improved quality of life, or lower cost of living. Those in search of care or support often return to their native states. The younger, more affluent retirees move to Florida, Texas, or Arkansas. Some move permanently; others move to escape the northern winters, dividing their year between a permanent home and a retirement community.

The long-term impact of this type of economic activity in rural areas is not yet known. Retirees do bring income in the form of transfer payments, such as Social Security or pension funds. They also spend much of their income in the local community. Because transfer funds are relatively stable sources of income, they shield local businesses from some of the ups and downs of manufacturing layoffs or drops in commodities prices.

Many researchers do question whether communities will be able to afford the increased demand on services needed as these young retirees continue to age. In addition, there is some evidence that the jobs created by this type of economic activity are primarily in the service sector where salaries are typically low and job turnover is high. As the U.S. population continues to age, intergenerational competition for scarce public funds will increase. Communities may find themselves split between the needs of the longtime residents and the relative newcomers.

Who Pays for Change?

Judy sees Atwood as a community with limited job opportunities. Miners in McDowell County see the same thing. Railway workers along abandoned routes, loggers in the Pacific Northwest, oil-field workers in Texas—all see communities with limited job opportunities. The skills each person developed through either education or work experience seem no longer needed.

Economists and sociologists can point to the factors that help explain this change. As technology enabled capital to replace labor, fewer people were needed to cut trees or mine coal. Increased supply worldwide has made U.S. oil less competitive; the result is fewer jobs for oil-field workers. Changes in transportation have left many railways abandoned. Economists would explain these changes in terms of market efficiency, arguing that the market will now do a better job of linking goods and services with those who need them.

Sociologists point to a broader issue. When industrialization and the subsequent increase in the demand for coal made it profitable, mining companies imported labor and created communities in McDowell County. When political circumstances made it important for the federal government to settle the Great Plains, policies encouraged migration and land settlement. If market efficiency and political circumstances have changed, what are the responsibilities to the people left behind?

Those who mine coal, farm, or engage in other natural-resource–based activities also made choices. They did not choose where to be born, but they did choose where to stay and what type of occupation to pursue. If the circumstances under which those choices were made have changed, what responsibilities do those individuals have for their futures?

Chapter Summary

We often characterize rural communities in terms of their economic base, the primary economic activity on which much of the community's local economy depends. Historically, the economic base of rural communities was based on the extraction or distribution of natural resources.

A number of factors have changed the extent to which these economies can support rural communities. Technology has increased productivity but decreased the number of low-skill workers needed in many industries. Changes in transportation networks have left some rural communities isolated from the distribution of natural resources and manufactured goods. Finally, economic restructuring has created opportunities in the form of new jobs but threatened the health of locally owned businesses and services in many small towns.

A community's ability to diversify its economic base depends, in part, on the local labor force. Characteristics such as educational level, age, and gender influence the types of economic activities a community can support. In turn, the types of jobs available in the community—the opportunity structure—influence the types of people who remain in a community and their commitment to education.

The labor market of a community can be described in terms of primary and secondary labor markets. The primary labor market recruits people based on educational and skill level. Jobs pay good wages and are relatively stable. Jobs in the secondary market may require less skill. More important, they offer lower wages and are often unstable, because workers are less protected.

Rural communities have both formal and informal economies. Formal economies include businesses regulated by state and federal laws and typically include those individuals working in both the primary and secondary labor markets. Informal economies are largely unregulated and involve some of those working in the secondary labor market. Employment in rural areas is more likely to be in the secondary labor market.

Rural communities now support a wide range of economic activities. Nearly half of all nonmetropolitan counties still rely upon natural resources, including agriculture, forestry, energy, nonenergy mining, and fishing. Rural counties in the East and Southeast depend predominantly on manufacturing for their economic base. About 23 percent of all nonmetropolitan counties depend on government employment for their economic base. The newest economic base is derived from the rapid growth in destination-retirement counties.

Key Terms

Economic base is the core economic activity on which much of the community's local economy depends.

Formal economy includes economic activities that are regulated by laws and monitored through routine data collection.

Informal economy includes economic activities that are not regulated by laws, such as an exchange of labor or goods. Such activity is generally not monitored.

Labor market areas (LMAs) encompass both place of residence and place of work of a local population. An LMA is that group of counties in which most members of a population live and work.

Opportunity structure describes the types of jobs and investment opportunities available in a community.

Value-added process is any process that converts a raw material or natural resource into a usable good or service.

References

Castells, Manuel, and Alejandro Portes. 1989. "World Underneath: The Origins, Dynamics, and Effects of the Informal Economy." Pp. 11–37 in Alejandro Portes, Manuel Castells, and Lauren A. Benton (eds.), *The Informal Economy: Studies in Advanced and Less Developed Countries.* Baltimore: Johns Hopkins University Press.

Falk, William W., and Thomas A. Lyson. 1988. *High Tech, Low Tech, No Tech: Recent Industrial and Occupational Change in the South.* Albany: State University of New York Press.

Parcel, Toby L., and Marie B. Sickmeier. 1988. "One Firm, Two Labor Markets: The Case of McDonald's in the Fast-Food Industry." *Sociological Quarterly* 29(1): 29–46.

Stull, D. D., and M. J. Broadway. 1990. "The Effects of Restructuring on Beefpacking in Kansas." *Kansas Business Review* 14(1): 10–16.

3

Community and Culture

Carol and Buddy Drew have just moved to Grovers Junction, a medium-sized southern town where Buddy grew up. Buddy had grown tired of teaching. So they decided to move back home where he could take over the family business when his father retired. Buddy went to work with his father. Carol found a teaching job.

The local high school seemed to be pretty good academically, but Carol was concerned about the high rate of teenage pregnancies. All the teenage mothers dropped out of school. Carol also saw patterns developing in families. Girls whose mothers had dropped out of high school because of pregnancy had themselves become pregnant and dropped out of school.

The last school where Carol taught, a suburban school in the Midwest, had been successful with a couple of programs. Officials set up a daycare facility in the school so that the teenage mothers could continue school after they gave birth. Many teenage mothers then finished high school; some went on to college. The school also offered a comprehensive program of sex education to decrease the rate of teenage pregnancies.

Carol took her ideas to town leaders and the members of the school board, but was roundly defeated at every turn. Keeping teenage mothers in school would only set bad examples for the other girls, she was told. Having daycare would be rewarding them for having babies. Sex education would simply encourage other teenagers to become sexually active.

Carol was bewildered. At Valley View, these programs were adopted without controversy. Why was this rural town unwilling to respond?

Grovers Junction is not unusual. The townspeople care as much for their young people as do those in the suburban area where Carol taught last year. Like Carol, those in Grovers Junction are concerned about the unusually high rate of teenage pregnancy. Grovers Junction is unwilling, however, to implement the programs that Carol is recommending. Why? The answer lies in a network of assumptions and beliefs about what leads to teenage pregnancy as well as the different character of the two communities.

This chapter explores culture and its usefulness in understanding the choices that rural communities make. The culture of a region or community plays a strong role in determining how a problem, such as teenage pregnancy, is defined. How the problem is defined then influences what solutions are acceptable. In this chapter we define culture, examine characteristics of rural communities that explain how community cultures develop and are maintained, and explore the role community culture plays in addressing social problems.

Culture and Its Sources

In everyday usage, the term *culture* refers to sophisticated tastes in art, music, or literature. Sociologists use the term much more broadly, suggesting that it embraces an entire way of life—the pattern of daily life, strategies for performing daily tasks, rules for acceptable behavior—not just the way people express themselves in the arts. This section defines culture, explores its various dimensions, identifies some of its sources within a rural community, and describes how it is transmitted.

DEFINING CULTURE

At its most basic level, *culture* is the shared products of society. Some of these products are material, such as the clothing, utensils, or pottery that archaeologists retrieve from past cultures. In this sense, culture is very tangible. Some of the products of a culture, however, are not material. Ideas, governments, patterns of acceptable behavior, values, and myths are all examples of nonmaterial products. In this sense, culture is less tangible. What the products of a culture actually describe is a set of behaviors with which a group of people handle daily tasks and make sense of their experiences.

Robert Bierstedt (1963) suggested that we think of culture in terms of three dimensions: ideas, norms, and material culture. Ideas include the values held by a culture as well as the knowledge gained. Norms are the accepted ways of doing things, which often reflect both the values and knowledge available. Finally, the material culture consists of the objects created by people and used in daily life or enjoyed as art. In this chapter, we focus on the values and norms found in a culture.

VALUES AND NORMS

Values are the shared ideas about what is right and what is wrong, or about what is desirable and what is undesirable. Some of what we regard to be right or wrong evolves simply from experience—from what works in day-to-day life or within a community. Other ideas are drawn from a religion, a philosophy, or an ideology. In this sense, values often reflect our notions of what should be. However they are derived, values influence the social *norms*, the specific rules that govern how people act toward one another. Values are abstract concepts, whereas social norms describe the concrete guidelines for how people should behave.

Differences in values and norms are seen most easily across diverse cultures. Within the United States, contrasts between Native American and white cultures offer us some insight into the relationship between values and norms. The Navajo culture, for example, values a strong extended-family structure. Because people in the Navajo culture consider cooperation essential to maintaining that structure, cooperative behavior is the norm. Children are taught to help one another in such a way that no one person stands above another. By contrast, the white culture values individualism. Competition is the norm. It is seen as a productive way of stimulating individuals to their best performance. From an early age, children are taught to compete, and individual achievements are rewarded.

The contrast in norms between the two cultures was immediately obvious to white teachers placed in Navajo schools, as illustrated by an excerpt from field notes collected by McNeley (1975):

> For field day, we organized a race around the school yard. One boy easily outdistanced the others, winning with 30 yards to spare. When he saw that the others were still running, however, he simply started in running around the track again. The race quickly dissolved in chaos as the Navajo children had no concept of what it meant to win a race. They ran simply to share the enjoyment of running.

We often accept social norms so unconsciously that we hardly know they exist. When asked why we shake hands in greeting or keep our left hand in our lap while eating, most of us would simply say something like "That's the way it's done!" Over time, some norms become completely disassociated from their values, making us wonder why it is we do things that way.

In general, we notice departures from the norm far more often than the norm itself. Teenagers are acutely aware of the norms in their school.

When we visit other countries, we suddenly notice that the norms of our culture differ from those in another. Humorists and movie producers take advantage of this, building comic dialogue or entire movie plots around how foolish the norms of one culture can seem in another. Mick Dundee in *Crocodile Dundee* was funny because he applied the norms of rural Australia while living in New York City.

Social norms vary in the extent to which people are expected to conform to them. Some norms allow people a fair amount of leeway. People do not have to conform absolutely. Those who do not follow such norms are merely considered a bit strange or eccentric. Other norms are considered more crucial to maintaining social order, and communities do not tolerate departures from them. People who do not conform are seen as more than eccentric—they are considered immoral. This distinction among norms is explored further in the discussion about sacred symbols.

DEVELOPMENT OF COMMUNITY CULTURE

Most U.S. communities owe a bit of their culture to the many racial, ethnic, and religious groups whose members settled the land. Some communities in rural New Mexico have retained features of the Native American and Latino cultures. Many farming communities in the Midwest or mining communities in West Virginia were settled largely by European immigrants who brought their culture with them. Communities formed by those of a single nationality (Germans, Swedes, or Czechs) or religion (Mennonite, Hutterite, or Mormon) have retained some of their original culture. Communities are exploiting this history, organizing festivals or tourist attractions around the cultural legacy left by those who settled the area.

In addition to the culture people brought with them, community members developed ways of dealing with one another that reflected the environmental setting and economic base of the region. Those who homesteaded Iowa, for example, found cooperation essential to survival. Helping out a neighbor became part of Iowa's culture, expected of everyone who farmed. Plantations in Georgia, however, were largely self-sufficient, and cooperation among owners was far less critical to survival. Thus, cooperation among farmers is much less common in parts of the rural South.

Mining communities, such as those in McDowell County, West Virginia, reflect the fierce independence developed in the work environment yet the dependence encouraged by company towns. Because they were paid by the volume of coal they could deliver each day, miners were their own bosses. Mining companies owned the town, however. The company arranged for the water, sewer system, housing, and even some of the stores.

By contrast, these same decisions were handled by the people, either collectively or individually, in towns such as Mammoth Lakes, California, or Eatonton, Georgia. The fierce independence fostered by the work environment in the mines, coupled with the inexperience in managing community affairs, has made it difficult for towns in McDowell County to mobilize in response to the loss of jobs.

CULTURE AND ITS TRANSMISSION

Although each of us is born into a culture, none of us inherits a knowledge of that culture. *Socialization* is the process by which we learn a culture, the process of becoming human. There are several perspectives about how socialization takes place. One suggests that the core of the socialization process is for a person to take on the role of another. We learn to view ourselves as we think others view us in order to get clues about what kinds of behavior are appropriate. It is through this process that we come to accept the norms and, later, values of society or groups within society. Although our basic personalities are formed at an early age, socialization continues to take place throughout our lives as we encounter new circumstances, modify behavior, and change our values.

The process of conforming to norms and values is not automatic. We first assess what it appears we are expected to do. We then determine whether we agree with that course. Finally, we decide whether we will do what we think is expected of us. Anyone familiar with a rural community or a tightly knit family knows that it is usually not difficult to determine what is expected, but it can sometimes be hard not to conform. Thus, we often do what is expected of us without necessarily agreeing that it is appropriate.

Socialization takes place within the social organizations closest to us— the family, school, and church. Other institutions, including community organizations such as civic groups or social clubs, play a lesser role. Collectively, the social organizations through which culture is transmitted are called *agents of culture*. Examined briefly here are two of these agents, schools and churches.

We normally think of schools as the institutions charged with helping children develop the intellectual skills needed for adult life. Schools also play an important role in socializing young people through the values and behaviors that teachers reward in the classroom. The school as an agent of culture was certainly apparent to Native Americans at the turn of the century and was a key element in the government's efforts to assimilate them into the white culture. Children were not allowed to speak their native language or practice native customs.

Current concern about the effectiveness of public schools also makes clear how schools serve as an agent of culture. In describing schools,

Schools play an important role in transmitting culture (photo courtesy of the Ohio University Telecommunications Center).

educators point to both a formal curriculum and an informal, or hidden, curriculum. The formal curriculum consists of the content areas to be covered, the knowledge and skills children are to gain. The hidden curriculum consists of the values and behaviors reinforced by the way in which schools are structured. Today's schools reflect the industrial age: Children are taught to be punctual, obedient, organized, and patient with repetitive tasks; these are the same behaviors needed in an industrial work force. Educators now argue that schools need to socialize children for the information age. This new age requires different behaviors— creativity, the ability to solve problems, the capacity to collect and organize new information, and patience with a constantly changing work environment.

Rural educators have become acutely aware of the culture being transmitted through school. Efforts to ensure that all children have access to quality schooling have led to increased state-level control of schools at the expense of local control. Some researchers argue that schools have "inculcated rural children with urban values, urban aspirations and urban skills . . . [encouraging] out-migration while discouraging the preservation and improvement of traditional rural schools and communities" (Sher and Tompkins 1977, 41–42). Because urban and rural differences have been declining for a number of reasons, it is difficult to judge whether an urban bias does exist in schools. The fear that schools are homogenizing all cultural differences, however, is one shared by racial and ethnic groups.

Often one of the first organizations formed when a community is established, churches act as another agent of culture. Religious beliefs, shared and reaffirmed through the church, often help shape the culture of a community. These beliefs can be used to reaffirm the status quo or to advocate change. The role played by the evangelical Protestant movement in labor disputes during the 1920s (Billings 1990) illustrates this apparent paradox.

The evangelical Protestant movement was strong in rural West Virginia and North Carolina in the 1920s, especially in organizing various segments of the emerging working class. In the coal fields of West Virginia, the church played an active role in the fight for unionization. In the textile mills of North Carolina, however, the church successfully blocked unionization.

The different positions held arose from the position of the church in each community. In the Appalachian coalfields, workers abandoned the company church and formed their own. Miners served as lay ministers, which enabled miners to use the authority of the pulpit in support of unionization. In North Carolina, the church was deeply integrated into the community. This integration enabled mill owners to wield considerable influence through subsidies to the churches and, in some cases, to the ministers themselves. In times of crisis, the church traditionally acted to preserve the status quo. Agents of culture, such as the church, can preserve the past or work toward change; which course they take depends on the character of their relationship with the community.

Social history, environmental setting, economic base, and social organizations contribute to the culture of a community, but these factors do not entirely explain the different responses to teenage pregnancy that Carol met. In many respects, the culture of a small town seems clearer and more coherent than that in a suburban community, no matter what region of the country we are describing. The next section explores this difference.

Culture and Solidarity

Whether it be a community of scholars, a labor union, a high school class, or the town in which we grew up, communities respond chiefly to three social needs. They offer us a place in which to belong, an arena in which we feel we can make a difference, and a sense of security. Sociologists often contrast the strengths of communities by the extent to which these three needs are met.

Grovers Junction and Valley View differ not only in culture but also in the character of community each possesses. Grovers Junction is a small community made up primarily of families who have lived in the region over several generations. Valley View is like most suburban areas—made up of fairly diverse groups of people who generally have come from somewhere else. This section explores factors that encourage and maintain solidarity in a community.

CONTRASTING RURAL AND URBAN

No subject invokes more controversy than efforts to describe the differences between rural and urban communities. Clear differences may have existed once. Over time, however, these differences have been obscured. Most rural communities no longer rely solely on natural resources for their economic base. Villages that were once isolated now find themselves bedroom communities for nearby metropolitan areas. In responding to the tastes of its urban clientele, ski towns such as Mammoth Lakes, California, seem more cosmopolitan than quaint. Urban areas are not nearly as homogeneous either. Extended metropolitan areas include ethnic neighborhoods that share features of what sociologists once called rural. Despite the ambiguities, differences in the two social contexts help explain why solutions to social problems in one do not transfer to the other.

Two concepts introduced by Ferdinand Tönnies toward the end of the nineteenth century offered sociologists a framework from which to make such comparisons. As discussed in Chapter 1, Tönnies (1887) proposed the terms *gemeinschaft* and *gesellschaft* to distinguish communities. *Gemeinschaft* refers to communities where human relationships are personal, citizens' worth is based more on who they are than what they do, the culture is relatively homogenous, and people have a strong attachment to each other and to the countryside. *Gesellschaft* describes communities where most people do not know one another well, worth is based on what people do and not who they are, the culture is heterogeneous, and people have relatively little attachment to each other or to the community.

Idyllic images of rural communities offer yet a second framework capturing what some feel is being lost in urbanization. Rural and urban people alike often assume a set of values found in rural cultures—honesty, fair play, trustworthiness, good neighborliness, helpfulness, sobriety, and clean living. These values are translated into a series of norms, such as leading a wholesome family life, acting in such a way that your word is as good as a written contract, being active in church, and being friendly to everyone. Some of these norms reflect the cultures of those who settled many of the communities. Others offer insight into values that support and maintain small communities.

What Tönnies was proposing parallels what the idyllic images suggest: Some rural communities develop a social context in which individuals are known. People in small towns often say they know just about everyone in town, meaning that they are at least familiar with everyone. In communities dominated by a single economic base, people not only know one another socially but typically know each other's daily routine.

This intimate social context makes it more likely that values such as honesty and neighborliness will be embraced. Behavior reflecting that your word is as good as a written contract responds to the ideal of honesty. In a practical way, however, honesty becomes even more compelling when both your actions and your words can be known by others. Helping your neighbors undoubtedly has roots in many cultures, but this norm also acknowledges that you too might need help one day. Being known alters the way in which people behave toward one another.

A second feature of the social context in many rural communities is that most members see the community as a whole, not as a series of separate institutions. In suburban settings, it is possible to have one set of friends at work, a second set at church, a third set in the neighborhood, and a fourth set through your child's school. Because there may be little overlap from one social context to another, people often think of their job, church, neighborhood, and school as separate institutions.

In smaller communities, there will be considerable overlap in these groups of friends. The overlap can be so extensive that it becomes difficult to distinguish between the community and its institutions. Efforts at school reform, for example, often fail when problems are expressed simply in terms of the school. In rural communities, the school and community are part of the same social fabric. School reform thus is more likely to succeed when the problems are expressed in terms of both school and community.

SOLIDARITY IN A COMMUNITY

What we call *solidarity* describes the extent to which a community offers its members a place in which to belong. A sense of solidarity emerges when the community offers a clear, well-focused set of values, beliefs, or goals with which their members identify. Athletic teams share clearly defined goals and a value system based on the need for teamwork. Labor unions often create solidarity through conflict in the form of labor demands or a strike against the company. Rural communities maintain solidarity through their culture, although outside threats or the need to mobilize community resources can sometimes offer common goals.

One indicator of solidarity is the extent to which a community shares a common identity, a "we-ness" that characterizes its members. This we-

Groups like the Irwin Rhythm Band contribute to the solidarity of a community (photo courtesy of the Ohio University Telecommunications Center).

ness can be reaffirmed in slogans or symbols integrated into community life. York, located in south-central Nebraska, refers to itself as "Where the Best Begins." Mascots chosen for schools often reflect a town's identity, such as the one derived from miners in West Virginia. Symbols of pine trees are carved into chairs, woven into curtains, glazed into pottery, or integrated into the architecture of logging towns in the Pacific Northwest. Some communities retain their ethnic identity. Lindsborg, Kansas, refers to itself as "Little Sweden," while Wilson calls itself the "Czech Capital of Kansas." Speech patterns or clothing styles can also establish a sense of common identity.

SACRED SYMBOLS

Although the slogans and symbols suggest a sense of common identity, it is the culture that underlies these symbols that is important. When members of the community have grown up within a common culture or have, over time, accepted a common set of values and norms, an even stronger sense of solidarity emerges. The community develops a set of sacred symbols that reflect its most strongly held values.

Sacred symbols are either concrete objects or abstract ideas that represent strongly held community values. The term *sacred* means that the symbol represents more than just the commonplace or everyday, so it is treated with reverence and respect. In this sense, a sacred symbol often evokes powerful emotional responses. The symbol, of course, represents something else, typically an ideal that is embraced by the entire community. Examples of sacred symbols might be the flag as a symbol of patriotism or the two-parent nuclear family as a symbol of social stability.

In Grovers Junction, teenage pregnancy challenges a sacred symbol. The townspeople see it as a moral defect in the young women who become pregnant. Having assumed that, they then build a model to explain the pattern of teenage pregnancies. Because the problem often persists in families, the moral defect is assumed to lie with the girls' families. These families are often poor; poverty therefore must also stem from moral shortcomings. Thus, families that are poor have moral shortcomings. Because of these moral shortcomings, girls from those families are more likely to be sexually active before marriage and thus more likely to get pregnant. Of course, this is not necessarily true. Sexually active girls from middle- or upper-class families are simply better able to prevent pregnancy or quietly get abortions.

Carol sees the problem differently, in part because the community from which she came did not attach the same significance to teenage pregnancy. Carol sees teenage pregnancy as a mistake, not a moral defect. She believes that the pattern of teenage pregnancy in certain families may arise from the instability created by poverty. Those who get pregnant in high school are not allowed to finish, so are limited to very low-paying jobs. This can make their homes unstable, making it more likely that a daughter will seek affection outside the home and risk becoming pregnant. The principal's decision to exclude pregnant teenagers from school in effect punishes rather than helps them. From Carol's perspective, the principal and those who support him are part of the problem.

The solutions a community is willing to accept depend on the way in which the problem is defined. Because the town sees teenage pregnancy as a moral problem, it is more likely to accept solutions offered through the local church.

Sacred symbols are important for several reasons. First, they do not emerge unless the solidarity of a community is relatively strong. Second, those who violate sacred symbols offer their community an opportunity to strengthen its solidarity as community members close ranks in condemning immoral behavior. Because teenage pregnancy is a sacred symbol, it is seen as more than an immoral choice made by an individual. It becomes a threat to the morality of the entire community.

DEVELOPING SOLIDARITY

A number of factors affect the extent to which a community can develop high solidarity and a strong sense of sacred symbols. A quick comparison of Grovers Junction with Valley View suggests obvious differences in community size as well as the stability and homogeneity of the population. These differences actually enable a sense of social equality and role homogeneity to operate, both of which are important to building solidarity in a community. We will examine each of these concepts separately and then look at how community size, stability, and homogeneity allow them to operate.

To some extent, solidarity depends on the absence of clearly defined distinctions within the community. Players on a football team have to believe that they are equally important to achieving success, even though some players are team leaders or others receive more media coverage. In order for community members to assume a collective identity, they must believe they are socially equal in theory if not in reality.

One of the features common to many rural cultures is the notion that their members are all "just plain folks." Everyone is socially equal. If differences exist, they are a matter of circumstance. Those who perform manual labor or work for others are seen to be aspiring to white-collar jobs or their own businesses. Those who have little money or few possessions are seen to be aspiring to the same economic comforts as others in the community enjoy.

Such equality seldom exists, but communities develop a set of strategies to protect the illusion. Those who are wealthy, for example, typically live and dress far more modestly than they might in an urban setting. In parts of the rural South, where class differences are a very real legacy of the economic structure, those in the privileged class typically use nicknames such as Bubba (diminutive for brother), Sonny, or Sissy (diminutive for sister). These nicknames are used to break down the social distance that exists because of economic status or power. Social cohesion is maintained in the face of very real discrepancies in wealth and power.

A sense of social equality helps, but ultimately people build a sense of solidarity through interactions with one another. When these interactions occur frequently and across several different settings, the potential for solidarity is increased. Sociologists refer to density of acquaintanceship and role homogeneity as variables that describe the frequency and character of social interactions.

Density of acquaintanceship describes the extent to which community members interact with one another on a regular, informal, and relatively personal basis. A high density of acquaintanceship might mean that everyone knows everyone else by name or that most community members see one another and visit on a weekly basis.

Role homogeneity refers to the extent to which people interact with one another across a wide variety of settings. In Grovers Junction, for example, teachers interact with one another regularly in other community organizations, at church, and in shopping. Carol the schoolteacher is also Carol the choir soprano, who is also Carol the president of the gourmet-cooking club. Because people see one another across a range of roles, they develop relationships with one another based on all these interactions.

These features—a sense of social equality, a high density of acquaintanceship, and role homogeneity—are important to establishing solidarity. Rural communities, in part because of their smaller size, offer environments in which these features are likely to emerge. Moreover, communities in which the population is relatively homogeneous are also more likely to share the same culture, a context that allows sacred symbols to develop. Many rural communities were settled by ethnic groups or over time developed a homogeneity often not present in larger communities.

Not all rural communities have solidarity; conversely, solidarity is not restricted to rural areas. Some sociologists suggest that a strong sense of solidarity exists in ethnic or minority neighborhoods of the inner city. The two criteria, small size and cultural homogeneity, can be met within a city although the city as a whole might not be at all cohesive. Rural communities undergoing rapid growth sometimes lose solidarity, at least for a time. What seems generally true is that the smaller size, greater homogeneity, and greater stability often found in rural areas make a sense of solidarity more likely.

BOUNDARY MAINTENANCE

When the solidarity of a community is strong, community members differentiate between those who are in the group and those who are outside it, between the "us" and the "them." Rural communities do this in several ways. In *Small Town in Mass Society*, Vidich and Bensman (1968) point out that Springdale's residents define themselves vis-à-vis city life. Cities are places where crime occurs, traffic is heavy, air is polluted, or people are separated from nature and the soil. Springdale is everything the city is not—safe, uncrowded, clean, moral. This may, in fact, not be true. Local newspapers sometimes reinforce idyllic images by not printing negative news.

Many rural communities take this differentiation a step further, declaring themselves to be different from nearby small towns as well. Springdale, for example, will argue that it is not just any small town. It is unique. Strategies or solutions that work in a neighboring town will not work in Springdale.

Efforts to differentiate between those in the group and those outside it are called *boundary maintenance*. In a sense, boundary maintenance is part of the process by which communities build solidarity. Defining what a community is not is just the opposite of describing what it is. Contrasting themselves with urban areas and characterizing the community as unique are community members' general strategies for erecting boundaries. The sanctions imposed on those who violate sacred symbols are the more specific strategies by which communities develop and assert a common identity.

CULTURAL CONFLICT WITHIN COMMUNITIES

Until now, the discussion has focused on solidarity and agreement within communities. Many rural communities are homogeneous and have developed a strong sense of solidarity. Despite this sense of common identity, diversity of opinion can and does exist. Conflict based on different sacred symbols is also not uncommon. Other rural communities are diverse, home to substantial differences in culture and values.

The character of conflict in rural communities differs from one community to the next. Mammoth Lakes, California, is the locus of sharp differences between environmentalists and developers. Those concerned with the environment favor no-growth or slow-growth policies. Others see the area's natural beauty as a resource to be developed and marketed. Eatonton, Georgia, embraces two cultures—one black, the other white. Overt conflict appears to be infrequent, but different values are clearly held by the two groups. McDowell County, West Virginia, has seen conflicts between unions and coal companies, among racial and ethnic groups, and between mountaineers and miners. Even in what appear to be culturally homogeneous agricultural communities, such as those in Illinois, cultural differences among ethnic groups contribute to different views of farming (see Box 3.1).

Although many of these conflicts have economic and class roots, most are also the result of cultural differences. When we examine rural communities carefully, we find that cultural differences are often as important as in urban cities and neighborhoods. If rural communities appear more homogeneous, it is perhaps because they are more effective in hiding or suppressing those differences.

Community Culture and Social Problems

As pointed out in earlier sections, a community's culture can affect how social problems are defined and what solutions are considered acceptable. Across rural areas, cultures can differ tremendously. Native American and Latino communities have maintained or are retrieving much of their cultural heritage despite the more dominant white culture. Even

BOX 3.1 GERMAN AND YANKEE CULTURES

In looking at Illinois farm communities, Sonya Salamon found that the structure of agriculture varied with the ethnic background of the families. Two cultures, those of the German and Yankee farmers, capture how values influence farming practices and community structures.

German farmers are yeomen, committed to the intergenerational transfer of farming. To ensure that at least one child stays in farming, parents assume responsibility for setting up a son (but not a daughter) in farming. They prefer land ownership to land rental, expanding their enterprises only enough to incorporate their sons. Consequently, farms are relatively small.

Because German farmers prefer family labor to borrowed capital, they engage in diversified crop and livestock agriculture. This style of farming uses both land and family labor most creatively. Children live on or near the farm. Education is not emphasized, but practical training is. Farmers retire early to make way for children to take over the farm. Loss of the family land through reckless investment is avoided at all costs.

By contrast, Yankee farmers are entrepreneurs. Their goal is to manage a well-run business that generates the highest possible short-term profit. Because there is intergenerational competition, sons must set themselves up in farming. Yankee farmers expand the size of their farming operation in order to make efficient use of their equipment. They purchase land only when interest rates or land prices make it profitable to do so. Otherwise, they rent land in order to expand production. Yankee farm operations are typically larger than average.

Yankee farmers produce grain crops, often with very little diversification. This style of farming relies upon equipment more than family labor. Parents expect children to learn most skills from school; thus education is emphasized. Farmers retire according to their own personal desires rather than when it might be most beneficial to a child who would want to take over the farm. Loss of land is considered a normal risk encountered in running a business.

These different orientations toward farming affect the character and stability of surrounding communities. For the German yeomen, the community is a central focus of their lives. The population is relatively stable. Churches are strong and play an important role in reinforcing ethnic values. Nonfarmers in the community are generally related to farmers. Both farmers and nonfarmers participate in community activities. All-community activities are common.

By contrast, Yankee communities tend to be less stable. Isolated communities are among those now facing a decline in population. Communities near urban areas have become bedroom communities. Consolidation of schools and of churches is more common. Most farmers are uninvolved with the community, focusing their energies instead on state and national issues that affect the profits of their farming operations. Nonfarmers are also relatively uninvolved in the community. All-community events are rarely held.

Both types of communities rely upon agriculture for their economic base. The different values embraced by the two cultures, however, influence the type of farming operation and the character of the community. Cultural values affect how individuals view the family, how the family views the economy, and how community is defined by both family and economic relationships.

Source: Sonya Salamon. 1985. "Ethnic Communities and the Structure of Agriculture." *Rural Sociology* 50:323–340.

within the white culture, however, differences exist. Some rural communities develop a stronger sense of solidarity and a set of sacred symbols. These further limit the response a community makes to a problem. This section explores features of rural communities that limit their capacity to understand and act on social problems.

TWO FACES OF CULTURE

The features of a rural culture described in the last section lead to both positive and negative images of community. A small town can be at once supportive, stable, and friendly, yet prejudiced, intolerant, and rejecting. The solidarity that offers community members a sense of belonging also demands a certain amount of conformity. Boundary-maintenance activities strengthen solidarity but make newcomers feel like outsiders, at least for a time. What some find caring and intimate, others find judgmental and stifling. The very features that some describe in positive terms, others characterize in negative terms.

To some extent, this duality reflects societal views of rural communities that have changed over time. At the turn of this century, most people came from rural towns. Early descriptions of urban communities were often negative, and people decried the loss of community as most of them knew it. During the first half of the century, urbanization took hold; the population gradually became urban, viewing cities as liberating and a way to release people from socially static small towns. Descriptions of rural communities often became decidedly negative, as were the stereotypes of rural people. In the 1950s, rural areas were rediscovered when research suggested that people were once again seeking a sense of place or social connectedness.

In fact, the very characteristics that make rural communities appealing also block change or limit the choices communities consider in dealing with social issues. A few examples will illustrate some of the problems.

EXTERNALIZATION OF PROBLEMS

The whole process by which solidarity is maintained often makes it easier for communities to unite against outside threats than to acknowledge internal problems. As stated earlier, a sense of solidarity emerges when the community develops a sense of "we," an image of itself based on a set of common values and beliefs. Efforts to identify and resolve problems locally run the risk of reducing solidarity. People will have different views on what the problem is and how the community should address it. Moreover, the integrated social networks in which people function make individuals more susceptible to community controls. Thus, it is much safer to define problems as being externally caused. Local people, by the very nature of solidarity and how it is maintained, would risk too much in identifying problems.

Because of this risk, most rural communities find it much easier to organize against something from the outside. They might organize against suspicious newcomers or outside political interests. Rural communities often unite against government regulations or programs, whether they be nuclear-waste dumps, fluoridation of water, medical-waste incinerators, mandatory kindergarten, or inappropriately conceived farm programs. Organizing to protect against the "they" enables the "we" to remain intact. In essence, communities externalize their problems, identifying something outside the community as being responsible for the problem.

This feature of rural cultures explains why outsiders were needed during the civil rights movement of the 1960s. At that time, wealth and status were both distributed on the basis of race throughout the South. Solidarity and role homogeneity made it impossible for blacks or sympathetic whites to challenge the existing social structure. What were then called "outside agitators" came into communities and challenged this structure. Once the threat presented itself, local people could become involved. These individuals were generally independent of the white power structure—ministers of black churches who were supported by black congregations, for example.

The need to maintain community solidarity yet acknowledge problems poses a real dilemma for small communities. In some cases, such as the civil rights movement, outside agitators may be the only answer. States can also act as outside agitators when they threaten intervention if communities do not remedy certain conditions. In many cases, however, communities can and should develop strategies that enable them to explore problems safely. Needs assessments conducted by outside facilitators or planning processes that enable problems to emerge in a less emotional context may be effective.

ROLE HOMOGENEITY AND LIMITS ON CONTROVERSY

One of the features associated with rural communities is role homogeneity, the extent to which people interact with one another across many roles. High role homogeneity limits not only the extent to which individuals deviate from community norms but also the degree of controversy that can develop within the community itself. Grovers Junction gives us an example of how this happens.

Carol is concerned about the many teenage pregnancies because they in turn result in an increased dropout rate among girls in Grovers Junction. Other teachers in the high school share her concerns. She soon learns that in-school daycare and sex-education programs will anger many community members. What influences whether she and the other teachers go public with their concerns? Ultimately, the many roles each person plays in the community's social structure affects the teachers' actions.

Carol is a member of the choir of the local Methodist church. The choir director organizes local revivals and has taken a strong public stand against sex education in the schools. Carol's husband, Buddy, has just taken over his father's clothing store. The choir director is one of his regular customers. Buddy will soon need a loan to expand his sportswear division. The choir director's husband is the vice-president in charge of business loans at the only bank in town. Both couples are part of a gourmet-cooking club that meets monthly; the club is one of the few forms of recreation for young professional couples in town. In the summer, both husbands play on their church's slow-pitch softball team. To top it off, Carol's son is dating the choir director's daughter; they plan to go to the junior prom.

High role homogeneity means that more is at stake than Carol's position as schoolteacher. When an issue touches a sacred symbol, community members tend to see it only in moral terms. Carol's stand on sex-education programs and in-school daycare would violate a sacred symbol. Some community members would respond by questioning Carol's moral integrity. In a very real sense, Carol might jeopardize her family's social life and certainly could cost her husband's clothing store some business. Moreover, she puts some of her own social relationships at risk. Because of high role homogeneity, some rural communities simply gloss over or ignore controversy.

The fact that Carol does not express her point of view publicly does not mean she does not hold strong points of view. Regardless of where people live, they can hold strong points of view. The low role homogeneity often found in urban areas means that individuals will not endanger their whole social network by articulating those views. This does not mean that urban people are more courageous than rural people. It means that they have less to risk because they are not part of the close cultural web that exists in most small towns.

Low role homogeneity does not ensure that local problems will be addressed. There are rural towns in which community members do not relate to one another across several roles. In fact, those living in communities near metropolitan areas often spend a great deal of time commuting to the city and thus may not even know their neighbors. They may belong to few local community organizations and do only limited shopping in the town. In these cases, the low community solidarity results in problems simply being ignored.

The extent to which role homogeneity can suppress controversy limits community options. Newspapers sometimes avoid publishing information on the problem, and the lack of facts makes it difficult for community members to examine all sides of an issue. Individuals are often reluctant to step forward and offer leadership for discussions. Because open discussion cannot occur, alternate ways of defining or solving a problem do not emerge. When problems are finally acknowledged publicly, towns often become deeply divided.

Ruralness does not ensure role homogeneity or high role density, but it does contribute to these characteristics. The ability to analyze this factor and understand the strengths and weaknesses is an important part of understanding how communities can recognize and develop strategies for solving social problems.

NEGATIVE IMPACTS OF SACRED SYMBOLS

For many, a small town provides a sense of belonging that comes from its solidarity. You know the local pharmacist because he is also a member of the Kiwanis Club. He knows the members of your family because he has filled their prescriptions since you were a child. This sense of social and family connectedness helps you feel at ease when you need medicine in the middle of the night.

If you develop problems that violate sacred symbols, however, community solidarity becomes a threat to you. If the medication you need is for a sexually transmitted disease or for a mental illness, the moral judgements invoked by these illnesses make it dangerous to approach the local pharmacist. Those who lost their farms during the farm crisis speak of feeling they had been labeled failures by their neighbors. Those with limited reading skills fear participating in a literacy program because they would be labeled stupid. In short, sacred symbols and high solidarity can be as threatening to those with a problem as they are supportive to those in need.

Issues that might be considered narrow in an urban community become questions of moral worth in a rural community. For example, in the Red River Valley of North Dakota and Minnesota, sugar beet farmers are engaged in a feud with grain farmers. The grain farmers run smaller operations, require less capital, and see sugar beet farming as detrimental to the environment. They label sugar beet farmers as immoral and proceed to label others based on which side they support. How one stands on sugar beets then determines where one fits into the community on other questions. The tendency to ascribe moral character or worth as the result of a single behavior or opinion creates labels. Those labels then limit the extent to which community members can really know one another's true feelings about complex issues.

Expanding the Options

When Carol moved from Valley View to Grovers Junction, she changed community cultures. Solutions to the problem of teen pregnancy seen as acceptable in Valley View were quickly rejected in Grovers Junction. Carol's experience was not unique. Efforts to address problems or initiate change can often meet opposition in rural communities. The very features that make rural communities inviting places to live also make them seem unforgiving.

The more stereotypically rural a community is in terms of cultural and role homogeneity, the fewer options it may allow itself in defining and resolving social problems. When a problem is defined to be a personal moral failing, the community in effect decides that it bears no responsibility in solving it. When the solution is to punish the deviant, the community runs the risk that the problem will persist. Excluding teenage mothers from school, for example, makes it more difficult for them to gain the education needed to support their children. Making those with limited literacy skills feel they are stupid simply decreases the likelihood that they will seek help. The intergenerational effects of illiteracy are now well documented. Responses such as these tend to limit options—for the community as well as for the individual.

Rural communities and social service providers have found a variety of ways of coping with this dilemma. For some social problems, the simplest solution is to develop strategies that protect confidentiality. Rural people may drive 100 miles to the next mental health clinic rather than seek services within the community. Literacy providers locate their programs in community centers that people are likely to be visiting for a variety of purposes. The limits to such an approach are obvious, however, when the problem is teen pregnancy.

In the long run, rural communities need to understand how to exploit the strengths of community solidarity yet minimize its inherent weaknesses. Some rural churches, for example, took a careful look at their response to the farm crisis. Instead of simply blaming individual farmers for poor management skills, they developed programs to inform community members of the many external factors that were also contributing to farm failures. Such a response not only reduced the social stigma felt by farm families but mobilized community resources in support of those in need of help. Many families still lost their farms, but they did not lose their communities as well. Some families have gone on to make contributions to the community in ways other than farming. Choosing to look at a problem from more than one perspective opened up the options the community saw.

With the growth of mass society has come the impression that the power of the community for maintaining social control and transmitting social values has declined. This is true in some cases, but it is not uniformly true. In many parts of rural America, strong interactions within a community, often based on family, continue to have enormous impacts. The next chapter explores the concept of legacy.

Chapter Summary

Culture is the shared products of society, consisting of values, norms, and material culture. Values are the shared notions within a culture about what is right and wrong. Norms are the specific rules that govern how we behave. Material culture consists of the objects created by people and used in daily life. The culture of a community is derived from the culture brought by those who settled the land, the environmental setting in which the community lies, and its economic base.

Socialization is the process by which we learn a culture. It takes place within a community's social organizations, such as the family, school, and church. Known as agents of culture, these organizations provide the opportunity for social interactions that enable a child to learn how things are done within the culture. Agents of culture can be used to preserve the past or work toward social change.

Communities differ in terms of the solidarity felt among members. Solidarity emerges when the community offers a clear, well-focused set of values, beliefs, or goals with which their members identify. Factors important to establishing community solidarity include a sense of social equality among community members, a high density of acquaintanceship (frequent opportunities to interact), and role homogeneity (frequent interactions across a wide variety of situations). When community solidarity is high, communities develop a set of sacred symbols that reflect their most strongly held values. They also begin to differentiate between themselves and other communities through what is called boundary maintenance.

A community's culture can affect how social problems are defined and what solutions are considered acceptable. Communities with high solidarity often externalize problems—they define problems to be externally caused and then unite against the external agent. They may also define problems as individual rather than social. Such a definition allows the community to ignore the problem and instead insist that individuals solve their own problems. High role homogeneity and sacred symbols often limit the willingness of individuals to express sharp differences of opinion. The problem faced by many rural communities is to develop strategies that enable them to exploit the strengths of community solidarity yet limit the extent to which features of solidarity block meaningful responses to social problems.

Key Terms

Agents of culture are the social organizations through which people develop their personality and learn their culture. Examples include the family, schools, and churches.

Boundary maintenance describes a series of strategies by which community members differentiate between themselves and others.

Culture is the shared products of society, including the ideas, norms, and material objects that describe how people handle daily tasks and make sense of their experiences.

Density of acquaintanceship describes the frequency with which community members interact with one another on a personal basis.

Norms are the shared guidelines for acceptable behavior.

Role homogeneity describes the extent to which community members interact with one another across a wide variety of social settings.

Sacred symbols are either concrete objects or abstract ideas that represent commonly held community values.

Socialization is the process of social interaction through which people develop their personality and learn their culture.

Solidarity is the sense of common identity or commitment to common goals shared by individuals.

Values are the shared beliefs about what is right or wrong, desirable or undesirable.

References

Bierstedt, R. 1963. *The Social Order*. New York: McGraw-Hill.

Billings, D. 1990. "Religion as Opposition: A Gramscian Approach." *American Journal of Sociology* 96(1): 1–31.

McNeley, J. K. 1975. *A History of Ramah Navajo Education: Notes from the Ramah Files, 1930–1952*. Ramah, AZ: Ramah Navajo School Board, Inc.

Sher, J., and R. B. Tompkins. 1977. "Economy, Efficiency and Equality: The Myths of Rural School and District Consolidation." Pp. 41–42 in J. P. Sher (ed.), *Education in Rural America*. Boulder, CO: Westview.

Tönnies, Ferdinand. [1887] 1963. *Community and Society*. Trans. and ed. by C. P. Loomis. New York: Harper & Row.

Vidich, A. J., and J. Bensman. 1968. *Small Town in Mass Society*. Rev. ed. Princeton, NJ: Princeton University Press.

4

Legacy and Social Class

d
ave and Rosemary glared at each other. There had been some heated discussions around the dinner table recently. Dave opposes the local school bond. He is trying to save money in order to buy land, so he doesn't want property taxes to increase. Rosemary believes that the quality of the school must be maintained, so wants the school bond to pass.

Dave Stitz and Rosemary Turner met while in college. Dave was a fourth-generation farmer, the first family member to go to college. Rosemary's father was a county agent, her mother a school teacher. Dave and Rosemary married the day after graduation and moved to the Stitz family farm. Dave works the fields with his father, while Rosemary runs the custom seed business they started. In order to understand their different positions on the school bond issue, however, we need to look further back in time.

Ever since Dave Stitz could remember, he knew he was going to be a farmer. His great-grandparents came to western Kansas in the early 1900s by covered wagon. His grandmother married the son of a local farmer. By expanding their farm gradually, they acquired enough land for Dave's father. One of four children, Dave's father would be left with only one-fourth of the land when his parents died. That was not enough to pass on to Dave. So acquiring more land became a high priority.

Dave's parents bought more land during the expansive times of the 1970s, even though the land was priced higher than it could ever yield in crops. While Dave was in high school, land prices suddenly dropped, and the family struggled to make payments on their loans. Dave quit the football team in order to help out on the farm after school. His mother took a job as school cook in a nearby town, and his father worked hard with local bankers to refinance the farm. By making sacrifices, they were able to keep the farm. Dave had to pay his own way through college, however.

Despite the struggle, the effort was worth it to Dave's parents. The farm was their legacy to their child. They had provided him with the best set of tools they knew for a happy and productive life: access to land and the willingness to work hard at making that land productive.

Rosemary was the daughter of a county agent, so was no stranger to farming. Her parents had never made much money in their jobs. From the day Rosemary was born, however, they had put aside money for her college fund. They felt that the most important thing they could give their daughter was a college education. They, too, were thinking of legacy. A college education would enable Rosemary to support herself and maintain a comfortable way of life.

Given this background, it seems less surprising that Dave and Rosemary are on different sides of the school bond issue. Dave's parents certainly supported education. When hard choices had to be made, however, they emphasized the need to acquire land. By contrast, Rosemary's parents put a college education above everything else. In their reactions to the school bond issue, Dave and Rosemary are simply reflecting and continuing the legacies bequeathed them.

Both Dave's and Rosemary's parents gave them what they valued most—land and education. Like most parents, they were concerned that their children be able to earn a good living. As the example illustrates, however, what parents believe they should pass on varies from one family to another. This chapter examines legacy, the social and economic factors that contribute to the legacy a parent leaves, and how these factors are affected by issues of gender, race, and ethnicity.

Legacy in Transition

How does a family come to value one future over another—land over education, for example? What parents believe they should pass on to their children depends to a large extent on what the parents' experiences have been. These experiences depend on a number of features, among them the economy and the options the economy presents to individuals. Thus, legacy and the economy are closely connected.

LEGACY AND THE ECONOMY

We normally think of legacy as the money or property bequeathed to someone through a will, typically what parents leave their children. In reality, parents leave more than just material goods to their children. They

Legacy of the past (photo courtesy of The Permanent Art Collection, Kansas State University).

leave behind a set of values or behaviors that in turn affect the choices their children make. As used here, the term *legacy* has this broader meaning. *Legacy* is what parents seek to pass on to their children, including material possessions as well as values and norms.

From the parents' perspective, legacy is the tools needed for survival. Dave's parents saw land ownership as key to Dave's future in farming. Consequently, they were willing to risk nearly everything to ensure that Dave had that tool for survival. Rosemary's parents had never owned land, at least not beyond their house and the property on which it was located. Both had made a living based on their education. Thus, they scrimped and saved in order to ensure that Rosemary left home equipped with the tool that had been most valuable to them.

In a very real sense, then, legacy depends on the economy and the options the economy creates for families. Other factors, such as social class, race, or gender, further influence those options, as discussed later. Examined first, however, are two broad patterns of legacy created by changes in the national economy.

SETTLEMENT AND THE INDEPENDENT ENTREPRENEUR

Until the last quarter of the nineteenth century, the United States was committed to the Jeffersonian ideal that citizens should become owners of a farm or small commercial or manufacturing enterprise. Labor, including wage labor, was valued in terms of its capacity to improve the opportunity for an individual to become economically independent. Those who worked for wages typically saved as much money as possible in order to invest in property that would allow them to become independent producers.

This ideal of individual business ownership was reinforced by the opportunities created as new lands were opened and communities created. Many rural communities were originally settled by people who wanted to establish their own farms or small businesses. Even people who moved into a community as wage laborers, such as cowboys on the western frontier, miners in the Great Lakes region, and loggers in the Pacific Northwest, often took such work to earn the capital they needed to invest in their own business venture. People saw the possibility of eventually becoming independent business owners, either producing goods and services or distributing them to others in the community. They planned their life course and that of their children around those goals.

CORPORATE PRODUCTION AND THE WAGE EARNER

As lands were settled and communities stabilized, the character of production changed. Goods and services needed by more mature farms and communities could not be produced within small businesses. At the same time, local economies began developing stronger linkages to national and international markets.

These changes created a number of problems for owners of small businesses. As more complex production processes were developed, the capital needed for business start-ups increased beyond that typically available within the family. Linkages with national and international markets increased the risk assumed by a business. Businesses found themselves unable to control supply and demand for their products and thus might earn high profits one year and suffer substantial losses the next. Small production companies were especially vulnerable to market fluctuations.

In response to these changes, businesses gradually became larger. The problem of acquiring enough capital could be solved if several individuals pooled their financial resources or companies sold stock to the public. Companies adopted a variety of strategies to reduce the risk of market fluctuations. Some specialized in the production of single products and attempted to obtain a significant market share, while others diversified product lines.

In resolving the problems created by a changing economy, larger companies also changed the options parents saw open to their children.

Large companies required large labor forces. People were drawn increasingly into the labor markets of urban centers, and as they joined the ranks of the employed, they left behind most hopes for self-employment and independence. The legacy parents passed on to their children, then, became a set of values and behaviors consistent with getting and keeping a job with a large corporation. In rural communities, this legacy often included the belief that children would have to leave a rural setting in order to find work.

Stratification and Social Class

Differences in the type of economy, such as the entrepreneurial or corporate economies, do explain some of the differences we observe in legacy. The skills and attitudes needed to run a business are quite different from those people use in working for a large corporation. Within a given economy, however, differences in legacy continue to exist. Some of these differences arise from what we call social stratification and the result of it, social class.

In many social groups, including communities, resources are not distributed equally among their members. Some individuals have more prestige, power, or wealth than others. Sociologists disagree on how this unequal distribution takes place. Some sociologists argue that it occurs because what some people do is more important to society than what other people do. Others argue that it is not functional importance that gives some people more resources than others, but differential power. They say that certain groups have more power than others and use that power to maintain a higher position in a group or society. Both sets of sociologists agree that in U.S. society, those on top tend to have more income, wealth, power, and prestige. Other characteristics, such as age, sex, ethnicity, race, and religion, are associated with different positions in the hierarchy.

Sociologists have explored social class from a variety of perspectives. Two approaches offer complementary views useful in understanding how social class affects the character of rural legacies. One examines how social class is influenced by the way in which individuals make their living. The second looks more closely at issues of status, power, and prestige.

MARXIAN PERSPECTIVES

Writing during the industrial revolution of the nineteenth century, Karl Marx defined social class in terms of the economy. In order to understand his perspective, however, we need to look first at how a business functions and how individuals within that business accumulate wealth.

The goal of any business is to make money. Profit essentially represents the difference between the price of the product sold and its production cost, including the cost of capital, materials, and labor. Business owners receive the profits, either directly as proprietors or indirectly through dividends paid to investors. Those who own the business, then, accumulate wealth through business profits over which they have some control.

Those who sell their labor to the company, who work for the company, receive a wage in return. Only rarely do they receive part of the profits, as in a cooperative or in an employee stock ownership plan (ESOP). Consequently, they accumulate wealth through their labor and the savings it generates. Their bargaining power with business owners is based on their ability to make their labor scarce. They either acquire skills and knowledge that are in demand or collectively threaten to withhold their labor, through labor unions or employee associations.

Given this difference in the capacity to accumulate wealth, Marx identified two social classes: capitalists and proletarians. Those who own the means of production (the factories or offices) make up the *capitalist* class. Those who sell their labor for wages form the working class, or *proletarians*. Marx also identified a part of the capitalist class that he called the *petty bourgeoisie*. This class includes small shopkeepers and farmers— individuals who owned the means of production, managed the firms themselves, and often used family labor alone or family labor combined with hired labor. Marx saw the petty bourgeoisie as a remnant of the preindustrial economy. Consequently, he expected it to disappear entirely once the transition to the industrial age was complete.

We have now moved through the industrial age and beyond, leading some sociologists to revise Marx's early theory. As corporations grew increasingly larger, sociologists saw a class of people emerge that fit somewhere between the capitalist and proletariat classes. Called the *managerial class*, this group includes managers or professionals within businesses or who serve businesses, as well as public-sector managers. These individuals do not own the means of production, yet they enjoy more autonomy and control over the work environment than do members of the proletariat (Wright 1985).

A second modification is that the petty-bourgeoisie class has not disappeared. There was a substantial decline of small-business owners and farmers in most industrialized nations, but the numbers have recently begun increasing again. In the United States, for example, self-employment fell from nearly 42 percent of the work force in 1880 to just under 10 percent in 1973. Since the mid-1970s, however, this class has grown slightly. Steinmetz and Wright (1989) attribute this growth to two factors: First, industrial firms are beginning to downsize, subcontracting work out to smaller businesses. Second, employment is shifting to the service sector

TABLE 4.1 Social Class as Defined by Relation to the Means of Production

	Owns Business	*Hires Labor*	*Sells Own Labor*	*Provides Own Management*	*Legacy to Children*
Capitalist	Yes	Yes	No	Maybe[a]	Property (Firm/Securities)
Petty bourgeoisie	Yes	No	No	Yes	Property (Business/Land)
Managers, salaried professionals, and officials	No	No	Yes	Yes	Education
Proletarian	No	No	Yes	No	Hard Work and Discipline

[a]Those who are rentier capitalists manage their portfolios, not the firm in which they have interest. Entrepreneurial capitalists have a role in managing the firm (see Steinmetz and Wright, 1989: 979).

of the economy, a sector that consists primarily of smaller businesses. Thus, sociologists have concluded that the petty bourgeoisie is an integral part of the class system in this postindustrial age.

Today, Marx's perspective produces a description of four major classes, two of which own the means of production and two of which do not (Table 4.1). At the top are those who own the means of production and buy the labor of others. The middle, often called the middle class, includes two groups. The first consists of those who own the means of production but neither buy nor sell their labor, the petty bourgeoisie. Those in the second group in the middle class, professionals and managers, sell their labor but have some autonomy in their jobs. At the bottom are those who do not own the means of production, can survive only by selling their labor, and have little job autonomy.

WEBERIAN PERSPECTIVES

Marx defined social class in economic terms, but some sociologists have argued that other factors are equally important in defining social class. Writing in the late nineteenth and early twentieth century, Max Weber argued that people are also stratified by prestige, social status, and power.

Social stratification is the division of people into layers, or strata, based on a series of attributes. From the Weberian perspective, *social class* then describes the various layers. Social stratification seems to be a feature of all societies. What differs is the extent to which the system is open or closed. Closed systems are ones in which members are not free to move from one class to another. Open systems allow individuals and families to move across layers. *Social mobility* is the term used to describe the movement of an individual from one layer to another, either up or down.

In an effort to explore this theory, W. Lloyd Warner and Paul Lunt conducted interviews with community residents in Newburyport, Massachusetts (Warner and Lunt 1941; Warner et al. 1949). Warner defined social classes to be status groups having rankings defined by members of the community. In order to belong to a particular class, a family had to be accepted by members of that status group and participate regularly in their activities. By asking community members to rank individuals and identify groups that share common activities, Warner and Lunt were able to identify six classes—an upper and a lower stratum for each of the upper, middle, and lower classes.

The difference between Warner's concept of social class and Marx's earlier notion is important. In defining social class in terms of whether or not individuals own the means of production, Marx linked social class to something that could be seen objectively. Warner introduced a subjective component to social class, arguing that a part of what we call social class depends on people's opinions (Warner and Lunt 1941). Warner's work showed a general correspondence between economic position and status group. He argued, however, that economic position was not sufficient to define social class. An individual's membership in a social class must be crystallized through social acceptance by and participation in that status group.

Rural Legacies and Social Class

In preparing for their children's future, parents typically work toward three goals—a place to live, a means by which to earn a living, and personal fulfillment. In one sense, legacy stands at the intersection between what parents have achieved in their own lives relative to these goals and what parents see as possible for their children to achieve. As shown in Table 4.1, social class (as defined in Marxian terms) affects the legacy parents pass on to their children. However, there are more subtle gradations in legacy based on income, education, and associated power and prestige. This section examines the three legacy goals, how they have been affected by economic change in rural areas, and how they vary with social class.

Legacy is discussed here in terms of four rural class groupings derived from both Marxian and Weberian perspectives. The first group is independent entrepreneurs, the members of the petty bourgeoisie who manage their own businesses, hiring no one or only a small number of workers.

The second group is the so-called managerial class, which includes managers, professionals, and government officials—individuals who work for others but who have some degree of job autonomy. In Weberian terms, the managerial class and the independent entrepreneurs would be considered the rural middle class. The third group described is the working class, the upper-lower class. The fourth group is the poor, or lower-lower class. Those in poverty have much in common with the rest of the working class. Unstable, low-paying jobs and limited education lead to legacies that are different from those shared in working-class families, however.

Missing, of course, is the capitalist (Marxist terminology) or upper-class (Weberian terminology) families, however. Large capitalist firms are important in many rural areas. Examples include mining firms such as Pittston Coal, timber companies like Weyerhauser, industrial firms such as Sara Lee/Hanes, or retail merchandising firms such as Wal-Mart. Despite their importance, owners or principal investors in these firms typically live in metropolitan areas. Consequently, this class is quite small numerically and not treated in this discussion.

Given the diversity found in rural communities, let alone among families, it is impossible to generalize about legacies without seeming to stereotype. The discussion that follows is intended to show in very broad terms how parental legacies vary because of social class. Within each social class, however, there are wide variations. Consequently, it would be erroneous to assume that the descriptions apply equally to all rural people in a given social class.

INDEPENDENT ENTREPRENEURS

As described earlier, rural communities were settled by people who expected to run their own business—people we now call independent entrepreneurs. These businesses are often family businesses and make up a higher percentage of the work force in rural communities than in metropolitan areas.

Independent entrepreneurs are the backbone for the Jeffersonian view of the ideal society described earlier. That ideology promotes attitudes of industriousness, self-improvement, and optimism. People expressing these attitudes presumably work hard to attain long-term goals of economic mobility. Work is pursued with great personal sacrifice, oriented to improvement of self and family and to the accumulation of wealth. Wealth, however, is generally not sought for its own sake or for the consumption of luxury goods and services. Instead, wealth is needed to acquire or develop an independent business. Thus, attitudes of industriousness, self-improvement, and optimism lead to behavior oriented to economic activity, which in turn generates wealth.

The legacy these parents have for their children is influenced directly by the resources they have accumulated. Parents work hard to invest in farms or businesses. These in turn provide employment and housing for their children as well as a source of social status within the community. All the hard work is considered an investment in their children's future as well as their own. Dave Stitz's father had acquired land for Dave; it seems only natural that Dave is now acquiring land for a son yet to be born.

For those who farm or operate small businesses in rural communities, the three legacy goals are combined in a single place. A place to live is often part of the means by which a family makes its living. Consequently, houses are valued for their use, worth maintaining for long-term use by the family and community. Personal fulfillment comes from the family business and involvement in the local community. Consequently, the connection between legacy and place is enormously strong. When that legacy is blocked, as it was for many farm families during the 1980s, the loss can be especially difficult to accept.

Socialization, both within the family and through other institutions, involves this close association with place as well. Values such as industriousness, self-improvement, and optimism are certainly important to any business. Parents also develop a set of skills important to running their business and being accepted within a community. Although the knowledge important to running a business may transfer to other communities, understanding how to run a business in a single town may be specific to that town's culture. Consequently, knowledge important to economic survival in a given community is passed from parent to child.

MANAGERIAL CLASS

Throughout this century, the possibilities for acquiring land or starting new businesses in rural communities have become more limited. Farms have become larger, requiring substantial capital investment. Rural businesses have been linked increasingly to expansive national corporations. Consequently, parents are less likely to pass along a means of production to their children. More people have begun selling their labor in order to survive economically.

The managerial class includes those who sell their labor but retain some autonomy in their work. Rural communities have always collectively purchased the labor of certain professionals, such as ministers and teachers. Although these individuals did not necessarily earn much, they enjoyed the respect of the community. Then as manufacturing grew and people began purchasing more services, the need for managers also increased. Large manufacturing plants and service industries have become major employers, requiring managers and administrators to regulate the labor of workers and clerks. For the most part, these managers are relatively well paid.

These salaried managers and professionals share some characteristics with those who own the means of production. They have a high degree of autonomy on the job. They not only make decisions that affect others but they determine the schedule and content of their own work. This autonomy in turn reinforces self-esteem and enhances the value of independence and decisionmaking ability. Consequently, the most important legacy middle-class parents impart to their children is the ability to command a high price for their labor, based on the credentials they earn through formal education.

For Rosemary Turner's parents, who are themselves salaried professionals, education substitutes for the transmission of material wealth. Their approach parallels that of many others in this social class—they encouraged Rosemary and her siblings to do well in school, helping them with their homework and challenging them to question and discuss issues with teachers. Independent thought is valued as part of the education process and a trait important to making management decisions. The Turners believe they succeeded because of their education; thus they believe their children's hope for satisfaction also lies through higher education. These families struggle to save money for their children to attend college.

Families like the Turners expect that their children will become part of a regional or national labor force. To an extent, legacy is location-free. Parents are committed to and actively involved in the local school system, with the goal of assuring their children the preparation needed for college. Some parents are still able to pass on their house to a child, often a home they had paid for over many years. Independent entrepreneurs often have lived in their place of business—the farm or next to the store. For many in the managerial class, though, buying a home becomes an investment made for its exchange value. In contrast to the independent entrepreneur, however, for them the three legacy goals—a place to live, a means by which to earn a living, and personal fulfillment—are no longer linked together by a place.

WORKING CLASS

The growth of manufacturing and service industries in rural areas also increased the working class, those who sell their labor but have little autonomy or control over their work. Textile mills in the South, garment and shoe factories in New England, lumber camps in the Northwest and the upper Great Lakes, and the mines in various parts of the country all employed large numbers of workers. Many went to work in these industries with the hope of saving enough to open their own businesses. Some eventually succeeded. Others, however, found that the low wages and high expenses involved in living in mill towns, mining towns, or lumber camps made saving difficult. A strong labor movement later increased wages in some of these industries, especially mining and timber. Wages and business start-up costs rose to the point that workers could not afford to quit and start their own businesses. Many settled into depending on wages for their livelihood, and their children have continued that tradition.

In most cases, these jobs require skills that are learned on the job rather than through formal education. In some cases, such as mining or logging, workers receive substantially higher wages than those with jobs requiring a college education, such as teachers. Consequently, there is little incentive to invest in education. Eager to earn money for personal use or to help the family with debts, young people go to work at an early age. Homes are not purchased for their resale value but as a secure place to live. Because seasonal layoffs or changing patterns in national and international markets often make employment unstable, families seek security through home ownership.

Those in the working class value different characteristics in their children. Children still need to learn how to work hard. Instead of wanting their children to learn how to make independent decisions, however, working-class parents want their children to be able to follow orders. Parents who work in the mines and the mills know how easy it is to be fired for saying the wrong thing or not working hard enough or fast enough. In contrast to middle-class parents, who are more concerned that their children reason independently (Kohn 1963; Kohn and Sholler 1983), working-class parents want their children to conform to externally imposed rules. Thus, the most important legacy working-class parents believe they can give their children is discipline, not creativity.

For workers whose jobs depend on natural resources, legacy is often tied to a sense of place. In the early days, those in logging or fishing simply moved on when they tired of a particular job. Other jobs were always waiting, sometimes for better wages. The introduction of unions increased the wages paid in these jobs substantially, but at a cost to worker mobility. Those in McDowell County, West Virginia, have become second- or third-generation mineworkers or steelworkers. Their investments, in homes for example, are tied to a place. When the local economy declines, the value of their homes decline, making it impossible to recover the cash needed to relocate. Consequently, most workers try to weather periodic economic downturns and layoffs. Like independent entrepreneurs, those in the rural working class often see legacy and place as strongly connected. The loss of an industry can mean the loss of all three legacy goals.

THE POOR

Some working-class jobs in rural areas involve very low-skilled work. These jobs are unstable, low-paying, part-time or seasonal and sometimes require migration. The wage earned does not depend on a worker's skills but rather on the supply of workers willing to take the job. Because supply almost always exceeds demand, the state's minimum wage becomes the maximum wage for this group. In many cases, these individuals see little chance of accumulating enough money to buy their own businesses or homes. Particularly for seasonal or migrant workers, children are often needed to work in the fields to ensure survival of the family from one season to the next. Thus, education is sporadic. Most young people drop out before completing high school.

Little is known about poor parents' aspirations for their children because few studies have been conducted. It appears that parents see inner discipline as less important because keeping a job depends more on the labor supply or an employer's whim than on individual behavior. Those who are poor often feel they have little control over their environment. They perceive, often correctly, that hard work does not lead to wealth or high self-esteem. People are often pessimistic about their children's prospect for the future and may feel unable to influence children positively. The legacies they desire to give to their children are modest: finding steady work and staying out of trouble.

In contrast to the stereotype that poor people are lazy and do not want to work, a substantial number of the rural poor are among the working poor. Of those who were not ill, disabled, or retired in 1987, 70 percent of the rural poor worked all or part of the year. Even with full-time, year-round work, more than 42.1 percent of all nonmetropolitan workers currently below the poverty line would not earn a wage sufficient to keep a family of four out of poverty (Shapiro 1989). Given these statistics, it is difficult to argue that hard work necessarily leads to economic stability. The legacy passed on by the working poor is, in many respects, an accurate representation of the society they have experienced.

Transmitting Legacy

Like culture, legacy is transferred from one generation to another through social institutions. Institutions that control the means of production, provide education, reinforce values, or support personal connections all influence the legacy handed down. This section looks briefly at two of the institutions, the family and the schools.

Legacy bridges the past and the future (photo by Jan L. Flora).

FAMILY INFLUENCE ON LEGACY

Families are, of course, the primary means by which legacies are transferred. Parents exert a great deal of influence over the values their children adopt, the sense of self-esteem and self-worth with which children face the tasks of growing to adulthood, and the opportunities available to them. As described earlier, these legacies are a link between what parents have achieved and what they see as possible for their children. To some extent, however, these legacies also depend on whether parents expect their children to remain in the community.

Rural families are deeply affected by the opportunity structure present in their community. If parents expect or want their children to stay in the local community, then they are very much aware of the job opportunities and class structures within the community. The legacies they pass on to their children often perpetuate existing class structures and certainly reflect parents' experience in the workplace.

If parents expect their children to leave, the legacy passed on may be very different. Middle-class parents, who are managers or professionals, emphasize education. Working-class families desirous of seeing their children achieve a better life also emphasize education, realizing that job opportunities, class structures, or both will require that their children leave the community in order to achieve more. Those in declining farm communities or in manufacturing communities such as Eatonton, Georgia, often encourage their children to leave. Those in expanding communities, such as Mammoth Lakes, California, may see vastly different opportunities. Latinos migrating to the town for seasonal work see the chance to make ends meet. Middle-class families see the opportunity for entrepreneurial activities.

ROLE OF THE SCHOOL

The family is not the only institution that transmits legacy. Funded and staffed by community members, schools play an important role in orienting children to their future position in society. (For a description of one such example, see Box 4.1.) In turn, the legacies parents have for their children influence the character of the school.

In the rural Midwest, where small businesses are still somewhat prevalent, legacies reflect the sense of social equality that existed during the settlement period. Because everyone aspired to the same goal—owning a business—class differences were often ignored. Parents expect their children to manage a business or become salaried professionals; thus they want their children to develop independence and the work habits needed to make a living. Schools generally encourage participation by all students, regardless of class. Education may also be oriented toward out-migration as parents acknowledge the few jobs available locally.

In communities in other parts of the country, particularly in low-income counties in the South and Appalachia, parents see limited job opportunities for their children. As discussed earlier, they also see little connection between hard work and success. Consequently, their investment in education is not nearly as great. Dropout rates are high. Problems such as teenage pregnancy are also more prevalent. Parents and young people do not see any immediate advantage to remaining in school. Consequently, the sense of independence created by going to work, even at a low-paying job, is not offset by what seems to be the remote chance that education will lead to higher earnings. Unfortunately, high school dropouts experience higher rates of unemployment. In 1988, 26.7 percent of high school dropouts were unemployed, compared with an unemployment rate of 13.5 percent for high school graduates.

BOX 4.1 TEACHING AND REBELLION AT UNION SPRINGS

In 1967 I got a job teaching high school in a small industrial community in upstate New York. . . . One of my first discoveries was that most of my students, who looked like Wonder Bread children, were non-college-bound and hostile to school. I asked them why they hadn't quit when they were sixteen. Most replied, like a chorus, "Because to get a good job you have to go to school." They understood that the boredom and discipline were preparation for the future. . . .

After a few weeks of teaching, I began to discover that the school was designed to teach the majority of students to adjust to the lives already laid out for them after high school. It reinforced what they had learned at home and in grade school: to . . . accept boredom and meaningless discipline as the very nature of things. The faculty and the administration saw themselves as socializers in this process. . . .

The school was also designed to promote a definition of work that excluded emotional satisfaction. To the degree that the kids accepted this definition, they distrusted the very classes they enjoyed. Students would often tell me, "This isn't English, it's too much fun." . . .

John B. was a senior who planned to pump gas after he got out of the army. He also wrote poetry. He alternated between being proud of his work and telling me that it was "bullshit." He was threatened by his creativity because he could see nothing in his future that would allow for that creativity. . . .

By my second year at Union Springs, I was intensely sensitive to the repressiveness of the school system and my own role in it. My way of dealing with that was to make my classes more relevant to students' lives. I told them to write about what they felt in the language with which they were most comfortable. The first papers I received were filled with obscenity, but I criticized them on stylistic rather than moral grounds. In the second papers, the students' efforts to shock me changed into honest attempts at good writing. I told one class of seniors who were working on short stories that I would mimeograph and distribute some of their work. The most popular story was a satire concerning soldiers in Vietnam; it was sprinkled with obscenity. . . .

A few weeks later the principal told me that I would have to "cease and desist" from accepting students' work that made use of "poor" language. The principal also criticized me for playing rock music in my classes. . . . As a result of my classes, he said, students were becoming defiant and teachers and parents were complaining. He said that I was doing a disservice to students in allowing them a freedom that they were not going to have later on. . . . I told the principal that I could not comply with his order but would discuss the issue with my class. He warned me that I was close to losing my job and that he couldn't figure out why I wanted to be a martyr for the students. . . .

I did not come to Union Springs to be a political organizer. I came to teach. But I refused to be the teacher that both the administration and students expected me to be. I had rejected the role of cop and socializer, not out of any revolutionary commitment, but out of my need to relate to my students. This same need made me reject the labels: lower track, non-college-bound, or slow learner that were placed on my students. . . .

In May of that year, following student protests against the tracking system (Michaels supported her students' protests) and the participation of some students in protests against the Vietnam War, Michaels was fired. There were protests at her firing, but she concludes: "Those who are still in school write me that Union Springs is quiet again. The movement that speaks to the needs they experienced and acted on at Union Springs is yet to be created."

Source: Excerpted from Patricia Michaels. 1970. "Teaching and Rebellion at Union Springs," *Socialist Revolution* 1, 2 (March-April): 95–106.

Hollingshead's (1949) study in Elmtown looked at the extent to which social class, and thus legacy, was passed from parent to child through community institutions such as the school. In socially stratified rural communities, schools are also stratified. Hollingshead identified three mechanisms by which the social structure of the community was reproduced in the school. First, the social structure of the adult world was replicated by the young people through cliques and recreational activities. Second, those adults who had a direct impact on the children, including teachers, school administrators, and community leaders, systematically discriminated against children from lower classes. Finally, children from the lower class learned patterns both at home and in school that hampered them in educational and occupational attainment.

As social institutions that transmit legacy and culture, schools are an enigma. Rural communities have fought long and hard to maintain local control of schools, in part to ensure that the values and attitudes of the local community are respected and transmitted through education. State and federal courts, however, see education as a social equalizer, a means by which students willing to apply themselves in school can move into the middle and upper classes. Research such as that conducted by Hollingshead demonstrates the extent to which schools can block this mobility by replicating the social class structure in place in the community in such a way that those in the lower classes see no way to advance. Some rural communities are now looking very carefully at who does and does not succeed in school, asking themselves to what extent the school serves all students fairly.

Impact of Gender, Race, and Ethnicity

Although class and social status are important in shaping legacy, their impact differs depending on gender, race, and ethnicity. Aspirations parents have for their children vary greatly, depending on the sex of the child and the family's race or ethnic heritage.

Any discussion of these issues carries some of the same risks as those involved in analyzing the relationship between social class and legacy. It is extremely difficult to generalize across populations without seeming to stereotype. Differences in legacy based on gender, race, and ethnicity do exist, although they are complex. This discussion reflects some of the current thinking about how these differences occur. By no means, however, does it capture the full complexity of the issues involved or the diversity found across any given population.

Legacy varies with gender, race, and ethnicity (photo courtesy
of the Ohio University Telecommunications Center).

LEGACY AND GENDER

Traditionally, parental legacy varied by the gender of children. In earlier
times, when men and women assumed more distinct roles in society,
parents expected male and female children to need different skills and
values. Parents expected that male children had to be able to earn a living
capable of supporting themselves and their families. Men were socialized
to be independent, able to compete, and competent in some skill or
profession. Women were socialized to make the best marriage possible
and to rely on men for financial security. Maintaining an attractive
appearance and developing homemaking and social skills were considered
values and qualities important to that future. To some extent, the social
and homemaking skills women needed depended on their parents' assess-

ment of the kind of men they would marry. Thus, a farm girl would learn a variety of production skills, such as gardening, home canning, and sewing. A town girl, whose parents felt her future rested on marrying a middle-class professional, would learn music, arts, and leisure sports.

The Turners' commitment to Rosemary's education demonstrates how these expectations have changed dramatically since the 1960s. Women are now entering the labor force in increasing numbers, partly to achieve self-sufficiency and self-satisfaction. Economic conditions also require that many women work to help support their families, sometimes because they are single parents. In 1988, women represented 45 percent of employed persons ages 16 and older.

Women's increased presence in the work force has affected child-rearing patterns. Increasingly, women choose to or are forced to return to the labor force soon after the birth of their children. They are no longer willing—in some cases, they are unable—to stay out of the work force to raise a family. Of women ages 18 to 44 who gave birth during the twelve-month period from July 1987 to June 1988, 51 percent returned to the labor force within a year. The proportion returning to work that soon after the birth of a child steadily increased over the previous decade, rising from 35 percent in 1978.

LEGACY AND RACE

Despite advances in civil rights made during the past three decades, race continues to exert a dramatic impact on legacy. Blacks make up the largest racial minority in the United States, constituting nearly 12 percent of the population. Their history, shaped by periods of slavery, segregation, and the civil rights movement of the 1950s and 1960s, has left a variety of legacies, some positive and others negative.

Because of their roots in slavery and the persecution that followed emancipation, generations of blacks were unable to pass on significant material wealth to their children. Instead, many focused on providing children with a social and cultural heritage that allowed them to survive in an often hostile environment. Legacy for rural blacks meant stressing the linkages within the family and to the larger black community as well as the mutual obligations and support such linkages provided. Family relations, the value of family, and family links to the community and to church were all stressed by black parents, regardless of class.

Studies of social mobility before the civil rights movement show how few black parents were able to build on any social mobility they may have acquired for themselves. Discrimination had an overwhelming impact on the life chances of their children, often wiping out the success parents had achieved. Nevertheless, a small but growing middle class of black busi-

98

Legacy and Social Class

nesspeople and professionals was established by the early twentieth century, centered mainly in urban areas such as New York City and Washington, D.C.

Large-scale internal migration of blacks from the South to the industrial centers of the North began during World War I, as the flow of immigrants from Europe was interrupted. Migrants were pushed from the South by increased agricultural mechanization and pulled to the North by industrial growth. Employment opportunities expanded during the postwar years, as industry boomed and legislation restricted foreign immigration. After World War II, however, technological advances decreased the need for unskilled labor. Opportunities lessened, and racial tensions heightened in many parts of the country.

Since the civil rights movement, black parents have been able to pass on more of their social mobility to their children. As a result, legacies now reflect fewer differences based on race. The black middle class and blue-collar families place a high value on education. Working-class families in rural areas pass along to their children a strong work ethic as well as continued commitment to family and the black community.

Dignity in the face of continued racism is an important part of legacy for blacks. Ways of responding to racism without resorting to violence or becoming the object of attack are important components of the skills parents foster in their children.

LEGACY AND ETHNICITY

In addition to gender and racial differences, ethnic heritage influences parents' identification of suitable legacies for their children. An ethnic group is a population that shares an identity based on distinctive cultural patterns and common ancestry. The United States is often referred to as a melting pot that has blended the diverse ethnic origins of immigrants and Native Americans. In reality, distinct ethnic subcultures continue to exist.

For example, there are about 1.5 million Native Americans now living in the United States. Almost half live in rural areas or on reservations, mostly west of the Mississippi River. They represent the poorest ethnic minority in the country. Despite the rich history and culture of the various tribes, Native Americans today can offer their children only a bleak legacy. As of 1987, 30 percent of Native Americans lived below the poverty line, more than twice the national rate of 13.5 percent. The average length of schooling is only eight years, and the high-school dropout rate is twice the national average. Alcoholism is a pervasive and persistent problem; the rate among Native Americans is nearly five times that of the nation as a whole.

Even in the face of such devastating statistics, Native Americans strive to maintain and convey pride in their heritage. Schools on some reservations, once used as a tool to eliminate the Native American cultures, now incorporate native and white culture in their curriculums (Spears et al. 1990). Efforts to stimulate economic development on native lands are also beginning to reflect native values and orientations toward the land. Increasingly, Native Americans seek to transfer a legacy that respects their own culture but equips young people to function more effectively in the white world.

Latino is used to refer to people of Spanish-speaking ancestry, but this is clearly not a homogeneous group. Of the approximately 15 million Latinos living in the United States, about 9 million are Mexican Americans, 2 million are Puerto Rican, close to 1 million are Cuban, and the remaining 3 million are drawn from many countries of Central and South America. Latinos are the fastest-growing ethnic minority in the United States and are expected to surpass blacks as the dominant minority within the next several decades.

Many Latinos in the West and Midwest can trace their residence in the United States for generations, but the vast majority arrived during the period after World War II. Significant immigration continues today, particularly from Mexico and countries of Central America such as El Salvador, Honduras, and Guatemala. Latinos tend to reside in national enclaves, to an extent resisting assimilation into the wider culture. For many, the level of job opportunities is low, a function in part of inadequate English-language skills. Many are drawn into low-paying service occupations in rapidly expanding rural communities. These typically offer few opportunities for advancement. Like the black community, Latinos value family loyalty, respect, obligation, and commitment to mutual support.

About 7.2 million U.S. residents, 2.9 percent of the population, claim Asian heritage. Like Latinos, they are a diverse group. Among the most numerous are Chinese, Japanese, and Filipinos. There are also significant numbers of Indians, Pakistanis, Koreans, and Vietnamese, however.

Asian immigration began on a large scale during the late nineteenth century, as Chinese were recruited to serve as cheap labor for the developing industries of the West, such as mining and construction. Although Chinese immigration was legally suspended in 1882, a diminished but continuous stream of Asians made their way to the United States. Many settled in California or in large cities such as New York and Chicago. Changes in immigration laws in 1965 resulted in increased flows once again, particularly from war-torn areas of Vietnam, Laos, and Cambodia. Today, many Asian Americans reside in rural areas, settling in small towns in states such as Kansas, Minnesota, and Massachusetts.

Although the different nationalities represented among Asian Americans value different characteristics and behaviors, there is a general appreciation for education, industriousness, and family cohesion. Until such time as material success is widely available to these ethnic groups, these qualities will define the principal legacy bequeathed to Asian American children by their parents.

Inequality: Whose Legacy?

Rosemary and Dave Stitz received different legacies from their parents, legacies that contributed to their different stands on the school bond issue. Heated discussions aside, both inherited a legacy capable of helping them maintain a stable lifestyle and contribute to the community. What of other communities?

Why have rural communities throughout the South, Appalachia, and the Southwest remained poor despite efforts at stimulating economic development? How can Native Americans escape the legacy of what some call "ethnostress," the "paralyzing conviction that one's place in society is pre-determined, permanent, and paradoxically, one's own darned fault" (Margolis 1986)? Are black families able to pass on whatever social mobility was achieved by parents? The answers to these and other questions are complex.

To some extent, social inequality is a part of legacy, which we have described as the material goods and behaviors parents pass on to their children. One line of research looks at the values parents pass on to children by virtue of their social class (Kohn 1963; Kohn 1969). These studies suggest that inequality is related to parental values derived from occupation and social orientations. Current work looks at the role these values play in the way parents socialize their children (Alwin 1989; Alwin 1990; Slomczynski et al. 1981). Furthermore, sociologists have found that the material legacy parents pass on to their children is a function not only of parents' wealth but also of parental values (Salamon 1985; Steelman and Powell 1991).

In other ways, inequality arises within the community and the institutions by which it socializes its youth. Society in general has chosen to attack inequality through the schools in the belief that education is key to social mobility. Hollingshead's (1949) research suggesting that schools can replicate the social structure of the community calls into question the capacity of the schools to overcome social stratification. Research into illiteracy suggests a strong correlation between the literacy skills of parents and their children, despite the intervention of schools (Sticht and McDonald 1989). Educators in their efforts to combat illiteracy now look at the parent and child as a unit, believing that help offered to parents may have more impact than help offered only to the child.

To whom does inequality belong? Is it part of a past, never to be overcome? Is it part of the present, capable of being changed for both parent and child? It is clear from sociological research that the answer lies somewhere in between. Such research can assist in devising programs aimed at increasing opportunity and decreasing inequality.

Chapter Summary

Legacy is what parents seek to pass on to their children, including material possessions as well as values and norms. Legacy depends, to some extent, on current economic opportunities. Parents' social class also affects legacy. Sociologists define social class either in terms of how individuals relate to the means of production or in terms of their social status within the community. When social status differences are large, a community or society is said to be highly stratified.

Membership in a given social class often affects the legacy passed on to children. Those who are small-business owners or entrepreneurs often pass on land or a business to their children. Legacy is thus strongly linked to place. Although desiring that their children take over the business or farm, other small-business owners or farmers realize that such a legacy may not be realistic in the current economy. They therefore encourage their children to get a good education.

Those in the middle class, particularly managers and professionals, typically invest in their children's education and value independent thinking and the capacity to make decisions. Limited to the manufacturing or natural-resource jobs available in the local community, working-class parents value discipline and want to ensure that their children can adapt to externally imposed rules. Some working-class parents find that their salary is not sufficient to keep the family above poverty. Those who are persistently poor often feel they have little control over their environment; consequently, they see little connection between hard work or education and a better future.

Legacy is transferred from one generation to another through social institutions. The family serves as the primary social group through which legacy is transferred. Schools can either reinforce existing class structures or offer opportunities that increase social mobility.

The relationship between legacy and social class is often modified by issues of gender, race, and ethnicity. In earlier times, men and women had distinct roles that affected the legacy bequeathed to each gender. Racial discrimination often prevents black parents from passing acquired social mobility on to their children. Native American people struggle with the legacy left by decades of oppression. Social inequalities continue to exist, inequalities that limit communities as well as individuals.

Key Terms

Capitalist class includes those who own the means of production.

Legacy is what parents seek to pass on to their children, including material possessions, values, and behavioral patterns.

Managerial class includes individuals such as managers, professionals, and government officials who sell their labor but maintain considerable job autonomy.

Petty bourgeoisie includes those who own the means of production but rely primarily on their own labor rather than the labor of others.

Proletarians include those who sell their labor for wages.

Social class has two distinct meanings. It describes people with similar relationships to the means of production. Alternately, it refers to a particular layer or stratum in a social stratification system.

Social mobility is the term used to describe the movement of an individual from one social class to another.

Social stratification is the division of people into layers or strata based on a series of attributes related to social status.

References

Alwin, Duane F. 1989. "Social Stratification, Conditions of Work, and Parental Socialization Values." Pp. 327–346 in Nancy Eisenberg, Janus Reykowski, and Ervin Staub (eds.), *Social and Moral Values: Individual and Societal Perspectives.* New York: Erlbaum.

———. 1990. "Cohort Replacement and Changes in Parental Socialization Values." *Journal of Marriage and the Family* 52:347–360.

Gordon, Milton M. 1963. *Social Class in American Sociology.* New York: McGraw-Hill (first published by Duke University Press, 1950).

Hollingshead, August B. 1949. *Elmtown's Youth: The Impact of Social Classes on Adolescents.* New York: John Wiley and Sons.

Kohn, Melvin L. 1963. "Social Class and Parent-Child Relationships: An Interpretation." *American Journal of Sociology* 68:471–480.

———. 1969. *Class and Conformity: A Study in Values.* Homewood, IL: Dorsey.

Kohn, Melvin L., and Carmi Sholler (eds.). 1983. *Work and Personality: An Inquiry into the Impact of Social Stratification.* Norwood, NJ: Ablex.

Margolis, Richard. 1986. Quoted in J. D. Spears, *Proceedings 1986: National Invitational Conference on Rural Adult Postsecondary Education.* Manhattan, KS: Action Agenda Project.

Salamon, Sonya. 1985. "Ethnic Communities and the Structure of Agriculture." *Rural Sociology* 50:323–340.

Shapiro, Isaac. 1989. *Laboring for Less: Working but Poor in Rural America.* Washington, DC: Center on Budget and Policy Priorities.

Slomczynski, Kazimierz M., Joanne Miller, and Melvin L. Kohn. 1981. "Stratification, Work, and Values: A Polish–United States Comparison." *American Sociological Review* 46:720–744.

Spears, J. D., J. P. Oliver, and Sue C. Maes. 1990. *Accommodating Change and Diversity: Multicultural Practices in Rural Schools*. Manhattan, KS: Rural Clearinghouse for Lifelong Education and Development.

Steelman, Lala Carr, and Brian Powell. 1991. "Sponsoring the Next Generation: Parental Willingness to Pay for Higher Education." *American Journal of Sociology* 96:1505–1529.

Steinmetz, George, and Erik Olin Wright. 1989. "The Fall and Rise of the Petty Bourgeoisie: Changing Patterns of Self-Employment in the Postwar United States." *American Journal of Sociology* 94(5): 973–1018.

Sticht, T., and B. McDonald. 1989. *Making the Nation Smarter: The Intergenerational Transfer of Cognitive Ability*. San Diego, CA: Applied Behavioral and Cognitive Sciences, Inc.

Warner, W. Lloyd, and Paul S. Lundt. 1941. *The Social Life of a Modern Community*. New Haven, CT: Yale University Press.

Warner, W. Lloyd, Marcia Meeker, and Kenneth Eels. 1949. *Social Class in America*. Chicago: Science Research Associates, Inc.

Wright, Erik Olin. 1985. *Classes*. London: New Left.

Part 2

Economy and Society

5

Capital and Community

eorge Martin, a former construction contractor and water-treatment franchise owner, says he used to be able to borrow $10,000 on his signature alone from his hometown bank in Marshall. That didn't happen when he opened a lumberyard last year. "Our banks didn't help much. I couldn't borrow penny one from them," he says.

Roy Kimsey, an independent oil man and longtime customer of First City Bankcorp of Texas, wanted to get into the increasingly lucrative ostrich business. He needed $10,000 to buy a male to mate with the two females he keeps behind the house. Owned by a big bank holding company in Chicago, First City couldn't quite bring itself to offer the loan. The locally owned United Bank stepped forward instead. (Allen 1989)

Marci Snell needed help in buying brand-name clothing on credit until sales recovered the cost. Her children's clothing store in Bend had a volume of sales too small to interest big city banks. She ended up paying cash for her shipments.

What these and hundreds of other entrepreneurs face is problems in acquiring capital—capital in the form of money needed to finance a new business, diversify a farming operation, or purchase merchandise to be sold later in the year. Difficulty in acquiring capital is neither new nor unique. Most of us have run across the problem from time to time, whether it be to buy a new car, finance an education, or start a new business. In the case of these rural entrepreneurs, however, problems in raising capital affect their communities as well as them. Failed businesses mean weaker economies.

Capital is important because it allows labor to be more productive. George Martin, Roy Kimsey, and Marci Snell each needed capital in order

Investing in ostriches? (Photo courtesy of the Ohio University Telecommunications Center.)

to convert their ideas into a business profit. Yet for rural communities and businesses alike, there is a crisis of capital availability. Lured by higher profits outside the local area and facilitated by new laws making it easier to move from one place to another, capital is becoming more and more mobile. This is not a new problem. Even at the turn of the century, thoughtful commentators such as Liberty Hyde Bailey, dean of the College of Agriculture at Cornell University, wrote (1911, 20): "The city sits like a parasite, running out its roots into the open country and draining it of its substance. The city takes everything to itself—materials, money, men— and gives back only what it does not want; it does not reconstruct or even maintain its contributory country."

As capital becomes more mobile, rural communities lose control. Bankers in Chicago did not understand the potential value of Roy Kimsey's ostriches; the local bank did. Bankers in New York did not understand why Marci Snell could not use her own cash to pay for the clothing shipment—the volume in which she dealt was far less than that of their usual clients. George Martin's hometown bank may no longer be locally controlled. Many rural banks have been bought up by larger banks.

This chapter examines capital and its various forms. The extent to which communities depend on capital is explored, as are the various institutions created to provide loans to businesses. Traditional sources of capital are contrasted with the new sources rural communities must develop to adapt to the changing rules of the financial playing field.

The Concept of Capital

The term *capital* is often used to mean money—the money needed to start a new business or the money that flowed from one currency to another. Money is not always capital, nor is capital simply money. Social scientists actually use the term more broadly. This section explores the definition of capital, the various forms capital can take, and both the public and private character of capital.

DEFINING CAPITAL

Although capital is more than simply money, some examples based on money are helpful in building a definition of capital. Money can be used for a variety of purposes. We use it to buy things, such as a new stereo, food for dinner, a ticket to a movie, or trash-collection services. Money can also be used to make more money. Money invested in a savings bond, for example, generates more money in the form of interest. People invest money in business because they expect to receive part of the profits in addition to the money they originally invested. Money is a form of capital when it is used to make more money.

Capital is any resource capable of producing other resources. This definition forces us to distinguish between consumption and investment. If you buy a car for personal enjoyment, the car is not considered a form of capital. But if you buy a car in order to run a shuttle service, the car becomes a means for generating income. A resource (the car) is capable of producing other resources (your salary).

FORMS OF CAPITAL

Because any resource can be considered a form of capital, it is helpful to organize resources into a few broad categories. We typically think of four forms of capital: (1) capital goods, (2) land, (3) financial capital, and (4) human capital. The first three types have tangible forms. The fourth, human capital, refers to the knowledge, skills, and talents people bring to any activity. In some respects, human capital is less tangible.

The tangible forms of capital are relatively easy to identify. *Capital goods* include the physical objects (cars, machines, buildings) that individuals or businesses invest in. A sawmill in Oakridge, Oregon, invests in the equipment needed to saw timber. The meat-packing plants in Garden City, Kansas, invest in the buildings, feedlots, and transportation equip-

Capital goods include the farm machinery that farm operators
now invest in (photo courtesy of the Ohio University Telecommunications Center).

ment needed to move cattle in and processed meat out. *Land* becomes an
investment because of the resources it has or the development space it
offers. Timber companies purchase land, in part for existing stands of
timber but also for the land's capacity to sustain new growths of timber.
Real estate agents buy land, hoping to realize a profit if the land increases
in value. Finally, *financial capital* includes stocks, bonds, market futures,
and letters of credit as well as money.

The other form capital takes is *human capital.* The notion that investments in people can produce additional profit or resources was first
proposed by T. W. Schultz (1961). In contrasting economic output across
countries, Schultz noticed that the education and training of the work
force played a dominant role in explaining different levels of output. This
concept has been broadened to include health care and other social

services as well as education. Businesses invest in preventive health care or education because they expect both to make their employees more productive. In completing high school or going on for postsecondary education, we make investments in ourselves; we expect these investments to pay off in the form of increased income.

PUBLIC VERSUS PRIVATE CAPITAL

Capital can be further classified in terms of who invests. When individuals or groups invest their own resources, they have used *private capital*. Land, buildings, equipment, and the inventory associated with a small business are part of its private-capital stock. Land owned by farm families, timber companies, or oil companies is private capital. The investment you make in your education is also an example of private capital.

Public capital refers to the resources invested by the community. Tax dollars are used to build roads, install sewer lines, maintain public parks, and finance schools. Governments raise the needed funds and then authorize their investment on behalf of the public good. Capital goods are then owned by the public, typically at the level of government involved in the original purchase. Communities own their street system or industrial park. Counties own courthouses, county road systems, or landfills. The state owns its state road system or state universities. The federal government owns national parks and federal lands.

Public capital and private capital are often linked through partnerships. For example, some logging companies in the Northwest harvest trees on land owned by the National Park Service. The logging companies gain access to federal lands in exchange for fees paid to the government. Postsecondary education is funded by both public and private capital. When individuals pay tuition to attend colleges and universities, they are investing private capital in their own development. However, tuition covers only a fraction of the costs of maintaining public institutions. State tax dollars support public colleges and universities. City or county taxes support community colleges.

MOBILITY OF CAPITAL

These various forms of capital differ in how easily they can move. Land and many forms of capital goods, such as buildings and roads, are not mobile. Thus, individuals and communities have to figure out how to make these forms of capital productive. By contrast, financial and human capital are quite mobile. Money can move to wherever it can earn the highest return. People can move to where they earn the best salaries. The mobility of both causes problems for rural communities.

Financial capital has become increasingly mobile. Electronic transfers of capital can take place in seconds not only between communities on either coast but from a rural community to an urban center halfway around the world. Wealth created in Iowa can end up as an investment in California or Malaysia, as savings deposits in the local bank become financial capital attracted to where the money can earn the highest rate of interest.

For example, a farmer in Iowa (Figure 5.1) may sell a truckload of hogs when prices are high and costs of production low. The profit made becomes savings that the farmer can now invest. That farmer phones a broker in Des Moines who buys shares in a New York–based mutual fund by computer. The mutual fund then invests in a garment factory in Malaysia, where the funds receive a higher return than they would have had they been invested in a garment factory in rural Iowa. Capital created in Iowa has become wages paid in Malaysia.

Human capital has also become increasingly mobile, and this factor has raised concerns about public investments in education. From the beginning, the concept of human capital embraced both private and public investments in education. Individuals are encouraged to invest in education because it enables them to generate more income for them and their families. Communities are encouraged to invest in schools because a well-educated citizenry is fundamental to economic growth. The rate at which rural youth migrate to urban areas, however, has limited the extent to which this type of public investment has resulted in local economic growth. Some communities are asking whether the school curriculum could introduce students to opportunities within the community as well as prepare them for work elsewhere.

Capital and Community Needs

Nearly all rural communities depended on capital from their very founding. Capital not only helped individuals set up homes and businesses but enabled local governments to provide roads, schools, sewers, and other services needed by community residents and businesses. This section examines the public and private needs for capital and describes the role played by rural financial institutions.

PUBLIC AND PRIVATE NEED FOR CAPITAL

Seeking to expand and protect its boundaries, the federal government encouraged settlement of the frontier by making capital available in the form of land. Although many families homesteaded, much of the public lands went to large companies such as railroads. The government encour-

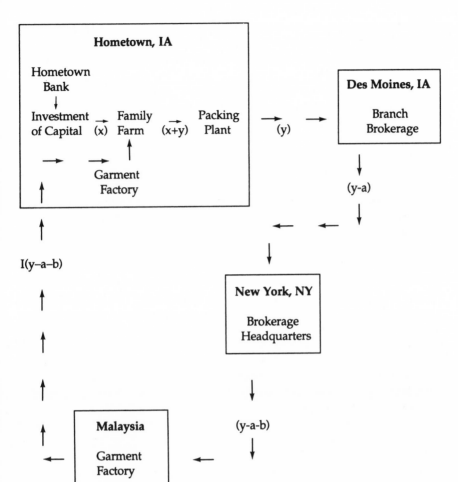

Capital created in Iowa becomes wages paid in Malaysia. The hometown bank provides investment capital (x) to the farmer. When the hogs are delivered to the packing plant, the farmer returns the investment capital (x) to the bank and retains the profit (y). The profit (y) is transferred to a nearby brokerage firm, which then transfers it to the firm's headquarters in New York. Both brokerage offices take commissions (a and b respectively) for handling the investment. The actual amount of money invested in the Malaysian garment factory is (y-a-b). The farmer eventually receives a portion of that investment in interest. Thus, the farmer's return on investment is: Return on y = I(y-a-b) where I is the interest rate offered by the brokerage firm. Meanwhile, the local garment factory has trouble accessing capital.

FIGURE 5.1 Mobility of Capital

aged the privatization of land by removing it from the public domain and selling it to private holders at reduced prices. This policy encouraged the development in rural communities of private capital held by businesses as well as individuals.

From its inception, the U.S. government recognized the role public capital played in community development and growth. First through the Northwest Ordinances of 1787, the federal government gave newly established communities land on which to build public goods (schools and roads) considered necessary for a community to exist and the nation to prosper. Further, the United States and Canada are among the few nations of the world that grant local governments the power to raise public capital through local means, such as property taxes. This ability to tax gave communities a powerful tool by which to become self-reliant, unlike rural communities in other countries that have had to depend on the central government in order to get roads, schools, or a water system.

The increasing cost of public services, combined with a decreasing population and tax base, has made rural communities more dependent on state and federal sources of funds. This dependence has, in turn, made communities less able to control their capital investments. For example, a school district that needs to introduce Spanish because of an influx of new migrants might instead find itself creating a gifted program, because federal funds are available for the gifted program but not for the Spanish program. Despite the need to improve a local water system, a county board of supervisors might decide to lengthen a local airport runway, again because of the availability of federal funds. As communities find it increasingly difficult to raise capital locally, the locus of control for capital investment shifts to the state or federal level. Communities find themselves acting on state or federal priorities rather than local ones.

To develop, communities require private capital other than land. Many rural communities were originally dependent in one way or another on farming. Agricultural production, unlike industrial production, is consecutive. Farmers must plow before they plant and plant before they harvest. There are long periods between the major production activities, particularly in crop production. Consequently, selling is done well after initial production decisions are made. That means that many farming communities have erratic income flows—a lot of money comes into the community when the harvest is sold, but little is generated at other times.

During the settlement period, women often sold eggs and cream throughout the year in an effort to even out income flow. When crops failed or a buyer could not be found, however, local residents created other mechanisms for generating capital. Individuals and groups formed banks or cooperative financial institutions to provide credit for both consumption and production loans. These institutions were especially important in communities dependent on agriculture, timber, and mining because fluctuations in production—and therefore in income—were often typical.

RURAL FINANCIAL INSTITUTIONS

The names of many small-town banks, such as Farmers and Drovers Bank and Farmers Bank, reflect the character of the needs that led to their creation. Capital was also needed for small businesses (Merchants Bank) and for workers seeking credit between paydays (Union Bank). Rural banks generally had local roots and functioned as other local businesses, either individually owned or as cooperatives.

Because of the amount of capital and risk involved, banks generally formed corporations that separated the owners' assets from those of the bank. Incorporation is a legal strategy often used to limit personal liability. Banks that were incorporated were required to be chartered by the state or federal government. *State* in a bank's name means it is chartered under state law. The term *national* or *federal* in a bank's name means it is chartered with the federal government.

Banks make loans to individuals on the basis of risk. The lower the risk, the more inclined the banker is to advance the capital. Common factors used to assess risk include (1) net worth, (2) cash flow, and (3) personal knowledge of the borrower.

Although some rural residents are wealthy in terms of land, that wealth has low *liquidity*—it cannot easily be converted into cash. This feature of land gave rise to the saying that one could be land-rich and money-poor. When these individuals need money to invest in their businesses, they use their capital assets (land, livestock, or machinery) as collateral to guarantee the repayment of a loan.

When loans are made on the basis of net worth, collateral is compared with indebtedness. Collateral is important to the lender, because if the loan is not repaid, the property can be claimed and sold to repay the loan. Loans based on net worth (the value of collateral minus outstanding indebtedness) are relatively safe loans to make, despite the fact that the lender assumes the assets will retain their value. Consequently, net worth is a traditional criterion for making a loan. One problem with this criterion is that it introduces a bias into the flow of capital. Those who already have wealth are best able to acquire capital.

More adventurous bankers make loans based on a borrower's ability to repay. Determining ability to repay involves a detailed comparison of the costs of expanding production weighed against the increased sales that would result from expansion. Cash flow, not net worth, is the criterion for such loans. Determining cash flow involves gathering more data about a business operation than when the criterion for loaning money is net worth. It is also somewhat more inexact. Bankers have to estimate not only the future value of assets but also the future costs of needed inputs and future prices that will be paid for what is produced.

Basing a loan on a borrower's ability to repay avoids the bias created when net worth is used. Because the loan is based on an individual's future prospects for repaying the loan rather than on present assets, a person with few assets can secure a loan. However, loans based on the ability to repay introduce yet another bias. Those who can keep good accounts and work through cash-flow projections are more likely to receive loans. These loans favor the more educated individual. A number of farmers had to become more sophisticated in these methods when land values dropped and their net worth no longer justified the size of the loans they needed to continue operating. For the most part, loans made on the basis of cash flow are more speculative.

Bankers in rural communities traditionally have had a third criterion for making loans: knowledge of the character of the borrower. In a sense, this is a shorthand way of calculating ability to pay. A young person known to be thrifty and hardworking could get a loan based on a handshake, indicative of the faith a banker put in the individual. In small-town settings, such loans were often biased against women and minorities, who were traditionally excluded from those considered worthy of credit.

This criterion was especially important in allowing those with little property an opportunity to become small-business owners. For the most part, however, this informal way of assessing risk is disappearing. Although state laws on branch banking and multibank holding companies vary, personal knowledge of the potential borrower by the individual with authority to make the loan is declining. As control of rural banks shifts to metropolitan areas, personal knowledge of the borrower is no longer valued as a method by which to assess risk. George Martin with his lumberyard was a victim of this shift away from local control.

Sources of Capital

In order to create more productive capacity or to get the inputs needed for production, individuals and businesses need capital. One way to get capital is to sell an asset. Another is to spend less money than taken in and thus accumulate savings. But many people, companies, and communities need a large amount of capital at one time in order to purchase a farm, a business, or a major piece of machinery. They do not have enough assets to sell to finance the purchase. Even if they did, selling those assets means selling their productive capacity. Nor can they save enough to

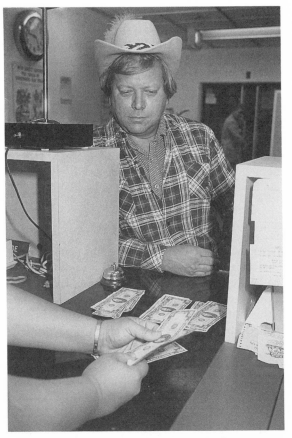

Money is the most familiar form of capital (photo courtesy of the U.S. Department of Agriculture).

purchase the capital asset in a timely fashion. Therefore they must borrow the money. Banks can provide this money in a number of ways.

SAVINGS

For most people in the world, income seems insufficient to provide for the necessary expenses of family maintenance and reproduction. Others are able to take in more money than they spend in a given period of time, so they save it. Some savings are voluntary; others are involuntary, such as the contribution to Social Security or other government-mandated pension funds. Regardless of whether they are voluntary or involuntary, savings represent a major source of capital.

In most communities, savers with moderate incomes tend to deposit their money in their local financial institutions. This money is then reinvested by the bank, savings and loan, or credit union to earn interest. Despite the fact that rural financial institutions often offer somewhat lower interest rates, rural banks remain a preferred investment for many citizens. Deposits in most rural banks steadily increased during the 1980s.

For a financial institution, money that is deposited is carried as a debit, or liability, on its books. A *liability* is an obligation to pay back on demand to depositors the amount credited to their accounts. A loan, on the other hand, is an asset because the bank is owed that money by a third person. An *asset* is money or property that can be used to repay a loan. For the bank, loans are assets that can be used to meet liabilities.

INTEREST

In lending money for a business, the lender generally secures the loan through the collateral of the capital goods acquired with the loan funds or a lien on the products produced. In short, banks have the right to collect the capital goods purchased or products produced by the business if it fails to repay the loan. There is also a charge to the borrower for use of the money, called the *interest*. A portion of that money goes to the individuals whose savings are used to provide capital. This encourages them to put the excess capital they have into the bank instead of under their mattress at home or into the purchase of additional consumer goods. A portion of the interest remains with the bank, credit union, or savings and loan. These funds are used to cover the costs associated with managing the loan and to provide the bank with a profit.

The *nominal interest rate* (interest rate charged to the borrower) varies according to the supply of money available for lending and the demand for money among competing borrowers. However, interest rates are not influenced by local supply and demand for capital. Even in isolated rural communities, interest rates are set daily through monetary and fiscal policies adopted by U.S. and foreign governments. This control decreases the ability of local institutions to redeploy capital to local investments.

In order to compete in the global financial market, projects must have high rates of return and low risk. Investments in rural communities are traditionally the reverse—low return and high risk. As interest rates become bound to global markets, capital leaves rural areas. Known as *capital flight*, this phenomenon describes the extent to which capital originally invested in rural areas eventually is moved elsewhere in search of a higher return.

Interest rates are one of the costs of capital. When interest rates are high, fewer people are able to borrow. When rates are low, more people may be inclined to borrow because it appears easier and cheaper to pay back the loan and interest on it. However, it is important to calculate the *real interest rate*, which is the nominal interest rate minus the rate of inflation. This is the real cost of capital.

In periods of high inflation, nominal interest rates are high, but they are often exceeded by the rate of inflation (Figure 5.2). In this case, it pays to borrow. The interest charged for the loan is less than the increased value of whatever was purchased. Savers, on the other hand, often lose money on bank deposits, bonds, and other ordinary financial investments. Consequently, they often look for investments the market price of which will rise at a rate likely to equal or exceed the inflation rate. Commodities or real estate are frequent choices. During the 1970s, for example, farmland and urban real estate prices escalated at an extremely rapid rate as investors sought inflation-proof investment opportunities.

For larger or more risky investments, local banks cannot provide the required capital. The risk may be too great, the amount needed too much, or the banker may simply lack the expertise to judge the appropriate loan period and rate of return. Rural banks accustomed to making agricultural loans may be unsure when asked to finance a cabinet factory. Agricultural loans are equally difficult for urban banks to evaluate, as illustrated by the problems Roy Kimsey had in securing a loan to expand his ostrich operation. There are several other sources of private capital for such undertakings, such as bonds and equity capital.

BONDS

When a large amount of capital is needed for a long-term capital investment, loans can be made in more formal contractual agreements such as bonds. Bonds pay interest and are issued by governments or business corporations. They pay interest and constitute a promise of repayment of a designated amount of money (often more than the amount received as a loan) at the end of an established period of time, usually twenty or thirty years. Businesses can pledge securities or future income to repay the money raised through bonds.

In the 1980s, deregulation of U.S. financial markets allowed the marketing of junk bonds. *Junk bonds* are high-risk, high-interest securities that are often sold at a deep discount, an amount well below their face value. The money raised by these bonds was converted into equity capital in new or established businesses. Because the businesses were risky, the bonds paid high rates of interest. Most such ventures were in urban areas; this drew capital out of rural areas. When the businesses failed, many savings and loan institutions, which had invested in venture-capital firms and in urban real estate, went under. Rural people contributed to the bailout of urban savings and loans through their taxes.

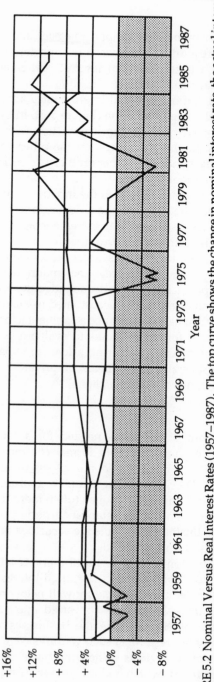

FIGURE 5.2 Nominal Versus Real Interest Rates (1957–1987). The top curve shows the change in nominal interest rate, the actual interest paid to the investor. The bottom line shows the change in real interest rate, the nominal interest rate minus the rate of inflation. During times of high inflation, the real interest rate may dip below zero. *Source:* Adapted from *The Wall Street Journal.*

Governments, including rural towns and counties, can issue *municipal bonds* to seek investments in public capital. Usually state law disallows use of bonds to pay operating expenses of local governments, schools, and hospitals but permits their use to support buildings or structural improvements. These bonds are guaranteed by the good faith and taxing power of the issuing government. The U.S. government feels so strongly that these local financing mechanisms should be in place that interest earned from personal and corporate investment in these bonds is usually tax free; this feature provides additional incentive to make capital available to local communities.

Bonds are an important mechanism by which rural communities raise capital but retain local control. Industrial revenue bonds, for example, can provide investment capital for a local firm. Too often, however, the money raised by such bonds goes to attract a business from another area rather than to create a local firm. Communities run the risk that the business will eventually move, despite local efforts to make it financially attractive for the firm to stay. Privately issued, publicly regulated bonds can provide an important source of seed capital for new firms or investment capital for local firms wishing to expand.

EQUITY CAPITAL

Sometimes a business has neither enough capital assets to provide collateral for a loan nor the proven excess of income over expenses to ensure a steady repayment of further indebtedness. In this case, other sources of capital must be found.

One mechanism is to "go public"—sell shares in the company to the general public through the stock market. Individuals with savings (or other access to capital) invest in shares of the company. In exchange for their capital investment, these individuals receive a portion of the company's profits in the form of dividends paid on their shares. Stockholders can also make (or lose) money on their investments by selling their shares on a stock exchange if the company goes public.

Once a business has decided to sell stock, the company no longer belongs solely to the business owner. However, the assets of the company have increased as a result of the capital investment of the new shareholders (or partners in the case of a partnership). The *equity* of the business is still defined as the total assets less the total liabilities, but that equity is now held by the partners or stockholders. In exchange for the capital invested in the company, the partners or stockholders share in determining who will manage the company.

The market price of the stock is largely dependent on the company's earnings. Stocks are of two types. Preferred stock guarantees a dividend of a specified rate and a specified portion of the assets if the corporation is liquidated. Common stock has a rate of return that fluctuates depending on the corporation's profits. Stockholders have voting rights in choosing the management of the company. Their votes are weighted according to the amount of stock owned. These votes are used to select the board of directors, which then sets policy and names the chief executive officer of the corporation. In seeking capital through selling equity, a business owner gives up management control.

Once companies have started up, they often need a high level of initial capital investment in order to upgrade technology and develop markets. Further, they need capital that comes from investors willing to take risks and be patient as they wait for a return. This kind of equity capital is referred to as *venture capital*. Some have argued that a shortage of venture capital stifles would-be entrepreneurs and hence retards growth and development. Venture-capital investment remained at about $3 billion a year during the 1980s. However, the funds were increasingly used for leveraged buyouts of growth companies rather than for investments in new enterprises.

Although selling stock is a useful strategy for raising business capital, it is not always viable in rural areas. In order to sell stock on a stock exchange, a business must meet several requirements related to financial disclosure. For small businesses in rural areas, putting these statements of financial disclosure together can be expensive relative to the amount of capital being raised.

The Changing Rules of Capital

One of the reasons banks were chartered by states or the federal government was to ensure that capital would be available locally for local investments. But the control exercised by government and thus the risk involved for the rural community have varied over time. Entering banking was easier when the National Bank of the United States (a forerunner of the Federal Reserve banking system) did not exercise disciplinary and restraining influences; control was loose during the periods 1781–1791, 1811–1816, and 1837–1863. State charters were the exclusive method for creating banking corporations during these periods. During the era of unregulated banking between the 1830s and through the 1920s, any entrepreneur who could meet minimal capitalization standards to set up a bank could obtain a state charter. Banks proliferated, particularly in rural communities, peaking at 30,000 banks in the United States in 1921.

THE AGE OF REGULATION

Over 10,000 banks failed during the Great Depression of 1929–1933. A large proportion of the failed banks were in rural communities. More demanding criteria for charters were then established by the Banking Act of 1933, including tougher requirements for capitalization and management based on the convenience and needs of the community along with competitive circumstances.

Other limitations were placed on banks in 1933. These regulations set lending limits, limited insider lending, and restricted bank investments. Interest-rate ceilings were established, and interest on *demand deposits*, such as checking accounts from which account holders could withdraw their money at any time, was prohibited. In 1933, the *Federal Deposit Insurance Corporation (FDIC)* became a supervisory agency for all national banks and state banks seeking FDIC insurance protection for their depositors. Federal deposit insurance offered borrowers insurance on deposits up to $100,000 in banks that agreed to be supervised by the FDIC. Few rural banks were established once the regulations were enacted, but few banks failed. In regulating banking activities, the government played a major role in reducing the financial risk to society.

These regulations, which were in effect between the mid-1930s and the early 1980s, specified that different organizations should specialize in different financial functions. For example, banks could not engage in real estate brokerage. Thrift institutions (savings and loans) were forbidden from offering demand-deposit accounts. These prohibitions had two major purposes: (1) to further certain social goals, such as home ownership, and (2) to prevent conflicts of interest within individual firms. As Anthony Downs (1985, 41–42), an economist concerned about the real estate capital markets and real estate finance, points out:

> Congress apparently believed that the average patron of each financial institution should not have to pass prior judgment on the quality of that institution's management in order to have confidence that the institution's assets would be prudently handled. Such judgments would require knowledge and expertise far beyond the capabilities of the average citizen.

Federal regulatory agencies were therefore established to provide collective supervision of financial institutions—to oversee the safety and socially responsible use of capital.

Bank regulation provided a governmental mechanism whereby public trust could be maintained in the major institution that linked capital to producers and consumers. In return for the security provided to savers through state and federal deposit insurance, capital was made available to borrowers. Public trust in banks and thrifts was gained not only through the insurance of savings but through the oversight provided by the federal and state regulatory agencies.

Under the Federal Reserve Board's "Regulation Q," the amount of interest that could be charged for loans or paid out on deposits was limited. This restriction tended to subsidize borrowers. Bankers in rural communities laughingly reminisce about the good old days of country banking, when the "3-6-3 rule" applied: 3 percent interest paid on deposits, 6 percent interest charged for loans, and on the golf course by 3 p.m.! This system provided security for lenders and borrowers, as long as the cost of money (the real interest rate) remained constant. Regulation tended to favor rural banks and made banking relatively straightforward. In order for this system to work, however, economic conditions had to remain generally stable. The instability of the 1970s undermined the effectiveness of the regulations for bankers and led to growing pressure to decrease regulation and increase the flexibility offered all financial institutions.

DEREGULATION

With the shift in the world economy, which involved devaluation of the dollar in 1971 and the rise in oil prices in 1973, there was a substantial decrease in the real cost of money as a result of inflation. Savers found they could get higher yields from financial institutions that were not controlled by putting their money into newly developed financial instruments, such as *money-market funds*. Banks found that they did not have the capital to lend at the rates they were legally able to offer; in other words, they were no longer competitive.

In the 1970s, rural areas found their locally owned and controlled financial institutions competing with nonfinancial institutions not restricted by banking regulations, such as Sears and Merrill Lynch. These institutions, which are multinational in character, channeled capital out of rural areas by offering investment opportunities such as money-market funds. A capital exodus from traditional banks, including rural community banks, occurred as savers increasingly sought higher interest rates elsewhere.

Additionally, the savings and loans, which had traditionally lent money for long-term real estate purchases, found that the short-term interest rates they had to pay to attract depositors far exceeded the long-term rates they were charging borrowers. In the early 1980s, savings and loan institutions were given the right to engage in activities formerly reserved for other institutions in an attempt to shore up their profitability. These changes offered short-term help for savings and loans, but rural banks lost their competitive edge. The Depository Institutions Deregulation and Monetary Control Act of 1980 phased in uniform reserve requirements for banks and savings institutions and provided for the gradual elimination of the Federal Reserve Board's Regulation Q limits on interest rates.

Banking deregulation involves a decrease in the degree to which the government limits and oversees (1) the costs of credit and services, (2) the geographic location of financial institutions, and (3) the variety of services offered by financial institutions. The goal has been to increase the *efficiency* of distribution of financial capital. What the lawmakers mean by efficiency is that funds be able to move to where they offer the investor the greatest possible return consistent with the risk involved in their use. With deregulation, return on investment is assessed on an increasingly shorter time frame.

Deregulation has made it relatively easy for financial institutions to capture savings from rural areas and add these funds to a national pool of capital that can be directed wherever the highest short-term profit can be made. From the rural perspective, it has become increasingly difficult to keep local capital invested locally. Facilitated by a variety of national policies, capital now flows easily from one city to another or from one country to another. This international capital market has increased the outflow of capital from rural areas.

When they compare other options, bankers and other lenders see investments in rural communities as having high risk and low payoff. Deregulation has increased the relative cost of credit for rural areas as compared with urban areas and decreased the availability of credit for rural borrowers. It has further decreased the availability of financial services for the rural poor. As Gary Green (1991) points out, "Banking deregulation has privatized the profits and socialized the losses associated with structural changes in the financial system." The balanced exchange of public trust through regulation and deposit insurance has been moved off center. Green, a rural sociologist who has studied rural banking extensively, advocates a return to regulation of a type that permits greater flexibility in the form and content of banking practices and organizational structure in return for social responsibility on the part of banks, including reinvestment in rural communities.

Business Capital and Community

For the most part, capital has always been less available in rural areas than in urban areas. Changes in the U.S. financial market have recently made it increasingly difficult for rural areas to attract and retain capital. This section explores some of the strategies by which capital can be attracted to and retained in rural communities.

KEEPING CAPITAL LOCAL

In many ways, banks and other lending institutions are like other businesses in rural communities. They also require investment capital, not just savings, to get started. Individuals wanting to start a bank or purchase an existing one take out an individual or business loan from another financial institution.

Starting or acquiring a bank often requires more capital than can be obtained through the usual loan procedure. Increasingly, banks require equity capital gained from stockholders. As more and more of those stockholders and owners come from outside the community, concern mounts that decisions on the use of savings deposited in the bank will be based on what benefits the shareholders but not necessarily the community. Under the previous ownership pattern, local owners were more likely to perceive benefits that were more consistent with those of the community.

Because banks and thrifts enjoy special privileges from the public sector in terms of deposit insurance and oversight, many think that banks should be required to serve the public good as well as stockholders' short-term interests. For banks, however, it is difficult to argue that the interests of the stockholders, who may now live anywhere in the world, are identical with those of the community. Stockholders tend to encourage capital use that favors short-term gain, which pays them higher dividends and makes their stocks worth more. This conflicts with the needs of communities, which often need "patient" capital that can be invested locally. This use of capital emphasizes long-term gain in recognition of the multiplier effect such capital can have in the community. By "multiplier effect" is meant the extent to which money is recirculated in the local economy; such recirculation enables each dollar to have an impact beyond its face value (see Figure 5.3).

The extent to which capital leaves a community can be seen in the declining loan/deposit ratios among rural banks. A decreasing ratio means that less of the money deposited by community residents is being reinvested in the community through loans. Instead, the money deposited is exiting the community through urban municipal bonds, certificates of deposits at larger banks, and government securities. The farm crisis significantly reduced traditional loan opportunities in rural communities, and bankers have not found it easy to identify nontraditional loan options.

The economic base of the rural community has a great deal to do with the readiness of bankers to reinvest locally. For example, the loan/deposit ratio in retirement counties in the United States in 1987 was nearly 33 percent higher than in farming-dependent counties. The implication is that bankers felt retirees created a business climate more favorable for

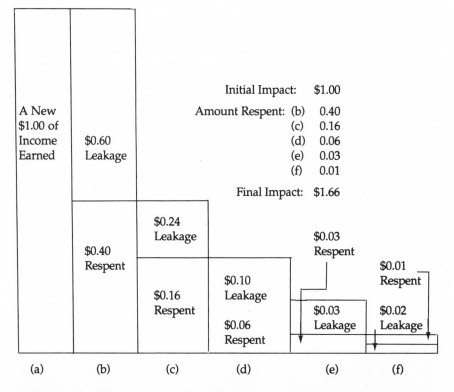

FIGURE 5.3 Income Multiplier. Each dollar of new income is respent five times, such that part stays in the community and part "leaks" outside of the community. The amount respent in the community multiplies the value of that income to the community. In this example, each dollar of income has an impact of $1.66.

investment than farmers offered. The return on investment derived from increasing services for retirees is much higher than the return on investment from increasing the productive capacity of farmers. Thus, capital remained in the retirement communities. Figure 5.4 shows the change in loan/deposit ratios over time as well as contrasted for retirement and farming communities. The third line shows the average loan/deposit ratios for all nonmetropolitan communities.

The Community Reinvestment Act of 1977 encouraged banks to invest their capital within the local community. The legislation was aimed primarily at poor urban areas, and few rural banks were forced to reinvest in rural communities under the terms of the act. Until the farm crisis of 1982, lack of rural reinvestment did not appear to be a major problem.

128

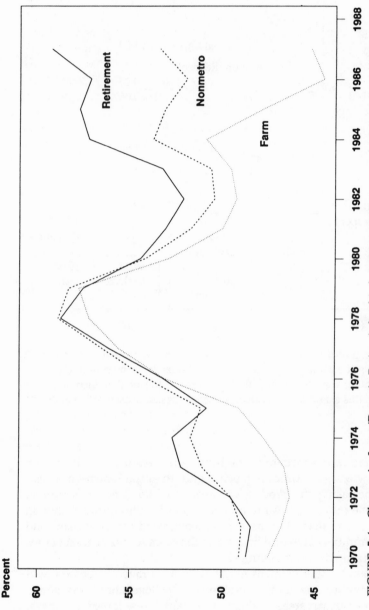

FIGURE 5.4 Change in Loan/Deposit Ratio. A bank's loan/deposit ratio is an indicator of the extent to which local capital is being invested locally. The higher the ratio is, then the more successfully the local bank is reinvesting the community's money. This graph contrasts the change in the loan/deposit ratio in retirement and farming communities. Clearly, banks are more comfortable reinvesting their funds locally in retirement communities. *Source:* M. Drabenstott and Charles Morris. 1991. "Financing Rural Businesses." In Cornelia B. Flora and James A. Christenson (eds.), *Rural Policies for the 1990s.* Boulder: Westview Press. Reprinted by permission.

Rural banks were eager and able to make agricultural loans locally and often diversified with energy-related loans.

With the farm crisis and the following worldwide drop in commodity prices came a marked decline in borrowers' ability to repay loans based on natural-resource extraction (agriculture, mining, fishing, and timber). Because rural banks could no longer extend the kind of loans they had traditionally made locally, they tended to decrease local lending dramatically and invest their deposits in government securities. Government securities were a far more secure investment, but they failed to recirculate capital within the rural communities.

A strategy by which the federal government borrows money, government securities are used to finance the federal debt. *Government securities* are either short-term or long-term securities sold by the federal government, such as U.S. savings bonds. Rural banks have a much greater percentage of their assets in government securities than do urban banks. That the federal deficit is disproportionally financed by rural areas is particularly ironic. The sectoral shifts in government spending during the 1980s, when the debt rose most dramatically, directed capital toward urban areas. Even the high agricultural subsidies that were paid out in the mid-1980s did not balance the decrease in federal capital inflow that had occurred in previous decades under social programs. As rural communities invested in government securities, they helped fund programs in urban areas.

NEW SOURCES OF CAPITAL

Traditional ways of generating capital for rural communities now appear to be inadequate. Indeed, the flow of capital from rural areas seems to have exceeded the out-migration of people. Governments as well as private entities and new public-private ventures are attempting to generate investment capital in new ways. By 1987, thirty-seven states had implemented targeted investment programs for rural areas.

State programs to create seed capital and venture capital use both tax dollars and forced savings (particularly state pension funds). These programs attempt to pool risk in directing capital to rural areas for housing or businesses. The problem with many of these programs is that they are labor-intensive. For each loan, data must be gathered regarding the potential risk, the collateral available, and the credit history of the borrower. It is as costly to give a small loan as a large one, and many rural enterprises do not require huge capital investments, only patient ones. These strategies, as in the cases of several federal programs, depend upon the development of community organizations with the capacity to manage the loans.

Federal Community Development Block Grants, for example, use an initial infusion of federal funds that can be recirculated within a community guided by local development organizations with private status but local government sanction. The key to this capital-transfer program is that loan repayment is recycled within the community, with community groups providing technical assistance and oversight, often with help from outside agencies as well. Small businesses can borrow capital for start-up or expansion at below-market rates. Technical assistance is then provided by fellow businesspeople.

There are in place a number of public-private partnerships through which state governments make available their idle funds (pension funds or reserves). When matched by private investment capital, these funds can provide businesses with needed start-up capital. Generally, such arrangements are desirable where available capital is insufficient to generate growth. The most successful of these funds have formed strong partnerships with local community development corporations to create private nonprofit entities having some local public funding. In these programs, as in other mechanisms of increasing capital availability in rural areas, social organization is more important than local savings in ensuring that capital investment for community development takes place.

CAPITAL RETENTION THROUGH RISK REDUCTION

Another way that risk to commercial banks on any given loan can be reduced is through the use of secondary markets for rural business loans. Secondary markets allow rural banks to package together a number of business loans, which they initiate and service; investors who purchase those securities bear the risk. Such secondary markets have been in place for many years for home mortgages and were initiated for farm loans in 1989. This approach to sharing risk could help rural banks recirculate local capital within the community.

Another way to make loans less risky is to provide technical assistance in such areas as personnel management, marketing, accounting, and planning. A recent study of rural West Virginia banks (Boggs et al. 1988) strongly indicated that banks should be more aggressive in providing such services if rural development is to occur. Both the Small Business Administration of the federal government and the Cooperative Extension Service at the state and local levels have programs that aid small businesses and that can be tied to capital investment.

Loan guarantees by the state and federal governments spread the risk of capital investment in rural areas between the public and private sectors. Such guarantees function much as the student loan program in which private banks make the loan. The individual who borrows the money is obligated to repay the capital plus interest, usually at below-market rates. The federal government guarantees that the lender will be repaid at least a certain percentage of the initial loan if default occurs. This strategy is cheaper than if the government makes capital investment directly, and it allows capital to be invested in a far greater number of enterprises.

GOVERNMENT'S INDIRECT ROLE

Another way that government directs capital is through tax concessions. Tax abatements reduce taxes for investments that are made in certain business ventures deemed socially desirable. Alone among developed countries, the United States has viewed home ownership as so socially desirable that its tax code allows a federal tax deduction of all interest and local taxes paid on home mortgages.

Other laws reduce the tax burden of those who invest in specific geographic areas by starting new businesses or expanding existing firms. Governments offer tax abatements in an effort to attract industry. The problem with this strategy is that although it benefits private capital investment in a specific area, it may not increase total capital investment in the nation. Further, the tax breaks given often increase the need for public capital investment in the form of schools, prisons, fire stations, sewers, and roads. The reduced taxation offered new businesses erodes the tax base needed to support the public capital investments.

More and more communities are trying to retain capital locally by stopping capital leakage and forming local corporations and cooperatives to generate capital and invest it locally. When successful, these enterprises build on the strengths of an area and the solidarity of its citizens. Such mechanisms of capital generation increase local control. They also tend to have a longer-term time frame than do firms brought in from the outside that have stockholders who provided capital in the hopes of reaping short-term gains.

Firms recruited from the outside are often branch plants of large multinational firms that seek some advantage—cheap land, lower wage scales, and the like. A recent study commissioned by the National Governors Association (John et al. 1988) points out that these transplants often create real difficulties for local capital formation in rural communities. Among the problems are low-wage employment, few purchases of local inputs for production, and cutbacks and shutdowns that are more frequent and likely because of the absentee nature of ownership and management. Still, the allure of such an option for a desperate rural community is great.

Recent studies have pointed to the weakness such a short-term approach has inserted into community development efforts. Rural communities are being forced to address the problems created by rapid capital movement to capture short-term gain. As rural areas organize to create alternatives to provide the needed public and private capital for their communities to function, they may provide alternative models of capital investment that strengthen the economic base of the country.

Organizing for Capital?

George Martin, Roy Kimsey, and Marci Snell are all rural entrepreneurs. All three need capital in order to function in the economy. All three have met resistance from the traditional social organizations—banks—created to offer access to capital.

Sociologists have been intrigued with the interaction between social organization and economic organization. Some theorists (Weber 1978) have suggested that how money was accounted for can be linked to the emergence of capitalism. In earlier days, the most common form of accounting had been cash accounting—a bookkeeper simply kept track of the money coming in and going out in a business. There was no way to keep track of exchanges in which money is converted to capital goods, such as when a business invests in a new plant or accumulates an inventory. When accountants began keeping track of assets rather than simply cash, capitalism as a form of economic organization began to emerge. More recent research is exploring double-entry bookkeeping (Carruthers and Espeland 1991).

Clearly, a number of social organizations have to be in place in order for a modern economy to emerge. The people in those organizations and the conventions they have for keeping track of assets and evaluating loans play an important role in influencing who has access to capital. Do we need new conventions—new ways of keeping track of capital in order to support rural economies? Deregulation of banks, coupled with the increased mobility of capital in a global economy, suggests that we need something.

Chapter Summary

Capital is any resource capable of producing other resources. Capital exists in four forms: (1) capital goods, (2) land, (3) financial capital, and (4) human capital. When individuals or groups invest their own resources, they have used private capital. Public capital refers to the resources invested by the community. The forms of capital differ in how easily they can move. Land and some forms of capital goods are not mobile. Both human capital and financial capital are highly mobile.

Nearly all communities depend on capital, either for private investment in local businesses or public investment in community services. Communities have often relied on federal and state governments in gaining access to capital for local improvements. Individual businesses have turned to local banks. Traditionally, rural banks have made business loans based on the individual's net worth, cash flow, and familiarity with the banker. As control of rural banks shifts to metropolitan areas, this last criterion becomes less important.

Capital is available from a number of sources. Businesses take out loans for which interest is charged. Businesses can also choose to sell stock in order to raise the capital needed. In exchange for making capital available to the business, stockholders participate in selecting the management of the company and share profits generated. Municipal bonds are typically used as a device by which communities borrow the larger amounts of money needed for capital improvements.

Deregulation of the banking industry in the early 1980s changed the economic environment in which rural banks now function. In limiting the interest rates that could be charged for loans or paid out on deposits, banking regulations were more favorable to rural banks. When the regulations were dropped, capital began moving to where it could earn the highest short-term return. Capital began to flow out of rural areas. Rural communities are working to retain local capital, reduce the risk associated with local investments, identify innovative sources of venture capital, and enlist governmental help in making capital available to rural businesses.

Key Terms

An *asset* is money or property that can be used to repay a loan.

Capital is defined as resources capable of producing other resources.

Capital flight occurs when funds originally invested or generated in a particular area are moved in order to take advantage of increased earning elsewhere.

Capital goods consist of objects used to produce other goods or resources.

Demand deposits are deposits in commercial banks and savings institutions that may be withdrawn upon demand.

Efficiency describes the goal of allocating capital in different places so as to maximize the return on the investment, given the level of risk.

Equity is the net worth of a firm or corporation (total assets less total liabilities) belonging to the partners or stockholders.

Federal Deposit Insurance Corporation (FDIC) is an agency created in 1933 to provide insurance for bank depositors and supervision of insured banks.

Financial capital includes stocks, bonds, market futures, and letters of credit as well as money.

Government securities are either short-term or long-term securities sold by the federal government, such as U.S. savings bonds.

Human capital describes a form of capital that results when investments made in people produce other goods or resources. These investments are made chiefly in the form of education and training.

Interest is the charge made for borrowed money.

Junk bonds are high-interest, high-risk securities that are often sold at a deep discount, an amount well below their face value.

Land is a form of capital when it is used to produce other resources.

Liability describes the claims of creditors.

Liquidity describes the difficulty and cost of converting assets into money. The greater the degree of liquidity, the faster and cheaper the conversion process.

Money markets are financial markets for short-term, highly liquid, low-risk financial instruments, such as U.S. Treasury bills, federal funds, and commercial paper.

Municipal bonds are debt obligations of a state, locality, or municipal corporation. Interest on these bonds is exempt from U.S. income taxes.

Nominal interest rate is the stated or published percentage cost or return on capital, not corrected for inflation.

Private capital is capital owned and controlled by individuals or groups of individuals.

Public capital is capital owned and controlled by governments or communities, such as schools or bridges.

Real interest rate is the nominal interest rate minus the rate of inflation.

Venture capital is the capital provided by investors willing to take a higher than average risk for an anticipated higher than average profit in an expanding but capital-short enterprise.

References

Allen, M. 1989. "Midland Malaise: Out-of-State Bankers Tight with a Dollar Rile Old-Style Texans." *Wall Street Journal* August 10: A1–A4.

Bailey, L. H. 1911. *The Country Life Movement in the United States.* New York: Macmillan.

Boggs, Bruce S., David F. Sorenson, and Andrew M. Isserman. 1988. *Commercial Lending Patterns and Economic Development in West Virginia.* Berea, KY: Mountain Association of Community Development.

Carruthers, Bruce G., and Wendy Nelson Espeland. 1991. "Accounting for Rationality: Double-Entry Bookkeeping and the Rhetoric of Economic Rationality." *American Journal of Sociology* 97:31–69.

Downs, Anthony. 1985. *The Revolution in Real Estate Finance.* Washington, DC: Brookings Institution.

Green, Gary P. 1991. "Rural Banking." Pp. 36–46 in C. B. Flora and J. A. Christenson (eds.), *Rural Policies for the 1990s.* Boulder, CO: Westview.

John, DeWitt, Sandra Batie, and Kim Norris. 1988. *A Brighter Future for Rural America: Strategies for Communities and States.* Washington, DC: National Governors Association.

Schultz, T. W. 1961. "Investment in Human Capital." *American Economic Review* 51 (1): 1–17.

Weber, Max. 1978. *Economy and Society.* Vols. 1 and 2. Berkeley: University of California Press.

The Global Economy

(6)

Susan stared at the notice. AT&T was closing the Fairlawn plant and moving its production facilities to Thailand and Mexico. Susan was offered the chance to go to Matamoros, a small town near the Texas border, to help train the new workers. That involved only another three weeks' work. Then what would she do?

Susan Cox loved growing up in Hiwassee, a small town nestled in the hills of southern Virginia. A natural athlete, she had been offered tennis and volleyball scholarships from colleges all over the country. Because her mother's health was poor and Susan was not particularly fond of school, she decided to take a job at the AT&T plant located in nearby Fairlawn instead. AT&T was a solid international corporation, and the plant offered plenty of room for advancement. Within a couple of years, Susan was taking home $50 per day along with a good benefits package negotiated by her union.

The New River Valley Economic Development Alliance had worked hard to attract the Fairlawn plant. When members learned that AT&T was looking for a production site, they persuaded the county to offer property tax abatements over the first ten years of the plant's operation. Combined with federal tax relief programs that allowed the company to depreciate the factory more rapidly, AT&T had been able to build the plant at essentially no cost to itself.

Housing construction in the surrounding communities boomed, as homes were needed for the executives transferred to the new facility. In addition, the valley had not been able to supply all of the nearly 1,000 production workers needed. So others moved into the region. Everyone seemed to profit. AT&T had a state-of-the-art production facility. Fairlawn and surrounding communities grew. Susan and others like her now had the option to stay in the area, with access to good jobs.

The plant opened in 1981. Compared with other companies in the region, AT&T paid relatively well. Like most international corporations, AT&T was unionized. Over time, however, working conditions gradually worsened. In 1990, the workers went out on strike. Much to their surprise, the company quickly agreed to all their demands, asking only that the new benefits package not be implemented until January 1991.

It was October when Susan got her notice. Some workers would be transferred to Dallas, while the bulk of the manufacturing would move to Thailand and Mexico. Many of the plant's tax advantages would expire by the end of 1990. The new benefits for workers at the Fairlawn plant would never be implemented. Susan would be replaced by a teenager in Matamoros, who was willing to work for 50 cents an hour. AT&T claimed it had no choice—labor costs were too high in the United States. Susan now feels that she, too, has little choice.

Susan's experiences are not unusual, nor are they unique to rural people. Businesses such as AT&T constantly seek to increase their profits. Strategies used to cut costs and increase profits focus on using cheaper inputs (land, labor, capital, raw materials) or making the existing inputs more efficient. As shown in Table 6.1, communities can contribute to these strategies. They can lower the price of land by reducing property taxes or by installing roads and utilities needed by the plant. Communities reduce the cost of business capital by offering government-guaranteed bonds or government grants and loans, enabling the firm to pay below-market interest rates. They can also reduce labor costs by keeping out high-wage unionized industries or by making it difficult for labor to organize.

For more than thirty years, U.S. and foreign-owned industries have moved production facilities to rural areas. Lower labor costs, subsidized plants, few environmental laws, and tax benefits offered by the communities have encouraged the growth of rural manufacturing. In the 1970s, this growth was often at the expense of urban areas. Labor unions, run-down buildings in need of major renovation, strict pollution controls, and high taxes had discouraged further investment in urban facilities. Ironically, many of these same firms are now moving their production facilities to developing countries, in search of still cheaper labor, freedom from labor-law enforcement, and fewer pollution constraints.

These changes are part of a broader economic restructuring that is occurring worldwide. Not only are rural and urban areas alike being drawn into a world economy, but the character of the economy has changed. Capital, the money industry needs to finance its operations, can

TABLE 6.1 Options for Reducing Costs

Costs of Production	Changes at the Firm Level	Changes at the Community Level
Labor cost per item produced	Introduce machinery to make each worker more productive (capital).	Provide cheap capital for more efficient machinery.
	Reorganize to make each worker more productive (management).	Offer management consulting.
	Improve quality of workers through training or education.	Offer continuing education programs for employees of firms.
	Reduce wages.	Absorb some labor costs through subsidized housing and welfare programs
Regulation		Pass less stringent health, safety, and environmental controls.

now be moved easily from one country to another. Thus, the price of money, not the price of raw materials, is driving many business decisions. Labor has also become more mobile. This chapter explores (1) traditional linkages between rural areas and international markets, (2) changes that have altered the character of the world economy, (3) the impact these changes are having on rural communities, and (4) the opportunities and problems this new economic environment creates.

Rural Linkages to a World Economy

Newspaper accounts and after-dinner speeches often characterize the world economy as though it were something new—as though the U.S. economy had been previously insulated from world events. Although the character of our economy has changed, we have always been linked to other countries through trade. In the case of rural communities, past linkages occurred primarily through the natural resources they exported and the labor they imported.

Raw logs are shipped to overseas markets (photo courtesy of the Ohio University Telecommunications Center).

EXPORTING NATURAL RESOURCES

As mentioned in Chapter 2, international trade has always been a part of the U.S. experience. Early European settlements in the New World were financed by trading companies eager to profit from the natural resources the new land offered. New England communities found furs, fish, and lumber to be their most productive exports. The South depended on cotton and tobacco. For the colonies, these international linkages were so important that the tariff England imposed on American tobacco was among the causes of the Revolutionary War.

Nearly all natural-resource–based economies move through cycles, some influenced by nature but others affected by trends in world markets. Mining towns have gone through boom-and-bust cycles as mineral prices fluctuated on the international market. In the 1870s, the silver streaming out of Nevada nearly ruined Germany, which had a currency based on silver. During World War I, cotton prices soared in response to the demand for uniforms. Once Europe recovered in the 1920s, however, prices dropped to historic lows. Increased grain production in Europe sent American wheat prices plummeting in the 1870s and 1890s and again during the 1920s. Until railroads opened up markets to the Midwest and East, Oregon lumber interests depended more on foreign than domestic markets.

More recently, oil towns from Texas to Montana prospered when members of the Organization of Petroleum Exporting Countries (OPEC) limited their oil production in 1973. The OPEC cartel represents the interests of major oil-producing countries, most of which are located in the Middle East. Decreased oil production in the Middle East meant increased prices worldwide, high enough to encourage the development of domestic oil reserves. This stimulated an economic boom that had not been equaled since the days of the gold and silver rushes of the last century. Less than a decade later, however, these same towns in states such as Texas and Oklahoma were struggling. Increased oil production from the OPEC nations had reduced sharply the price of oil worldwide, making our domestic oil no longer competitive.

IMPORTING LABOR

Early linkages with the world economy also included labor—the people needed to harvest the vast natural resources available in the New World. New England's furs, fish, and lumber were harvested by European immigrants seeking to escape religious persecution or simply get a new start on life. The labor used to harvest cotton and tobacco in the South was provided by slaves recruited involuntarily from Africa. The need for low-cost labor to perform domestic work along railroad lines or in mining camps led to heavy recruitment among the Chinese. Mine owners in West Virginia recruited experienced miners from Eastern Europe. Farms throughout the Midwest were settled by Europeans eager to own land.

The need for labor, especially in rural areas, was so great that the United States maintained open borders for nearly 100 years after independence. Immigration hit an all-time high in the first decade of the 1900s, leading some to propose that limits be put in place. In 1921, Congress passed the first quota act, limiting the annual number of immigrants from each country to 3 percent of the number of people born in that country and residing in the United States as reported in the 1910 census. The Immigration Act of 1924 was even more restrictive; it used the national origin of each individual in the United States in 1890 as the basis for allocating the flow of immigrants. It was not the numbers of immigrants but their racial and cultural backgrounds that inspired these exclusionary efforts, which were clearly aimed at reducing immigration from Asia and Eastern Europe. Over time, some attitudes have changed. National-origin limitations were lifted in 1965, but numerical limits remained in place until 1986. Although our recent history has been shaped by immigration restrictions, it is important to remember the extent to which economic activity in rural areas depended on labor imported from other countries.

The Growing Importance of Capital

Rural linkages to world markets are not new, but the character of those linkages has changed dramatically. *Commodities*, the natural resources or manufactured products bought and sold on markets, once drove the economy. The country that could mine copper or weave quality cloth at the lowest cost would export the most. Consequently, national industries sought to make their operations more efficient in order to remain competitive.

Today, it is the flow of capital from one currency to another that drives the economy. Corporations have become multinational, moving their operations to where the financial conditions 'are most profitable. As a result, local areas have less control over what happens to them economically. To understand how this came about, we need to examine (1) changes in international monetary policy, (2) changing supply-demand relationships, and (3) impact of a nation's internal fiscal policy.

INTERNATIONAL MONETARY POLICY

As World War II drew to a close, world leaders met in Bretton Woods, New Hampshire, to grapple with the problem of how to reestablish trade. Most felt that the economic chaos of the 1930s had contributed to the Nazi takeover in Europe; thus, they were anxious to develop mechanisms that would ensure stability in the world economy. The Bretton Woods Agreement created a system of fixed exchange rates among national currencies. *Exchange rates* set the value of countries' currencies relative to one another and are thus important in facilitating trade among nations. Under the agreement, the United States fixed the value of the U.S. dollar to gold at $35 per ounce. Exchange rates of other countries were then fixed relative to the U.S. dollar. This system of *fixed exchange rates* did not allow the dollar to fluctuate on world markets.

During the 1950s and 1960s, the United States enjoyed economic predominance worldwide. Its economy grew steadily, filling the trade gaps left as the nations of Europe and Japan turned their attention to rebuilding what had been destroyed during World War II. The United States favored open trade of its products and enjoyed a trade surplus, exporting more than it imported. The dollar occupied a unique position in the world economy as the standard against which the values of all other currencies were fixed.

As the world economy recovered and other nations strengthened their industrial base, the United States found its exports facing increased competition. By the early 1970s, the United States was importing more than it was exporting, in part because the dollar was valued much higher than other currencies. There was a net flow of dollars out of the United States and into countries from which we were importing goods.

When the dollars held by other countries exceeded the gold reserves we had with which to buy back those dollars, financiers assumed that the United States would increase the price of gold. In other words, increasing the exchange rate for gold from $35 per ounce to $40 per ounce in effect would decrease the value of each dollar relative to gold; this is called *devaluation of the dollar.* Financiers began trying to unload their dollars on world currency markets, hoping to sell the U.S. dollars before they were devalued. The flood of dollars on currency markets forced the United States to do just what the financiers feared—devalue the dollar. In August 1971, the United States also suspended the conversion of dollars into gold.

Efforts to establish a new fixed exchange rate failed. In May 1973, President Richard Nixon negotiated what became known as the Smithsonian Agreement. This agreement established a *floating exchange rate,* allowing currency values to fluctuate and find their market values. Central banks, including that of the United States, could no longer fix exchange rates except in cases when a nation's currency began fluctuating widely. In general, national controls on currency were reduced and cross-country banking restrictions were eased.

Financial capital, the money available for investment, now moves more easily from one country to another. This allows private speculators to buy and sell different currencies in an effort to make a profit as exchange rates fluctuate. Capital markets established through this exchange of currency generate a flow of money that is thirty times as great as the money exchanged when countries import or export products. Whether a nation's copper is competitive on the world market, for example, depends as much on the current exchange rate of its currency as on the local costs of mining the copper. A strong dollar discourages foreign tourists from visiting the United States, but U.S. tourists travel enthusiastically to other countries. When the dollar is weak relative to other currencies, visitors flock to the United States.

EFFECT OF INCREASED PRODUCTION ON COMPETITION

The 1970s brought a second milestone in the transition to a global economy. As mentioned earlier, OPEC decided to limit oil production. In making oil more scarce, OPEC effectively increased the price of oil. Urban people in the United States remember long lines at gasoline pumps and occasional fistfights as motorists jockeyed for position to buy the scarce gasoline at unbelievably high prices. Rural people remember $5-per-bushel wheat and $12-per-bushel soybeans—prices two to three times higher than usual.

BOX 6.1   THE GLOBAL ECONOMY AND ITS IMPACT ON THE ENVIRONMENT

OPEC's decision to limit oil production increased the prices for nearly all commodities. Although this stimulated most rural economies, it had a devastating impact on the environment. In the United States, more farmland was put into production. Windbreaks were plowed up, as were terraces that had been put in place back in the 1930s in an effort to conserve soil and water. Wheat, raised primarily in the Midwest and Northwest, was added to crop-rotation cycles throughout the country. U.S. Secretary of Agriculture Earl Butz urged farmers to plant fence row to fence row. Developing countries also responded. Because of the higher commodity prices, land that had earlier been unprofitable could now be pressed into production. Rain forests were cleared and prairie soils plowed. If roads were needed to provide access to this land, countries simply borrowed money from the oil-rich nations.

The rapid increase in the production of commodities had a number of impacts, some good and others bad. The U.S. economy boomed during the 1970s, in part because of the commodities rural areas were able to export to meet high demand and offset an ever-decreasing dollar value. A number of developing nations, able to improve their road and trade systems, became much more active exporters. Ultimately, however, the environment suffered. Rain forests and fragile prairies were destroyed. Peasants who had colonized land in their countries were often pushed out by developers, whose primary interest was in profit and not settlement of the land. Land-conservation principles were cast aside and are only now being reintroduced.

In order to understand how the price of oil is related to the price of wheat, we need to look back at capital markets. The sudden increase in oil prices meant that the oil-producing countries developed a trade surplus. The money they received from the oil they exported exceeded the money they spent on imports. Oil-producing nations had petrodollars to spare and were suddenly able to import more goods. The Soviet Union, for example, was a major exporter of oil. It also needed food and feed grains with which to support its people. The trade surplus created by higher oil prices enabled the Soviets to purchase larger quantities of basic commodities such as wheat and soybeans.

As OPEC nations created a higher demand for commodities, the price those commodities brought also increased. Higher prices made it more profitable for others to enter the market. Production increased rapidly, with both good and bad outcomes (Box 6.1).

NEW LINKAGES OF NATIONAL ECONOMIES

The increased price for commodities that followed set off a period of worldwide inflation. *Inflation* occurs when the currency in circulation or the availability of credit increases, leading to a sharp rise in prices. The devaluation of the dollar made U.S. exports extremely competitive in world markets. Percentages and volume of crops exported were higher than they had been during the past fifty years. By the end of the 1970s, U.S. economic growth depended on the rest of the world, particularly as a market for agricultural products. Like many developing nations, the United States moved into a period of stagflation—high inflation with no real economic growth.

Efforts to curb inflation in the United States focused on internal fiscal and monetary policy. In 1979, the Federal Reserve Board, the governing body that sets monetary policy for the U.S. central bank, withdrew dollars from circulation in the economy. This strategy reduces inflation. People have less money to buy products, which reduces demand and stabilizes prices.

In addition to the Federal Reserve Board's action, the Reagan administration decreased the federal income tax and, despite making spending cuts in many areas, increased spending for defense and farm programs and allowed interest rates to rise. Massive tax cuts were made in 1981, with the high-income and corporate sectors of the economy being the primary beneficiaries. The rationale was that tax cuts would free up money for investment in the domestic economy and stimulate economic growth. Increased economic growth did not occur at the projected rate, however. As a result, the federal deficit increased rapidly. The United States became the largest debtor nation in the world, borrowing money from foreign countries rather than raising taxes or cutting spending.

The United States took these actions in an effort to deal with its internal economic problems. As it turns out, however, these actions had an enormous impact on the world economy. Economic theory predicts that if the money supply is reduced, the economy will slow down in what economists call a recession. A *recession* occurs when the currency in circulation or availability of credit decreases, resulting in decreased business activity. The trade-off is reduced inflation. The actions taken by the Federal Reserve Board and the Reagan administration slowed inflation. As expected, a recession also occurred. The recession was not limited to the United States, however. It was worldwide. Dollars withdrawn from the national economy were also dollars withdrawn from the world economy.

Why should action taken in the United States to cure its economic ills affect the world economy? The answer lies, in part, with how easily capital flows from one country to another. Removing dollars from the money supply makes them more scarce and hence more valuable. The growth of the federal deficit meant that the federal government itself was competing for scarce dollars. Interest rates increased substantially.

High interest rates make U.S. government securities a good investment. Foreign capital flowed into the United States because the U.S. government needed to borrow so much money to service the debt. The U.S. deficit

The new markets are "global" markets, as U.S. commodities compete with those of countries throughout the world (photo courtesy of the U.S. Department of Agriculture).

became something of an international "black hole," pulling in any and all liquid capital. This made capital scarce for others, and a worldwide recession occurred. The spiral of increasing demand and thus higher prices for commodities came to an abrupt end. Prices of commodities on the world market dropped dramatically.

National economies are now linked with one another. The ease with which money can move from one country to another means that steps taken to manage one country's internal economy now affect the world economy.

THE NEW CORPORATION

What is the impact of these changes? The world economy in which we now function has features that have changed significantly. Companies have become multinational. Competition within natural-resource industries has increased substantially. The flow of capital, not commodities, affects international trade.

The change in corporate structure has been especially dramatic. No longer confined to one country, many of today's corporations have developed branches and subsidiary companies in countries throughout the world. These diversified locations ensure that the company has access to local markets and the flexibility to move resources quickly in response to changes in capital and labor markets. The organizational structure of these companies reflects the multinational character of their operations. Stockholders reside all over the world, as do the board members who make decisions on behalf of the company. Individual countries can do little to control the activities of these new corporations. At this point, no international controls exist.

Impact on Rural Areas

Any discussion of capital flows, increased commodities prices, floating currency exchanges, and foreign investment seems abstract until their collective impact on rural areas is examined. Two examples, one drawn from agriculture and the second from rural manufacturing, illustrate how rural areas were affected by the changed global economy. Discussed also is the changing character of the rural labor force.

THE FARM CRISIS

In many respects, the history of U.S. agriculture is one of increased efficiency yet dwindling significance in the economy. In 1790, 95 percent of Americans were farmers. Today less than 2 percent of the population is engaged in farming. Farm exports accounted for 80 percent of U.S. exports during the decade after the Civil War, but this value had shrunk to 32 percent by 1932. In 1988 farm exports were only 12 percent of the nation's exports.

Mechanization that began in earnest in the 1920s accelerated after World War II, changing the character of farming operations. Farms became more mechanized for a variety of reasons. The rapid industrialization that developed to serve war needs and later support European and Japanese reconstruction drew many rural people to urban jobs. Because there were fewer people to work on farms, the cost of labor increased. In the South, civil rights efforts eventually influenced the wage paid to blacks who picked cotton. Rather than pay the higher wage for hand picking, owners turned to cotton-picking machines. Throughout the 1960s and 1970s, technology continued to offer increased assistance through bigger tractors, more effective herbicides, or more productive hybrid seed.

Ultimately, however, mechanization in any industry means that costs shift from labor to capital. Instead of paying wages to farm workers, farmers pay interest on loans for these technological advances or for more land. Consequently, money needed to be available for farmers to borrow at relatively low interest rates. A variety of economic conditions and government programs made this capital available.

The economic environment created by OPEC's decision to limit oil production in 1973 favored both expansion and mechanization. As mentioned earlier, higher oil prices ultimately increased the demand for nearly all natural resources. As the demand increased, prices for these commodities rose to all-time highs. Because the best way to profit from high prices was to acquire more land on which to grow more crops, more and more land was pressed into production. The price of land rose quickly. The real value of land, when controlled for inflation, nearly doubled during the 1970s. When the effects of inflation are added in, the price per acre nearly tripled during this same time period (U.S. Department of Commerce 1986).

A number of factors affect a person's ability to borrow money. First, an applicant must have collateral, or equity—something the bank can keep if the applicant is later unable to repay the loan. For most farmers, equipment and land serve as collateral against loans. Second, interest rates must be low enough that the borrower can afford to pay them and still make enough to live on. Because interest rates typically reflect the availability of money, an ample money supply will keep interest rates low. Third, using money to buy more land or equipment must appear to be more profitable than simply putting the money into savings.

Economic conditions during the 1970s encouraged farmers to borrow money. Land was rapidly increasing in value, giving farmers more equity in the land they already held. The shift to floating exchange rates and devaluation of the dollar made U.S. products very competitive in world markets. Business was booming, and capital was readily available. Moreover, inflation was outstripping interest rates. If inflation averages 10 percent and interest rates are only 8 percent, it makes sense to buy land or equipment rather than put money into a savings account. Land itself became an excellent investment and a hedge against inflation.

Actions taken in the late 1970s and early 1980s to control inflation and stimulate the domestic economy brought this expansion to an abrupt end. As real interest rates climbed and the value of the dollar rose, those who had borrowed money found themselves paying more interest with increasingly scarce dollars. When commodities prices fell so dramatically, both crops and land lost much of their former value. Land prices dropped by more than 50 percent, reaching the point where farmers no longer had the equity to justify loans that were still outstanding. In short, a great many farmers faced financial ruin. By 1985, the number of farm foreclosures, forfeitures, or loan defaults reached levels not seen since the Great Depression.

Farmers were not stupid, nor were banks greedy. Both applied tried-and-true investment principles to the economic environment created by the floating exchange rate and increased oil prices. Monetary and fiscal policies initiated by the federal government (decreasing taxes) and the

Federal Reserve Board (cutting the money supply) simply changed that environment.

U.S. farmers now function in a changed economy. The increased production stimulated by high commodities prices of the 1970s has flooded the market. In an earlier day, the United States competed with Canada and Argentina in exporting wheat and with Argentina and Australia in exporting beef, for example. Today U.S. farmers must compete with dozens of nations in nearly every agricultural export. Access to capital for investment in land or equipment has dwindled. Government willingness to fund programs to tide farmers over has decreased in response to demands from other sectors for government funds. The farmer in Iowa now competes with the car manufacturer in Japan as capital moves easily from one country to another. Finally, the worth of a farmer's produce has become as much a function of currency markets as it is of the inherent productivity of the farm operation.

RURAL MANUFACTURING

Economic conditions that encouraged farmers to expand also stimulated the growth of rural manufacturing. About 1960, relatively mature industries began looking to rural areas for cheaper land, an ample labor supply, and lower wage levels. This trend was bolstered by decisions to devalue the dollar and shift to a floating currency. The cheaper dollar made U.S. exports more competitive in world markets. This country's products also became more competitive within domestic markets because it was less costly to manufacture some products at home than import them from Germany or Japan. The rapid increases in commodity prices that followed OPEC's decision to limit oil production put money in the hands of many developing nations. Their greater purchasing power further increased demand for U.S. products.

Growth in rural manufacturing employment continued during the 1970s, increasing at an annual rate of about 1.4 percent until 1976. By contrast, manufacturing employment in urban areas was declining at a rate of 1.1 percent per year. The availability of low-wage, hardworking, nonunionized rural labor forces attracted many light-manufacturing plants, such as the AT&T plant that hired Susan Cox. Rural communities invested heavily in industrial parks and infrastructure developments designed to attract industry. Tax abatements, new-job tax credits, training programs, low-interest loans, and a host of local, state, and federal subsidies added more incentive. High demand, low wages, and inexpensive capital made it profitable for industries to relocate their more routine production activities to rural counties. By 1979, manufacturing had become the largest employer of the rural work force.

148 The Global Economy

Actions taken to control inflation and stimulate the domestic economy brought this expansion to a halt. Between 1979 and 1982, employment in rural manufacturing dropped 5.6 percent as nearly every state in the nation lost manufacturing jobs. Recession hit the U.S. economy. As the 1980s progressed, the money supply tightened, thereby increasing the value of the dollar. U.S. goods became more expensive on the world market.

By the mid-1980s, rural areas found themselves in a totally different economic environment. Electric transformers that had been produced profitably at the AT&T plant in Fairlawn, for example, now cost more than parts imported from elsewhere. The strong U.S. dollar made it more difficult for products manufactured in the United States to compete on world markets. To maintain its profits, AT&T felt it necessary to move the plant to the developing nations of Mexico and Thailand, where labor could be acquired still more cheaply.

Experts differ as to whether manufacturing will rebound in rural areas. Features of the changed world economy, however, do make some issues clear. First, the competitiveness of goods manufactured in the United States depends as much on the relative value of currencies as on labor productivity, plant operating expenses, or raw material costs. Ultimately, rural manufacturing has been drawn into the same global economy as commodities production. Second, rural areas of the United States can no longer rely on cheap labor as the device with which to encourage manufacturing development. Developing nations such as Mexico or Thailand can supply labor even more cheaply. Rural communities will need to find innovative ways to adapt to the new global division of labor.

AN INTERNATIONAL LABOR MARKET

As discussed earlier, rural areas historically depended on imported labor. Immigration limits were not imposed until 1921. In the two decades after World War II, only a little over 60 percent of the legal quota of immigrants entered the country. Labor was needed, however, as the economy expanded.

Permitting temporary immigration offered one solution to the problem, and this was provided through the Bracero Program, a series of bilateral agreements that temporarily admitted agricultural workers to the United States from Mexico, Barbados, Jamaica, and British Honduras. Migrant workers harvested fruits and vegetables, providing low-wage labor at crucial times in the production cycle. Illegal immigrants, those without any formal documentation, also began moving into both urban and rural areas.

As international capital flow increased, so did international immigration to the United States. The United States took in more legal immigrants in the 1980s than in any decade since the great wave of European immigration at the beginning of the twentieth century. Despite a temporary decline in illegal immigrants after the amnesty law of 1986, illegal immigration to this country is again high. Immigrants now represent 10 percent of the U.S. labor force, twice the proportion of twenty years ago. In the 1980s, one in four new workers was an immigrant. Most labor economists predict that proportion will increase in the 1990s.

Agriculture in many parts of the United States depended on migrant labor at planting, harvesting, and weeding time, but both service and manufacturing communities now increasingly employ immigrants also. Packing plants in the Midwest, such as a plant in Garden City, Kansas, hire mostly Latinos and Southeast Asians, many of them women. The town of Lynd, Minnesota, recently brought in Southeast Asian immigrants from the Twin Cities area to fill a labor shortage at a local turkey-processing plant. In rural Montana, an innovative project combines the work of Hmong women, Native American women, and displaced home-makers in high-fashion clothing design, construction, and sales.

Imported labor will continue to be a feature of rural community life. Rural areas have benefited from the immigration of medical doctors and nurses from developing countries, gaining access to professional skills that have been scarce. The majority of the new immigrants, however, have relatively few skills and limited education. They are viewed as hard workers and thus are often favored over U.S.-born workers of equal skill levels. This keeps wages low among unskilled workers. In good times, immigrant labor helps rural areas deal with a labor deficit. In bad times, immigrants compete with native workers for jobs and present communities with a complex set of social problems. Indeed, the press has noted that the price of more open borders is being paid by those workers least able to afford it.

Long-term Restructuring

Most experts now agree that the world economy has changed and that the U.S. economy is restructuring in response to these changes. Rural communities have become part of this transformation, and although they exert limited control over the nation's fiscal policies and even less control over what are now worldwide capital markets, they can make intelligent choices. Those choices need to be based on a firm understanding of what drives the global economy. This section examines features of the new global economy and what these features suggest for rural communities.

FEATURES OF THE CHANGED GLOBAL ECONOMY

The shift to floating exchange rates for currencies and the economic response to OPEC's actions in the early 1970s led to a series of features that now characterize the global economy. According to Drucker (1986), these features are that (1) the industrial economy has become uncoupled from the primary-goods economy; (2) production has become uncoupled from employment; and (3) the movement of capital has replaced trade as the driving force of the economy.

The first feature refers to the fact that manufacturing and other sectors of the economy no longer seem to change in response to prices for natural resources. In the past, the economic health of the industrial sector was linked to the economic health of raw materials or natural resources. Now U.S. industrial firms get fewer of their raw materials from U.S. sources and sell fewer of their products back to the producers of primary goods. Our industrial economy appears to be functioning independently of our raw-materials economy.

The second feature of the changed world economy is that manufacturing production has become uncoupled from employment. Again, traditional models of the economy predicted that as manufacturing production increased, manufacturing employment increased. For example, when Henry Ford increased wages at the Ford plant, workers were able to buy more cars, thus increasing production. Expanding the industrial base of the economy created more manufacturing jobs.

The relationship linking worker to market to manufacturer has now changed. Manufacturing production increased by nearly 40 percent from 1973 to 1985, but manufacturing employment decreased over that same period. Paralleling the economic uncoupling of raw materials from industry, this uncoupling between production and employment results from both a decreased dependence on labor and a shift in the types of manufacturing producers. As an alternative to moving operations overseas to where labor costs are lower, industries are looking for ways to mechanize their operations and reduce labor needs. In addition, newer industries are more dependent on knowledge and information and consequently use less labor.

Production itself is growing more international. Capital-intensive parts can be made where capital is the cheapest, and parts can be assembled in countries having low labor costs. Workers also move to areas of potential labor demand, whether the work is in an assembly plant along the border at El Paso or a meat-packing plant in rural Kansas.

Finally, the movement of capital rather than the movement of goods and services drives the global economy. Traditional economics teaches that the relative value of goods and services is what determines exchange rates. Financial transactions once occurred as a function of trade. The growth of capital markets now means that most financial transactions occur independently of trade. These transactions are what determine exchange rates and hence the extent to which a nation's products are competitive on the world market.

RURAL COMMUNITIES IN THE GLOBAL ECONOMY

The changed global economy has a number of implications for rural communities, some of which have already become obvious. The collapse of commodities markets and the flight of manufacturing industries during the 1980s suggest that no single economic activity offers stability to rural communities. Urban areas were affected by these same changes—Pittsburgh had the steel slump, Detroit lost automobile manufacturing jobs. Because they typically have more diversified economies, cities and surrounding suburban areas are often better able to adapt. Clearly, rural communities need to broaden their economic base as protection against the increased uncertainties created by the changing global economy.

Low-wage labor and natural resources, traditional strengths in rural economies, today offer little advantage. Most natural-resource–based industries, especially agricultural production, are experiencing increased competition internationally at a time when markets are already flooded. The flight of manufacturing jobs to developing nations demonstrates that rural labor has been drawn into competition with labor in other countries. The overall decline in blue-collar jobs underscores the futility of capturing low-skill manufacturing industries, in any case. Although natural resources and light manufacturing will probably continue to be important contributors to rural economies, the character of these enterprises must change in response to the changed global economy.

The rate at which many natural resources are being depleted has become alarming. Communities relying on natural resources for their economic well-being are beginning to emphasize constructive measures, such as replenishing those resources. In 1991, for example, the Chesapeake Bay oyster industry called for a three-year ban on oyster harvesting. The oyster beds, a source of food and income for Maryland communities around the bay for centuries, had been reduced to less than 1 percent of their estimated original stock. Without a complete ban on harvesting to allow the oyster population to reproduce, the entire economic role of the bay would be altered permanently. People are beginning to acknowledge the need for economic practices that maintain rather than deplete finite resources. Choices, both private and public, are being made accordingly.

Natural-resource industries, including food producers, are beginning to expand into value-added activities or look for market niches. Logging communities, for example, are adding small wood-manufacturing operations to existing milling facilities. This enables the community to capture the economic benefit from value-added activities as well as that realized from the extraction of natural resources. It also diversifies the local economy.

Other communities are beginning to make imaginative use of the resources at hand. After decades of trying to rid their fields of milkweed, some farmers in Ogallala, Nebraska, are now harvesting it. The pods are separated from the stalks, and the fibers within are extracted. This "Ogallala down," as it is called, is then used as filler for pillows, quilts, and other household products.

Local economic planning now takes place within a new context—constant change in a global economy. The world is becoming smaller; people are now global citizens. Cyclical trends in national and global economies affect the stability and growth of even the smallest, most remote rural community. At the same time, improved transportation and communication linkages have increased rural-urban connections, fostering regional and national economic integration. To be successful, local planning must strengthen the international competitive position of local businesses and take advantage of the new opportunities for employment, marketing, tourism, and local cooperation.

Is It Progress?

When the New River Valley Economic Development Alliance put together a package of tax incentives for AT&T, little did it realize that ten years later the plant would stand empty. When Susan Cox decided to go to work for AT&T, little did she realize that a few years later she would lose her job to a teenager in Matamoros. Both town and citizens have been affected profoundly by events on a global stage that involve economic factors and financial actors far removed from Fairlawn.

What happened to Fairlawn happened earlier to several urban areas abandoned by AT&T in 1981. Economic factors encouraged AT&T to move its plant to Fairlawn in an effort to decrease labor costs. AT&T is now moving the plant to Mexico in search of still lower labor costs. Is this progress? For whom?

The larger issue that concerns many social scientists is the relationship between development and equality. Can the shift to a global economy lead to greater equality among people? One perspective, called "modernization," assumes that economic development eventually leads to greater equality. Jobs in Matamoros do lead to improved income and living standards for those working. The modernization perspective would argue that this improved standard of living changes values and norms, leading to continued economic development. The gap between developing and developed nations can begin to close.

A contrasting viewpoint argues that the global economy is reaffirming current inequality. Current economic conditions simply increase the extent to which developing nations depend on developed nations as well as reinforce inequalities internal to each country. In the United States, for example, rural communities continue to have lower income levels and higher incidences of poverty than urban areas, despite continued efforts in economic development. AT&T's move to Fairlawn did not, ultimately, leave Fairlawn economically improved. Those who hold this perspective argue that Matamoros will not find itself significantly improved either.

Increasingly, sociologists are looking at the impact that investment and trade dependence have on indicators of quality of life—nutrition, health services, mortality, and education. Some studies compare developing nations at various points in time (Wimberley 1990 and 1991). Others offer longitudinal case studies of specific nations (Wallerstein 1983; Chase-Dunn 1989). These studies suggest that development, if defined as increased linkages to the world system, does indeed increase inequality.

Chapter Summary

Rural communities are being affected by economic restructuring that is occurring worldwide. Historically, rural areas have been linked to international markets by the natural resources they exported and the labor they imported. The character of these linkages has changed dramatically in recent decades.

Since the close of World War II, national economies have been moving toward integration into a global economy. The shift from a fixed standard (Bretton Woods Agreement) to a floating exchange rate (Smithsonian Agreement) reduced controls on international currency. Capital now moves easily from one country to another. OPEC's decision to limit oil production in the early 1970s eventually led to increased production of commodities, drawing more competitors into international markets. Finally, steps taken to control inflation and stimulate the U.S. economy ultimately led to an economic recession worldwide. National economies are now linked to one another.

The events that signaled the transition to a global economy have had an impact on rural communities. The farm crisis was triggered in part by the same series of events. The expansion in commodities production created by OPEC's decision to limit oil production encouraged farm lending. Steps taken to control inflation and stimulate the local economy later made it impossible for those who had expanded their farm operations to service their debt load. Similar conditions encouraged manufacturing companies to move their operations to rural areas and then, more recently, to foreign countries. Imported labor has become a feature of rural community life.

Most experts now agree that the world economy has changed and that the U.S. economy is restructuring in response to these changes. Features of the new global economy are that (1) the industrial economy is less dependent on the natural-resource economy; (2) manufacturing production is less dependent on labor; and (3) the movement of capital is the driving force in the world economy. In this changed economic environment, rural communities need to diversify their economies, be creative in locating market niches or finding new uses for existing resources, and develop regional, national, and international linkages that help local businesses remain competitive.

Key Terms

Commodities are natural resources or manufactured products bought or sold on markets; examples are wheat, cars, televisions, and oil.

Devaluation of a currency occurs when the exchange rate changes such that it takes less gold to equal the same unit of currency.

Exchange rates set the value of countries' currencies relative to one another.

Fixed exchange rates establish a fixed standard against which one currency can be exchanged with another. The Bretton Woods Agreement fixed the price of the U.S. dollar relative to gold.

Floating exchange rates allow the value of one currency to change relative to another in response to the demand and availability of the currencies.

Inflation occurs when the currency in circulation or the availability of credit increases, leading to a sharp rise in prices.

Recession occurs when the currency in circulation or the availability of credit decreases, resulting in decreased business activity.

References

Bornschier, Volker, and Christopher Chase-Dunn. 1985. *Transnational Corporations and Underdevelopment.* New York: Praeger.

Chase-Dunn, Christopher. 1989. *Global Formation: Structures of the World Economy.* Oxford: Basil Blackwell.

Drucker, P. 1986. "The Changed World Economy." *Foreign Affairs* 64:768–791.

U.S. Department of Commerce. 1986. *Statistical Abstract of the United States.* Washington, DC: Bureau of the Census.

Wallerstein, Immanuel. 1983. *Historical Capitalism.* London: Verso.

Wimberley, Dale. 1990. "Investment Dependence and Alternative Explanations of Third World Mortality: A Cross-National Study." *American Sociological Review* 55:75–91.
Wimberley, Dale. 1991. "Transnational Corporate Investment and Food Consumption in the Third World: A Cross-National Analysis." *Rural Sociology* 56:406–431.

7

Consumption in Rural America

the Archer family has begun to settle into the Wednesday evening meal. Susan Archer works at the local manufacturing plant producing small metal parts for automobile air conditioners. Her shift began at 7:00 a.m. and ended at 4:30 p.m. Her husband, Dan, has just come in from his job as an auto mechanic at a local car dealership. They and their three children crowd around the Formica table. Jill, age six, says grace. Susan sets a large bowl of fresh salad on the table. The evening meal—and the conversation—begin in earnest.

Eric, thirteen years old, begins with a plea for some new sneakers. He will be trying out for the middle-school basketball team and says he needs a particular pair, a brand-name shoe endorsed by a professional basketball star. Dan grouses at this request. "Jeez, Eric, those shoes cost a bundle, and they aren't any better than a pair half that price. Besides, you'll grow out of them by spring." Eric goes through a list of the shoe's features and adds, "The other guys have already bought theirs!"

Susan finally intervenes on Dan's behalf. She points out that the pair Eric wants is equivalent to about twenty hours of work at her take-home pay. She then suggests that the family will pay what the department-store variety costs if Eric will pay the difference from his allowance. Eric quickly calculates the difference and estimates that the shoes will cost him about eight weeks' allowance. A deal is struck.

Dan is curious about where Eric is going to go to buy these sneakers, because none of the local merchants carry such expensive brands. Eric smiles and says at the Central City Mall, about an hour's drive away. Susan asks who is going to take him there. After a brief silence, Eric says he'll buy them on the next trip the family makes there.

He can wait—they usually go to Central City about every fourth weekend.

There is an insistent buzz from the microwave oven. The main course is ready. Susan gets up and pulls out a large frozen-food package of turkey and gravy and quickly puts in the vegetables. Then she scrapes the quick-rice out of a pot on the stove. She fills the pot with water from their well.

Jake, ten years old, makes his pitch for some new clothes that are popular at school. Susan asks what they look like. Jake refers to an ad on TV. "But Jake, the only thing different about those clothes is the label on the shirt." Jake doesn't contest this. Although he feels considerable pressure to wear what is in style, Jake is not willing to give up his allowance to make up the difference. But he does make it clear that he feels his secondary status in the family and at school has been confirmed. Dan then reminds them that when he was a kid he didn't worry about how he looked. A good pair of blue jeans and a flannel shirt were the style. Jake groans.

After cleaning up the dishes, Jake takes the day's trash out to the garbage can and then takes the can to the road for the Thursday morning pickup. The two bags join others full of discarded aluminum foil, newspapers, jars, and plastic containers. None of the garbage is sorted for recycling. The garbage will end up in a landfill about five miles away.

What we buy and consume has changed as dramatically as the way in which goods and services are produced. These changes have made rural-urban consumption patterns more similar than they were in the past. More things that once were produced at home are now available for purchase: bread, clothing, suntans, and even fingernails. We now live in highly automated and controlled environments, work in buildings with windows that do not open, process enormous amounts of information on personal computers, and assess the weather on the basis of satellite pictures only minutes old. Most people drive automobiles and rely on in-home, high-tech stereo equipment, video recorders, and television for entertainment. Our consumption habits today were not even imagined just a few years ago.

Consumption has many faces—inputs used for production, needs for day-to-day living, or preferences for leisure time. As the Archer family illustrates, consumption starts with inputs and ends with landfills, both of which are important to rural communities. This chapter explores how and why consumption patterns have changed in rural areas.

Why Is Consumption Important?

Fifty years ago, it was fairly easy to distinguish rural residents from urban ones. Rural residents, particularly those who lived on farms, tended to wear homemade clothes and eat food they produced and processed themselves. Urban residents often bought their food and clothing at the store. Urban residents were consumers; rural residents were producers. By the 1990s, consumption patterns no longer distinguished urban from rural residents. This section explores what factors contributed to increased consumption and the impact changing consumption patterns have had.

SOCIETAL TRENDS RELATED
TO INCREASED CONSUMPTION

A number of factors explain why consumption has increased. Economic expansion and the rise in real wages after World War II meant that more and more Americans could afford to buy a wider variety of goods. Increased demand meant increased variety. Producers no longer determined what consumer choices would be. Henry Ford's dictum about the Model A—that the consuming public can have cars any color they want as long as it is black—became a thing of the past. The development of commercial television in the 1950s allowed producers to shape but not dictate consumer tastes.

Our consumption patterns have also changed with the transformation of the labor force. As women entered the labor force in greater numbers after World War II, precooked frozen food became more readily available. Time once spent preparing food was given over to other work and leisure. Frozen foods, in turn, required electricity and a change in home-based food-preparation technology.

In the 1970s and 1980s, new methods of production also increased the variety of products we can consume. Flexible production, made possible because of the use of computers in operating machine tools, managing inventories, and scheduling transportation, has replaced mass production. The global economy makes it possible to produce clothing in Malaysia that will be available across the United States at the same time and for the same price.

These and other changes have had a direct impact on consumption patterns in both rural and urban areas. Although a number of economic and social forces have contributed to this change, five phenomena have had particular influence. All are nationwide trends, but each affects rural areas differently from urban areas. These are the five trends, each of which is examined in later sections:

- Market incentives to consolidate retail and service enterprises
- Changes in the labor force structure
- Mass advertising, market segmentation, and increased social inequality
- Environmental consumption and degradation, including the increased conversion of leisure activities into commodities

EFFECTS OF INCREASED CONSUMPTION

These changes have had a significant impact on the service industry, the environment, and people. The burgeoning service industry now responds to needs that were previously met within the household or the firm. Goods once produced at home have become commodities, items to be bought and sold. To the extent that they can be bought and sold, services also have become commodities. Activities once performed at home, such as laundry or sunbathing, have become commodities. Even entertainment is purchased rather than created at home. Leisure once involved visiting one's neighbors or reading. A growing sector of the economy now generates new alternatives for use of leisure time. Theme parks and other forms of instant entertainment have become quite popular.

Consumption that occurs in the process of producing commodities, goods and services, ultimately affects the environment. Costs to the environment are often ignored. Producers worry about the inputs they consume. For instance, fertilizers and seeds are inputs that are consumed in the production of a crop. Electrical power and computers are inputs that are consumed in the process of producing goods or services in an industrial firm or in an educational institution. These *inputs* are often included in the calculation of costs of production. Other things consumed in the course of production, such as the quality of water, soil, and air, are often ignored. Economists refer to these costs as *externalities*. Sociologists examine consumption in terms of its totality—inputs and externalities. Environmental degradation associated with acid rain, impure water, toxic-waste dumps, and soil erosion is a by-product of consumption.

Finally, differences that once characterized rural and urban residents have given way to differences based on wealth. Different amounts of disposable income limit what any individual and household can consume. Consuming, in terms of purchasing goods, is increasingly looked upon as leisure, as entire families go together for an afternoon at the mall. A family's income, however, limits what family members can buy and how far the parents can drive to buy it. There are different versions of consumption items for different economic groups, from Saks Fifth Avenue to Dollar Stores.

Certain key goods and services still are not universally available. Rural-urban distinctions persist, especially for the rural poor. For example, research comparing rural and urban North Carolina (Bunn et al. 1988) found that infant mortality was much higher in rural areas, a statistic suggesting lack of access to health facilities. The proportion of housing that was overcrowded was 49 percent higher in the rural areas, and the proportion of housing without adequate plumbing was 300 percent higher. These figures suggest very different patterns of consumption and well-being at the individual level.

Where we consume, what we consume, and why we consume certain types of commodities and services shape the quality of our lives. Our consumption affects the natural environment as well as our relationships with others.

CONSUMPTION AND CULTURE

What we consume determines in great measure not only our material well-being but also our cultural identity. For example, food preparation has been a significant part of the role women have played as homemakers. However, cooking a frozen dinner in a microwave oven is a profound change in the way we consume food compared with just a few decades ago. Our language and culture change as a result of this change in consumption patterns. The verb "to microwave" did not exist a decade ago.

More importantly, however, the character of the role of homemaker has changed from when Susan's grandmother cooked meals for a threshing crew. Whereas her grandmother was concerned with filling stomachs of hungry workers engaged in hard physical labor, Susan is concerned about nutrition and controlling calories. Susan's grandmother was known throughout the county for pie crusts made flaky by a generous use of lard; Susan includes low-fat yogurt in her children's lunches. Both women were viewed by their peers as outstanding preparers of good food for their families. The definition of good food and the time spent in preparing it have changed dramatically, however. More of Susan's food-preparation time goes into planning meals; most of her grandmother's time went into cooking meals.

An expensive pair of tennis shoes endorsed by a professional basketball star will not necessarily improve a person's basketball game any more than a much less expensive pair. Wearing them may bring higher status if not a higher vertical jump. What we consume can become a statement of who we are or want to be, whether in our eyes or the eyes of others. The group identity provided by consumption makes us painfully conscious of not having or being able to acquire the symbols that show we are "with it." This is particularly true of young people, who are changing rapidly and whose sense of self is still developing. Eric and Jake both needed to feel they were part of the group.

For those whose jobs are not inherently satisfying, being able to provide consumer goods and services for their families becomes a reason for working. Increased consumption can give meaning to work. Sociological studies show that an increasing number of people now work because of what their earnings allow them to consume rather than because of what they can produce.

In summary, changing consumption patterns are having a significant impact on rural life. The service industry has expanded to meet the increased demand for services once performed within the family. Increased consumption has placed added stress on the environment. The products and services now consumed have changed the pattern of daily life and influenced how young people define their identity; these factors ultimately affect the community's culture. Finally, wealth rather than place of residence now determines what and how much families consume.

Consolidation

Perhaps no other aspect of changing consumption patterns is more symbolic of rural social change over the past four decades than the loss of Main Street businesses. The Archer family's trips to Central City Mall are typical of the changing consumption pattern of rural families. This section explores the consolidation of rural businesses, factors that explain why consolidation occurs, and the impact consolidation is having on rural social services.

BUSINESS AND SOCIAL-SERVICE CONSOLIDATION

When the railroads pushed across the country, they facilitated mail-order buying, which led consumers to bypass local merchants who could not provide the wide diversity of products or take advantage of quantity wholesale discounts available to the mail-order firms. What was true then continues to be true today. Across most retail trade, rural businesses find it difficult to offer the diversity available in large central markets, such as urban malls. This has meant a loss in business for local merchants.

Consolidation has occurred across both the business and social-service communities. Many locally owned stores have disappeared or been bought out by larger retail chains. Locally owned banks are now members of regional consortiums or have been taken over by large regional banks. Department stores have either closed or moved into the suburban mall, leaving empty buildings on Main Street. Rural hospitals have closed for a number of reasons (see Box 7.1). Medicare reimbursement policies pay them less than urban hospitals to treat the same medical conditions; the result is lower revenues. They are also unable to purchase expensive medical technologies or attract trained healthcare specialists.

Local businesses and services have consolidated at different times and in different ways. Some small businesses have been replaced by nationally based chain stores. Mom-and-pop stores became franchises that later became national chains, especially in the hardware and automotive businesses. Family-owned and -operated firms were first replaced by franchises such as Western Auto, Gambles, and the like. The franchises are now fighting a losing battle with Wal-Mart and K-Mart, national firms that have incorporated hardware and automotive sections into their diversified merchandising stores. In the grocery business, local groceries and markets were replaced by regional chains, which were then bought out by chains that are national in scope. For example, small markets were purchased by Dillons Stores, a regional chain based in Wichita, Kansas. Dillons was eventually purchased by Kroger, a national chain.

In contrast, franchise convenience stores occupy an important niche and will not be replaced by direct-management national or regional firms. Their comparative advantage is convenience, not price. Consequently, their location is more important than the price they are able to charge. Because economies of scale are not a driving force, the parent firm has no advantage in directly managing individual outlets.

This transformation in retail trade is characterized by both a decline in the number of retail merchandising and service enterprises in smaller communities and by the introduction of firms that are national in scope, often in regional trade centers. This pattern is illustrated by a comparison of Iowa communities influenced by Wal-Mart with similar sized communities not affected by Wal-Marts. Kenneth Stone (1988) found that the introduction of a Wal-Mart store in ten small trade centers of 3,000 population and above resulted in a slightly greater increase in retail trade in those communities than for the state as a whole. However, the smaller towns within a twenty-mile radius of trade centers that had acquired a Wal-Mart within the previous three years showed a greater decline in retail sales than did comparable sized communities within twenty miles of trade centers without Wal-Marts. Apparently, Wal-Marts draw business into the regional center, decreasing retail sales in surrounding small towns. Table 7.1 summarizes those results.

The public sector also has responded to the need to maximize scarce revenue resources. Health, fire, police, public education, and other community services continue to undergo consolidation as rural areas address the increasing quality of service expected and their accompanying expenses. As with the retail sector, rural community health services have

BOX 7.1   THE CENTRALIZATION OF HEALTHCARE IN RURAL AMERICA

Since the mid-1980s, a disproportionate share of hospitals in rural areas have closed. The primary reason that rural hospitals are facing financial strain is that admissions are down sharply. Admissions to rural hospitals declined 22 percent between 1979 and 1985, whereas urban hospitals experienced a slight increase in admissions. Occupancy rates for rural hospitals are now below 50 percent, which makes it difficult for them to cover fixed costs. There are a number of reasons for the low occupancy rate: First, many rural areas are experiencing declining populations, and thus the patient base is reduced. Second, there is strong pressure from Medicare and other insurers to reduce hospital admissions and length of stay in the hospital. Third, medical technology is becoming increasingly sophisticated, which makes it difficult for small hospitals to provide the quality of care that many rural residents expect.

Two Medicare rules have disproportionately affected rural hospitals: First, the fixed-rate diagnosis-related groups (DRGs) system of hospital payments sharply limits the payments to be made for particular procedures; the system pays nonmetropolitan hospitals 25 to 40 percent less for a particular procedure than is paid to metropolitan hospitals, presumably because rural hospitals have lower operating costs. Second, the prospective payment system severely limits the length of a hospital stay for many illnesses or procedures. Because the rural population is aging and many rural people with other kinds of health insurance are going to urban areas for specialized procedures, there has been an increase in the proportion of admissions that are paid by Medicare. In 1980, 20 percent of rural hospital patients were covered by Medicare; by 1985, that percentage had risen to 37 percent. A related problem for the rural hospitals (and their patients) is that the proportion of nonmetropolitan residents under age sixty-five who lack health insurance is 20 percent higher than in metropolitan areas. Hospitals generally rely on fees from privately insured patients to cover some of the cost of Medicare patients because Medicare payments normally do not cover all costs.

Although 24 percent of U.S. residents live in nonmetropolitan areas, only 15 percent of physicians practice in rural areas. There is nothing inherently wrong with rural people going to urban areas for part of their medical care. However, a higher proportion of the poor live in rural than urban areas, and many do not have adequate means of transportation to go to urban areas for treatment. In short, many of those with greatest need for medical attention are further disadvantaged by centralization of services—more so than their urban counterparts. On the other hand, one burden that has not hit rural hospitals nearly as hard as it has hit urban inner-city hospitals is the AIDS epidemic. Overall, however, the problems of rural hospitals are more like those of inner-city hospitals than of suburban hospitals.

Some rural hospitals have survived and prospered, but they have had to respond proactively to the structural changes in the healthcare industry. An example is the Onaga Community Hospital that serves five small communities in Kansas. In 1981, the hospital provided 40 jobs and $500,000 in revenues. In 1990, the hospital reported 170 jobs and $5.5 million in revenues, including a $2.5 million annual payroll.

The Onaga Community Hospital was organized by residents of five small Kansas communities. To counter talk of closure in 1981, the board refocused the hospital's mission statement from strict illness-care to the total health needs of the five high-elderly-population base communities. What started as a hospital district in a single county has grown into a tricounty rural primary healthcare system with daycare, a community fitness center, an intercommunity education network, various mobile services, and a home healthcare network.

continues

Box 7.1 *continued*

Joe Engelken, the hospital administrator, describes the program services as a mini-mall of thirty-plus healthcare-related businesses that are not located under one roof. Examples include the community hospital in Onaga, a drugstore, an ambulance service in Onaga and St. Marys, a women's health center, a mental health center, a nutritious diner, a holistic birthing center, a small-wonders discovery center, "Better Breathers" respiratory care services, the foundation center, the grantsmanship center, and a mainstreet community encouragement center.

As hospital services grew, employees and doctors assumed active roles in community affairs. Staff identified community needs that could be addressed within the hospital mission. Members of the staff are now active proponents of community economic development through their participation in various community organizations that seek new avenues of job and income generation.

Sources: Rick Curtis, et al. 1988. "Health Issues in Rural America." New Alliances for Rural America, background paper submitted to the Task Force on Rural Development. Washington, DC: National Governors Association.

North Central Regional Center for Rural Development. 1991. "Self-Development Conference Highlights Grassroots Efforts in Rural Midwest." *Rural Development News* 15 (April): 8–11.

TABLE 7.1 Percent Change in Per Capita Sales

Number of Years After Wal-Mart Opening	Rural Towns Near Wal-Mart Towns	Comparable Towns with No Wal-Mart Nearby
1	− 6.3	− 2.0
2	− 7.6	− 7.5
3	− 13.1	− 7.5

Note: Changes are cumulative from base year.

Source: K. E. Stone. 1988. "The Effect of Wal-Mart Stores on Businesses in Host Towns and Surrounding Towns in Iowa." Unpublished paper. Ames: Iowa State University. Reprinted with permission.

found central trade centers siphoning off business that once supported local hospitals.

FACTORS FAVORING CONSOLIDATION

Why do businesses consolidate? Why do services eventually become regional rather than remain local? One explanation given for centralization is provided by central-place theory. *Central-place theory* proposes that population centers, whether small crossroads communities or large cities, are geographically organized into hierarchical retail and public service markets. Moreover, according to the theory, any particular hierarchy of places reflects a division of labor such that the larger places possess greater economic diversity of products and services for consumption than do smaller places. Correspondingly, the smallest places offer the fewest commodities and services. Thus, there is a system of nested markets.

The position of any particular community as a trade center is related to its place, or centrality, in the transportation network. In most cases, central places developed at intersections or other strategic places along railroads, canals, highways, and other transportation facilities. Trade increased with the rapid and comprehensive development of a transportation infrastructure that opened rural areas to larger markets. A rapidly increasing standard of living in rural areas and a tendency to close the gap with urban incomes, especially in the post–World War II period, contributed to the expansion of consumer demand in rural areas.

The expansion of trade had two immediate effects. First, it made it easier for local firms to sell their products outside the local area. Second, this expansion opened once relatively isolated rural areas to outside producers and retailers. However, the distance between buyer and seller continues to affect the price of commodities in markets that are isolated and have a low population density. Commodities cost more in isolated rural areas because of the costs of transportation.

Another factor favoring consolidation is economies of scale. Such economies occur when a greater volume of business can occur at one particular site—volume is a way to spread costs (of transportation, land and buildings, equipment, labor) over a larger number of products. Both distance and the small population in the market area make it difficult for rural businesses to take advantage of economies associated with scale. Thus, central-place theory suggests that there is a constant pressure to centralize economic activities in larger places.

The theory does not tell us why and when consolidation occurs in a particular sector. Other factors such as the opportunity to generate profit based on favorable macroeconomic trends, capital availability, and organizational innovation help explain why centralization occurs at a particular time in a particular industry. In retail trade, enterprises tend to spill over into rural areas when several elements are in place. New, more efficient forms of economic organization already fine-tuned in urban areas are introduced in rural areas when they appear to have promise for profit there as well. Centralization also occurs when capital is abundant and the marginal advantage increased urban investment offers is no greater than what rural areas present, or when cost of labor becomes critical and the cheaper labor available in rural areas is central to profitability or the accumulation of wealth.

Retail grocery chains reached into rural areas in the 1960s, after they had already organized the grocery business in urban areas. Grocery chains had developed a transportation system sufficiently well organized to move perishables from warm-climate areas to regions lacking year-round growing seasons. When rural consumers acquired incomes large enough to demand vegetables and fruits year-round, organization could be matched to new markets. The chains began appearing in rural communities.

Wal-Mart was a pioneer in bringing retail discount general merchandising stores to rural areas because it organized itself economically to support volume sales by attracting rural customers over a wide geographic area. Wal-Mart was able to offer lower prices and more diverse stock than the mom-and-pop stores and the more specialized franchises that preceded them. Improved transportation, of course, enabled them to draw in consumers over a larger region. Strategic site selection coupled with careful inventory control and organization of labor enabled them to be profitable. In general, Wal-Mart stores keep less inventory and use more part-time workers than traditional retailers. Labor costs less in rural areas, and using part-time workers has allowed Wal-Mart to pay fewer benefits.

This progression from mom-and-pop stores to franchises to the "Wal-Marting" of rural America has multiple impacts. The mom-and-pop stores had a limited variety of goods, purchased only occasional display advertisements in the local newspaper announcing a sale, and generally used family labor. When they did hire, these locally owned businesses paid low wages to employees, who often worked only part-time. In general, their work was not organized as efficiently as in the chain stores. Mom-and-pop stores generally had higher prices than either the franchises or the nationally based discount stores that replaced them. This was principally because their low volume required substantial markups and they could not take advantage of volume buying. The mom-and-pop stores provided a more personal atmosphere for customers, especially those who came from a similar social class as the proprietors. They also offered expertise about the features of competing products, provided repair services, and made it easy to find what one needed.

The franchises had features of both a family firm and a national chain. They offered variety of inventory and some of the same friendly helpfulness, although they often hired clerks who knew little about the products. They were able to use national advertising and had frequent sales. Their regular prices, however, were not discount prices.

National merchandising firms offer infinite variety and low everyday prices, but provide little in the way of customer service. For those who define shopping as recreation and for poor people and minorities who risked not being treated in a friendly manner by the proprietors of family firms, these changes have been acceptable. Others view the reduction in the number of clerks, the use of part-time labor, and the resulting lack of personal service as problems.

Changes in the Labor Force

Changes in the rural labor force have followed national trends since the end of World War II. Among these, two have had important consequences for consumption patterns of rural people.

ENTRY OF WOMEN INTO NONFARM LABOR FORCE

It now takes more than one income earner to make what one alone could earn in the 1960s. This reduced earning power has led to the entry of more women into the labor force. The increased proportion of women working outside the home has meant that less time is available for household chores they have traditionally performed, such as food preparation and preservation, the making and maintenance of clothing, housecleaning, and child supervision. That has contributed to an expansion of the service sector.

The Archer family is now the typical American family. Both parents work. This puts a strain on both spouses in fulfilling traditional role expectations, but it is particularly stressful for women. Women may have entered the workplace, but there is little evidence that they have transferred some of their traditional caretaker roles to other members of the family. Women are still the primary care givers. They continue to prepare meals, take care of the laundry, and look after the children. For women who are single heads of households, especially women in or near poverty, the burden of being both wage earner and care giver can be a tremendous source of stress. In order to cope with their increased time in the workplace while continuing to shoulder their traditional care-giving roles, women have changed their consumption patterns. Evidence of this is the growth of convenience foods and the popularity of microwave ovens, as can be attested to by Susan Archer.

GROWTH OF THE SERVICE SECTOR

The service sector has grown because service activities previously performed within firms and farms have had a price placed on them. In other words, services have become commodities. Services once performed within the household, such that no money exchanged hands, are now purchased. Consolidation has supported the growth of the service sector. As farms and rural businesses consolidate, they become so large that the work is no longer manageable within the family unit. These enterprises purchase goods and services that they once produced themselves.

In earlier times, farm women would prepare and take lunch to the field. Now it is much more likely that one spouse or the other will have an off-farm job and prepared meals will be purchased for whoever operates the tractor. In addition, if the family has small children, childcare will become a commodity part of the time; before, it was handled entirely within the family. Also, the application of pesticides to crops may be contracted out to a firm licensed to apply lethal chemicals; today's farmer is unlikely to obtain the training necessary to apply them as now required by law.

Whereas earlier the wife kept the books of the family farm or business, now bills and receipts may be sent to an accounting firm and sent back in the form of a computerized monthly balance sheet. If the family business has grown large enough, a full-time bookkeeper is hired. In either case, a price has been placed on the cost of keeping accounts—the activity has become a commodity.

Multiple job holding is practiced by both adult members of a family. Teenagers, too, often have jobs, thereby modifying family consumption patterns. Leisure time, an objective of these efforts to maintain or increase family income, ironically becomes scarcer. When young people work beyond a certain minimum, there is a resulting reduction in their effective consumption of education and of extracurricular activities.

In summary, the increase in the number of jobholders per family and the growth of the service sector of the economy have influenced household consumption patterns. Families have substituted prepared foods and fast cooking technologies, particularly microwave ovens, for the time once spent preserving and preparing food from scratch. Expansion of the service sector has led to the sale of highly processed food rather than of the raw ingredients once taken home for final preparation. The vast expansion of fast-food franchises and of salad bars and delis in grocery stores illustrates how important service has become.

Mass Advertising and Segmented Markets

Television introduced a powerful tool for marketing products. During the early days, advertising was directed at as broad an audience as possible. Mass advertising became a powerful influence on the consumption patterns of people, rural and urban alike. The introduction of cable television and the rapid proliferation of highly specialized channels now enable advertisers to use this tool to reach very specific audiences. For example, MTV and VH1 video television networks can be considered continuous mass advertising targeted to very specific groups. In this sense, markets have become segmented. Consumption patterns now reflect both mass advertising and the introduction of segmented markets. These two trends have affected those least prepared to deal with increased consumption, the poor.

MASS ADVERTISING

The Archer family conversation over shoes and clothes is one repeated among both rural and urban families. Decisions on what is consumed have moved beyond mere functional necessity. Eric Archer's willingness to spend allowance money on a pair of sneakers that he will likely outgrow in a short time is not driven by a rational comparison of competing brands. Rather, his decision is based on the social acceptance he gains by having the resources to consume the more expensive pair of sneakers. Although unwilling to commit his allowance money to designer clothes, Jake clearly feels the same desire for social acceptance. The difference in quality of the merchandise is probably not great enough to account for the magnitude of difference in price. The status that consuming particular styles of clothes bestows upon the consumer, however, does have meaning in school or at work. Such status is often given meaning through mass media advertising.

Since World War II, the use of multiple media to advertise commodities has expanded. This is particularly true of television. No other telecommunications technology has had such an immediate and profound influence on people's decisions to buy particular products. As Goldman and Dickens (1983) noted, "Like most sectors of the commercial mass media, advertisers' production of ideology is usually derivative from their principal agenda, the expansion of sales" (p. 586). Some observers suggest that the introduction of mass advertising was a calculated response to lagging consumption. Instead of responding to consumer demand, manufacturers now create a demand for a particular product or elaboration of a product. The effort has been so successful that this is one reason the United States has one of the lowest savings rates in the industrialized world.

Mass advertising often uses values that are deeply seated in popular culture to create demand. Goldman and Dickens, for instance, demonstrate how advertisers continuously employ the rural myth to create positive images of their products. Soft-drink commercials that celebrate the honesty of farm work, family, and the land seek to connect these values to consumption of the manufacturer's product. Others rely on status attainment. Designer tennis shoes and jeans advertisements propose that the consumption of a particular shoe or pair of pants will bestow a particular status on the consumer.

Mass advertising and the mass media in general have become a powerful influence on the consumption patterns of rural people. To the degree that mass media messages are successful in manipulating consumption patterns of a broad public, this cultural force has contributed to a leveling of differences between rural and urban people. There appears to be little difference in the consumption of rural and urban teens in clothes or of rural and urban adults in the consumption of processed food. Mass media can inspire universal demand for certain consumer products. However, economic differences within rural areas make such purchases extremely difficult for some families. Class replaces ruralness as the feature that distinguishes among people's consumption patterns.

SEGMENTED MARKETS

As mentioned earlier, television enabled advertising to be aimed at as broad an audience as possible. This was the case for several reasons, including the fact that broadcasting was concentrated into just three competing networks. The expansion of cable and satellite dishes has led to the proliferation of channels, many of which are highly specialized. Advertising can now be targeted to the specialized audiences those channels attract.

Similar targeting has occurred in the print media with the proliferation of professional, sports, hobby, and other types of magazines. The growth of desktop publishing, made possible by the continued miniaturization of computer technology, suggests that this trend will continue. An extreme example of targeting is a beef-industry magazine called *Beef Today*, produced by *Farm Journal*. The magazine is free but is provided only to cattle growers. It is virtually impossible for even a public library to obtain a subscription.

The information age is representative of the revolution currently under way in the quantity and availability of all kinds of information. Although we may or may not be consuming any more information now than did our parents, we are consuming much more specialized information.

Changes in the character and price of communications technologies have made it easier for the more wealthy rural residents to participate in telecommunications consumption, regardless of space. Indeed, some observers have argued that telecommunications technology represents the greatest leveling force for rural and urban residents. However, an Office of Technology Assessment report cautions that rural consumers of such technology are likely to be a relatively small proportion of the rural population (U.S. Congress 1991).

IMPACT ON LOW-INCOME FAMILIES

Inequality of income has been growing in the United States since the early 1970s. Incomes of the working class have been stagnant or on the decline since the mid-1970s. The purchasing power of the average hourly wage today is equal to that in 1965. Similarly, since the beginning of the 1980s, the lower price of primary goods (agricultural products, timber, and most minerals, except petroleum) has contributed to lower incomes for farmers, miners, and loggers.

The pressures to spend discretionary income are felt by all, although different groups are encouraged to buy different things. Discretionary income is quite unequally distributed. Among teenagers, this inequality becomes obvious as many take on part-time work in order to consume products such as the latest in tennis shoes or, in rural areas, to invest in a four-wheel-drive pickup truck. Often they work many hours a week, which has a negative impact on their studies.

What we consume is ultimately limited by income more than by point of sale. Outlet malls, for example, are a current growth area in retail trade. Initially these stores were located near factories to market flawed goods, called "seconds." Because factories were often located in rural areas, outlet malls offered inexpensive merchandise to rural consumers. By the 1990s, major manufacturers found that outlet malls enabled them to keep production and sales up in the face of continued economic downturn in the U.S. economy. In part because of the availability of cheap land in rural areas, and in part because the upscale department stores that feature their products dislike direct competition located nearby, the discount malls have continued to expand in rural areas. However, shoppers frequenting these malls are upper-income suburban residents seeking name brands at bargain prices.

Rural people in the immediate area shop the local Dollar Store or K-Mart. As economic conditions continue to decline in rural areas, people increasingly shop at used-clothing stores set up by churches and other volunteer groups. Families can indeed get quality clothes at these local shops. Teenagers, however, cannot buy the faddish items in the year they are fashionable. Level of income continues to affect consumption patterns.

Increased Natural-Resource Consumption

Per-capita energy consumption in the United States has increased greatly since World War II. Presently, the United States consumes approximately a quarter of the world's energy, but accounts for less than 5 percent of the world's population. There are few signs that the public will support a decline in standard of living. We could maintain a stable standard of living by increasing resource efficiency and decreasing use of resources, particularly nonrenewable resources. Yet as a society we have not made this a priority. Instead, we depend on relatively cheap foreign sources of energy. The sustainability of this level of resource use seems to be officially questioned only when the sources of cheap energy are problematic, as during the oil embargo in the 1970s or fleetingly during the Gulf war in the early 1990s.

Land and water are also consumables (photo courtesy of the U.S. Department of Agriculture).

A related question is the safe and environmentally sound disposal of the waste derived from consumption. The refuse created by production and domestic consumption must go somewhere, often to a rural landfill or incinerator. Rural Americans often have to discard their garbage into their own backyards. When the trash collectors pick up garbage in the suburbs, however, few urban residents could tell you its final destination. Rural communities are home to most waste dumps. Most rural people know exactly where refuse, theirs and that of others, is dumped.

Most environmental degradation is considered to be the externalized by-products of our production and marketing processes. The price of the commodities produced and consumed usually does not include the cost of correcting the environmental degradation caused by use or disposal of those products. In agriculture, for example, the price of the farm commodity produced will not include the costs of cleaning up the waterways or the inestimable health costs of a water table polluted by pesticides that have percolated from surface applications.

The consequences of these trends of production and consumption are of particular importance to rural people. First, their own quality of material well-being is now dependent upon high levels of consumption. Rural people do not differ greatly from city dwellers in their consumption levels. Second, rural people account for only a quarter of the U.S. population but live in 98 percent of the land area. That lower population density relative to urban areas makes it politically attractive for decisionmakers (politicians and technicians) to locate dumps for solid, toxic, and nuclear wastes in rural areas.

In general, the less densely populated the rural area, the stronger the inclination to select it as a waste site. From the technician's point of view, the fewer the number of people directly affected, the smaller the social impact. From the politician's point of view, the smaller and more dispersed the population, the less the likelihood of effective political organization in opposition to that particular site. NIMBY (not in my back yard) opposition may appear anywhere. All other things being equal, politicians would rather have a few rather than many people angry at them.

The increased conversion of leisure activities into commodities also creates environmental dilemmas. The number of visitors to the U.S. national parks each year has reached the point that the parks may no longer be able to remain the pristine environment the park system was designed to protect (Box 7.2). The proliferation of off-road vehicles for use in leisure activities threatens environmental damage that may take centuries to repair. Rural residents find themselves affected as consumers yet residents of the land being enjoyed. Communities find they must weigh carefully the economic benefits of tourism and recreation against the environmental costs.

BOX 7.2   YOSEMITE NATIONAL PARK: WILDERNESS AREA OR RURAL THEME PARK?

Yosemite National Park in northern California had 3.4 million visitors in 1989. Most came in their own cars. Although 94 percent of the park has been set aside for wilderness, environmentalists charge that Yosemite Valley has been turned into a theme park. Concessions have been contracted out to the Curry Company, a subsidiary of MCA. There are 17 acres of asphalt parking lots, 1,700 hotel rooms and cabins, 3 swimming pools, several tennis courts, numerous restaurants including a pizza parlor and a deli, a video store, 23 liquor establishments including a sports bar, and other similar enterprises. This development has occurred in spite of the fact that in 1980, environmentalists succeeded in gaining approval of a master plan under which the park would be deurbanized and nonessential services eliminated. Automobiles were to be banned and replaced by shuttle buses. The Curry Company pays the Department of Interior an annual franchising fee of $600,000. It grossed $85 million on its Yosemite Park operations in 1989. Environmentalists charge that the company blocked implementation of the master plan, a charge denied by Curry's top management.

Source: "All Things Considered." National Public Radio, October 24, 1990.

Who Are the Rural Poor?

Compared with families even a generation ago, the Archers consume an enormous number of products. In order to do so, they must both work. The trend toward two incomes is well documented and frequently cited as evidence of growing economic inequality. But the Archers are not poor. Who are the rural poor?

We often imagine the poor to be uneducated, unwilling to work, residents of the inner city, and responsible for or part of large families. Sociological theories of poverty have traditionally linked two of these variables—level of education and size of family—to the incidence of poverty.

The most recent data on poverty challenge both our stereotypes and theories. Data gathered in 1987 showed poverty rates that were higher in rural areas, 16.9 percent compared with 12.5 percent in urban areas (Porter 1989). The vast majority of the rural poor lived in a household whose head was not ill, disabled, or retired; 70.5 of these heads of households worked all or part of the year. More than a third of these (24.3 percent) worked full-time, year-round (Shapiro 1989). Although lower educational attainment contributes to poverty, recent increases in rural poverty have occurred at all educational levels.

Research on poverty in general confirms that the characteristics of poor households have changed. Family size is smaller, and more heads of households are female. Despite declines in family size and increased educational levels among young people, poverty levels persist (Duncan and Rogers 1991). Low wages and the increased numbers of female-headed households appear to be more potent in explaining poverty.

Sociological research does show a dramatic increase in inequality in the 1970s and 1980s (Phillips 1990). The variables now linked to poverty raise serious questions. The rural poor appear to be keeping up their end of the bargain—most are employed. But wages are low—low enough that a full-time job may not be sufficient to lift a family of four out of poverty. Is society keeping up its end of the bargain? Does increased consumption play a role in the increase in poverty?

Chapter Summary

What we now consume has changed as dramatically as the way goods and services are produced. Expanded earnings, increased presence of women in the work force, and the technical capacity to produce more varied products have both increased and changed the character of what we consume. These changes have made level of income more distinguishing than urban-rural residence and influenced our sense of identity.

Several economic and social factors have contributed to the change in consumption patterns. Current markets are forcing consolidation of both retail and service organizations. Changes in the labor force have increased the number of jobholders per family, stimulating the growth of the service and informal sectors of the rural economy. Mass advertising has led to the standardization of products. More recently, this advertising has been targeted to market niches.

The way we produce goods and services is linked with the way these commodities are consumed, where they are consumed, and why they are consumed. The life cycle of a commodity or service is much more than the points of production and purchase. The final resting places for many commodities or their remains are the landfills and toxic incinerators located in rural areas. As the national environment acquires greater importance as an issue, increases in our societal consumption patterns—and the consequent concerns about resources, the environment, and waste disposal—will become national political issues. These issues, though, are already personal and family issues for rural people and their communities.

Key Terms

Central-place theory proposes that population centers, whether small crossroads communities or large cities, are geographically organized into hierarchical retail and public service markets.

Externalities include the social costs of production not borne by the company producing goods. These might include the contamination of the soil, air, or water when waste products are released to the environment.

Inputs include the natural resources or raw materials needed in the production process.

References

Bunn, K., William Clifford, and Stephen Lilley. 1988. *North Carolina: Rural Profile.* Raleigh, NC: Rural Economic Development Center.

Duncan, Greg J., and Willard Rodgers. 1991. "Has Children's Poverty Become More Persistent?" *American Sociological Review* 56:538–550.

Goldman, Robert, and David D. Dickens. 1983. "The Selling of Rural America." *Rural Sociology* 48(4): 585–606.

Phillips, K. 1990. *The Politics of Rich and Poor: Wealth and the American Electorate in the Reagan Aftermath.* New York: Random House.

Porter, Kathryn H. 1989. *Poverty in Rural America: A National Review.* Washington, DC: Center on Budget and Policy Priorities.

Shapiro, Isaac. 1989. *Laboring for Less: Working but Poor in Rural America.* Washington, DC: Center on Budget and Policy Priorities.

Stone, Kenneth E. 1988. "The Effect of Wal-Mart Stores on Businesses in Host Towns and Surrounding Towns in Iowa." Unpublished paper. Ames: Iowa State University, November.

U.S. Congress. 1991. Office of Technology Assessment. *Rural America at the Crossroads: Networking for the Future.* OTA-TCT-471. Washington, DC: U.S. Government Printing Office, April.

Part 3

Community Resources

8

The Character of
Rural Governments

alcolm T. Porter was worried. According to local teachers, children were going to school hungry. He knew for a fact that many of the older people in town were surviving on one meal a day and the tea they made from local herbs.

Malcolm had heard of a government commodity program that distributes surplus food to communities. The communities, in turn, distribute the food to the poor. But there's a catch. A local government must receive and distribute the food. Coker had no government.

Coker is a poor, isolated community of fewer than 400 people. It has been without a mayor or town council for fifty-two years. Back in 1933, the Donovan family "just sat down around a table and decided we didn't want it anymore." The richest white family in town, the Donovans concluded that the town didn't need a government and closed it down.

A handful of the town's black residents, including Malcolm, decided to take matters into their own hands. They organized the Coker Community Club. Members sold fried chicken and fish dinners until they had enough money to construct a small house. The house served as a temporary city hall, recreation center, library, community, and voter-registration center.

By 1985, they were ready to elect a government. They held a town meeting, nominated a slate of officers, and elected the first town officials in fifty-two years. Just five hours after the election, however, the Donovan family filed suit in the county court. The local government was suspended pending the outcome of the suit.

181

Malcolm just couldn't imagine what they were going to do. People had worked long and hard to get the community center up and operating. More and more school children were going to school hungry. Without a town council, Coker could not receive the surplus food. Without a government, the people of Coker could not meet even their most basic needs.

Those in Coker understand why they need a government, though most of us do not really think about it. Why do we have town councils, county commissions, water districts, parishes, boroughs, and school boards? State legislatures are also beginning to ask this very question, wondering whether we perhaps have too many local units of government.

From a sociological perspective, local governments exist for at least three purposes. They offer an avenue for citizen participation, inviting those who live in a community to take part in making the decisions that will affect them. Local governments also provide the structure by which community needs can be met. Whether it be distributing food to the poor, constructing roads and bridges, ensuring safe water supplies, or maintaining schools, local governments provide the mechanism by which people can collectively meet common needs. Finally, local governments offer an arena in which issues of responsibility are explored. Food, roads, safe water supplies, and schools all cost money. Governments decide from whom that money will be raised.

Town councils, local school boards, water districts, and county commissions all represent different types of government found in rural areas. Their organization, legal powers, allowance for citizen participation, control of community decisionmaking, and provision of public services all differ markedly. This chapter explores how rural governments are organized, what they do, and what problems they face in providing public services. During the past decade, the balance among local, state, and federal governments has changed. These changes have had profound effects on the capacity of local governments to respond to rural needs.

Organization and Functions of Local Governments

Ultimately, control over taxation is the central issue for governments. The ability to tax enables a government to raise the resources needed to set an agenda and implement policies toward accomplishing that agenda. In this regard, the U.S. system of government differs from that typically found in other nations. This section explores the powers shared with local government, the different types of local governments found in rural areas, and the manner in which these governments are staffed.

POWER OF LOCAL GOVERNMENTS

Most countries have a unitary form of government, a central government that holds tightly the power to tax. Although there may be local units of government, these are unable to levy taxes on behalf of local needs. The U.S. system divides power, including the power to tax, between two levels of government. As provided by the Tenth Amendment to the U.S. Constitution: "The powers not delegated to the United States by the Constitution, nor prohibited by it to the States, are reserved to the States, respectively, or to the people." Just which powers are reserved to the states is often in question, and the resulting flexibility enables the balance of power to shift back and forth between the two levels. This form of government is referred to as *federalism*.

Local governments are not mentioned in the U.S. Constitution. They are, in fact, created by each state. Local governments derive their power either from grants of authority in state constitutions, known as home-rule provisions, or by general laws or statutes passed by state legislatures.

In theory, local governments provide the mechanism by which participation, needs, and responsibility are linked. They can allow for direct citizen participation in government, or they can provide representative government, in which local citizens elect officials to act on their behalf. New England town meetings are among the more famous examples of direct citizen participation. Town meetings held once a year enable all citizens to participate in setting the agenda as well as making decisions. Of the 16,691 townships in the United States, 6,081 conduct business through town meetings. Under representative government, local residents elect from their neighbors a group of people (town council, city commission, school board, or board of supervisors) who then make decisions. These decisions relate to (1) what services will be provided, (2) who will be hired to provide them, and (3) how the revenue will be raised to pay for those services.

When communities are small, as they are in rural areas, more people can play an active role in this process. Wide participation should allow services to be uniquely tailored to the needs of the local population. The fact that they have the power to tax enables local governments to ensure that the community accepts the responsibility for raising the revenue needed to provide the services the community deems most important. Theory often falls short of reality, however. Communities such as Coker can block participation of certain groups of citizens. Local resources may simply not be available to respond to local needs, at which point other levels of government often become involved.

TABLE 8.1 Number of Local Government Units, 1987 and 1962

	1987	1962
Total local governments	83,186	91,186
General-purpose governments		
County	3,041	3,043
Municipal	19,200	18,000
Township	16,691	17,142
Special-purpose governments		
School districts	14,721	34,687
Special districts	29,532	18,323

Source: U.S. Census of Governments. 1987. *Government Finance.*
Washington, DC: Government Printing Office.

TYPES OF RURAL GOVERNMENTS

Rural governments are as diverse as are rural economies. As shown in Table 8.1, the many forms of government can be sorted into two types: general-purpose and special-purpose governments. *General-purpose governments* are, as their name implies, governments created to respond to the general needs of a county, city, or town. They usually have the power to raise revenue and determine its use. State governments may restrict use of certain types of taxes or place ceilings on tax levels, as happened when taxpayers revolted in states such as California. *Special-purpose governments* are created to respond to specific community needs, such as schools, water, or medical services. They, too, can usually raise revenue, but only in response to well-defined purposes. Their freedom to tax is often severely restricted by state governments.

To complicate matters, public services in rural areas are also provided by public authorities. These include limited- or single-purpose enterprises created by general-purpose governments, such as municipal power and water companies (Berne and Schramm 1986). An important extension of rural governments, these agencies have grown rapidly in number since the 1960s.

There are almost 39,000 general-purpose governments, which include those for towns, townships, municipalities, and counties. Eighty-six percent of these serve populations of less than 10,000. Fifty percent serve populations of less than 1,000. The more than 44,000 special-purpose governments include 14,721 school districts and 29,532 special districts.

The relative importance of any one type of rural government varies by region of the country and from state to state. In some states, small municipalities are the most common type of general-purpose government. In the West and throughout much of the South, counties provide most local governmental services. Villages and towns are often not incorporated. In the West, where counties are much larger than in other regions of the country, county government can be essentially regional in character. In the states across the Great Plains, small municipalities and counties vie for political prominence, often providing complementary services. In New England and across the northern tier of states, townships are the most important general-purpose government. Differences in political traditions and state law are reflected in the diversity found in local governance (ACIR 1991).

One of the most dramatic changes in the structure of rural government has been the decline in the number of school districts since World War II. In 1942, there were about 108,000 school districts. By 1962, that number was down to just under 35,000 (Table 8.1). As of 1987, there were 14,721 school districts remaining. Current shortfalls in state revenues are leading many states to push for further consolidation of school districts.

School consolidation illustrates the tension that often exists between local and state governments. School district mergers were pushed by professional education groups and state departments of education in the 1950s (Sokolow 1982). Because professional educators were concerned about the quality of education in extremely small districts, they pushed for consolidation in an effort to standardize schools. States were beginning to assume more responsibility in funding education and were concerned that the system become more fiscally efficient. Small schools were seen as inefficient; thus, most of the decrease in school districts resulted from consolidation of rural districts.

Before the move toward consolidation, the small one-room schools scattered throughout the countryside each formed a single district. When students graduated from the elementary schools, they changed districts to attend high school in town. During the first phase of consolidation, these one-school districts were unified into kindergarten–twelfth grade (K–12) districts based in villages and cities. Initially these new school districts had multiple attendance centers, but gradually the attendance centers in the countryside were closed. All children attended school in town. A second wave of consolidation occurred in more scarcely populated areas. In that phase, some villages or towns lost their schools entirely. Often new high schools were built in wheat or corn fields, equidistant from two or more small towns, when towns could not reach agreement as to which would have the new school.

The consolidation of rural school districts has been accompanied by increased state control of education. The state of Vermont, for example, maintains firm control over nearly every aspect of the educational system, including the following matters:

- Controlling teacher certification and training
- Maintaining a list from which local school boards can choose superintendents
- Prescribing courses of study, the number of school days, and the age at which a child may leave school
- Establishing boundaries of superintendency districts
- Forbidding towns from seceding from union districts
- Demanding compliance with its approval standards for public schools

Although the educational system has become more standardized, some critics argue that it has become less responsive to local needs and resources. Given the extent to which state funds are now being used to support local schools, however, states may feel that they have little choice.

STAFFING RURAL GOVERNMENTS

Small governments are often led by citizen-officials who receive only symbolic remuneration and thus must have another source of income. The town mayor (paid for by local taxes) might also be the city postmaster (paid for by the federal government) and local fire chief (not paid at all). In contrast to their urban counterparts, rural governments are highly dependent on citizen volunteers as opposed to paid elected and appointed officials. In the United States, as Alvin Sokolow (1988, 28) notes, "The typical local government serving a small community is a small organization with few, if any, salaried employees and little in the way of formal structure. One in three general purpose governments in the U.S. does not have full-time employees."

Despite the limited time they can devote to their official duties, rural officials face many of the same issues as those faced by larger governments. Professional networks and associations can be helpful, but officials in rural areas are less likely to participate than are those from urban areas (Waltzer et al. 1986). Advisory councils and technical assistance available through state agencies often provide information helpful to policy decisions or offer training that will improve public management (Valente 1985). For example, small municipalities in Pennsylvania receive training and technical assistance in everything from financial investments to rural living. Assistance providers include the State Department of Community Affairs, Association of Township Supervisors, Cooperative Extension Service, borough associations, universities and colleges, private consultants, neighboring municipalities, Pennsylvania Economic League, and other sources (Cahill et al. undated).

Small city councils rely primarily on the advice and expertise of the few people who do hold paid management and consulting positions in

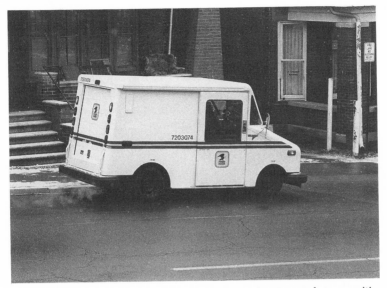

Federal government plays a role in delivering services to rural communities (photo courtesy of the Ohio University Telecommunications Center).

the local government. They include such people as the town clerk, the city attorney, the county engineer, and city treasurer (Snavely and Sokolow 1987). These individuals are extremely valuable to the community, but can exercise inordinate control over the decisionmaking process.

City or county attorneys and engineers, for example, can act as gatekeepers to the community. Because they often have exclusive control of technical expertise, these officials can limit the information shared on an issue or the extent to which outside resources are sought. Because they have paid positions in the local government, these officials can also spend more time on local affairs than can elected officials. Thus, paid technical staff can exercise a substantial amount of political control over inexperienced or part-time elected officials.

Problems in Providing Public Services

Rural governments face a common problem—providing adequate levels of public services with limited resources. The problem is common to all rural communities, whether they are experiencing growth or decline. Communities with growing populations must provide services for more people, despite the fact that tax revenue rarely keeps up with the increased demand. Declining rural communities grapple with the problem of providing continuing services in the face of an eroding tax base and less support from the state and federal governments. Poor communities have little tax base with which to provide any services, yet include people whose need for assistance is great.

A study of small counties in North Dakota illustrates how widespread this problem now is. In 1989, 84 percent of the counties had raised taxes in the previous two years in order to maintain services, and 79 percent reported a decrease in state aid. The counties were hit especially hard by cutbacks in the 1980s in federal programs for low-income people, the elderly, children, farmers, and the unemployed.

The struggle to provide adequate services in rural areas is complex. Some services are mandated by state or federal governments, yet may not be appropriate to rural communities. The mandates require that local resources be spent for those services, however. In other cases, the structure and management of rural communities make it difficult to provide adequate services. Finally, fiscal stress has become a constant companion of many communities.

MANDATED SERVICES

In theory, the services provided by local government are determined by the needs and demands of citizens in the local community. In reality, the type of services a local government provides is often a function of federal and state mandates. Local communities cannot choose whether to provide clean air, clean water, or schools that incorporate special populations. These mandates have developed from federal and state initiatives. The growth of federal assistance programs, especially during the 1970s, proved to be a double-edged sword. Increased federal assistance occurred, but was accompanied by increased federal mandates. Table 8.2 lists the mandates rural governments face in the 1990s.

The problems that arise from mandated services are graphically illustrated by the Safe Drinking Water Act enacted by the federal government in 1974. Subsequent revisions to that act require all community water systems using surface water as a water supply to filter the water in order to eliminate giardia, regardless of whether they are in a region where the organism is prevalent. Because giardia is an intestinal parasite resistant to chlorine, it cannot be eliminated by treating the water chemically.

In responding to this mandate, rural water districts have two choices. First, they can upgrade their water system to incorporate the filtering process mandated by the act. On a per-capita basis, this becomes an especially expensive process for small water systems. Although improved filtration systems are mandated by the federal government, federal funds are not widely available for upgrading local water systems. Alternately, communities can simply close down the public water system, forcing

TABLE 8.2 Federal Mandates and Obligations

Type of Mandate	Legislation
Clean water requirements	Federal Water Pollution Control Act (1972)
Groundwater protection	Safe Drinking Water Act (1974)
Solid-waste disposal	Resource Conservation and Recovery Act of 1976
Personnel	Fair Labor Standards Act of 1938
Floodplain development restrictions	National Flood Insurance Act of 1968
Prevailing wages	Davis-Bacon Act of 1931
Medicare	1986 Deficit Reduction Act
Election places	Voting Accessibility for the Elderly and Handicapped Law of 1986
Conditions of aid	Various Acts of Congress
Litigation	Civil Rights Act
Administrative activity	Various Acts of Federal Agencies (FCC, for example)

Source: Adapted from A. Sokolow. 1987. "Introduction: Small Governments as Newcomers to American Federalism." *Publius: The Journal of Federalism* 17 (Fall): 7.

members of the rural water district to obtain their drinking water individually. However, individual sources of drinking water are not regulated; in many respects, therefore, this alternative seems counterproductive to the intent of the mandate.

MULTIPLE STRUCTURES

The very organization of local government in rural areas presents special problems for the effective delivery of services. The multiple general-purpose and special-purpose governments that serve a single community can lead to conflict. Then, too, the types of services needed are becoming increasingly complex and sometimes highly technical. The capacity of local officials to deal with these issues is limited. Several examples illustrate the character of these problems.

In an effort to encourage regional cooperation, federal and later state governments created regional government districts. The Area Redevelopment Act of 1965 created a series of regional or multicounty districts through which federally supported area development efforts could be focused. States have also created multicounty strategies through which to deliver a wide range of services—regional planning, solid-waste disposal, health, mental health, aging, and so forth. In general, these districts have been created to distribute federal or state aid to local communities and to implement the program and planning requirements required in order to receive the funds.

Combined with local governments, these regional agencies create an enormously complex structure by which the needs of communities are met. One obvious problem is the conflict created when local and regional agencies both are addressing the same need. For example, Vermont recently required town governments to participate in Act 200, a comprehensive regional planning act. The act would require towns to work with county-level planning groups that would have the authority to veto the towns' planning proposals. Because many towns have their own planning efforts under way, it came as no surprise that more than two-thirds of Vermont's towns voted against the act.

Multiple and overlapping agencies also lead to fragmented efforts that may not necessarily respond to the community as a whole. To promote economic growth, for example, a general-purpose government may decide to use tax abatement as a strategy by which to attract industry. This abatement is typically in the form of property-tax relief. School districts, however, are heavily dependent on property-tax revenues for their operation, yet do not participate in the decisions made by general-purpose governments. The decision to lower or waive the property taxes charged to local industry has a direct impact on school budgets. Such a strategy helps to promote local economic development, but it can be harmful to local schools.

For example, the city commission of Manhattan, Kansas, used tax-increment financing to pay for the city's share of costs of building a downtown mall. This method of financing assumes that the development of a mall will result in increased valuation of the property being developed. The increased revenues expected from the higher valuation can then be used to pay off the bonds needed to finance construction of the mall. Two or three years after completion of the mall, citizens realized that tax-increment financing limited their short-term ability to expand school budgets or upgrade streets in response to new needs. Increased tax revenue had already been committed to the bonds used to construct the mall. One local government, the city commission, made decisions that affected another local government, the schools.

Issues local governments now deal with have become as complex as the structure of governments themselves. Despite the fact that they are typically volunteers, rural government officials are often responsible for a diverse set of services. They generally lack the expertise needed to deal with technologically complex issues such as hazardous waste, infrastructure financing, or healthcare. The limited size of rural communities also means that these officials are less likely to find a local expert to consult. Thus, the capacity of rural government officials to deal with multiple and complex issues may also make it difficult for local governments to organize needed services.

FISCAL STRESS

Many rural governments suffer from what is called *fiscal stress*. Fiscal stress occurs when available revenues decrease and the need for services increases. When jobs are lost, for example, tax revenue declines, but demand increases for community services such as job training, welfare, counseling, and housing.

Different services also require a certain minimum number of users before it becomes cost-effective to provide them. When a community's population starts to decline, the number of users may drop below that minimum level. Fixed costs must then be shared by a smaller number of remaining residents. At some point, local governments must decide to eliminate the service, allow it to be provided by a higher level of government, or arrange for it to be provided privately. For instance, townships in various midwestern states transferred the upkeep of township roads to county governments when farms were consolidated and the number of farmers declined. Acute fiscal stress frequently triggers decisions in which local governments give up services.

We can get a sense of the limited resources available to rural communities by looking at a sample budget. Table 8.3 lists the revenue sources for a recent budget adopted by a small town in Ohio. Revenue sources differ considerably from state to state and even within states because communities differ in terms of their eligibility or share in certain funds. This sample, then, is illustrative but not representative of rural communities.

As shown in Table 8.3, this community in fiscal year 1990 raised about 70 percent of its budget from local sources. Local revenue included funds raised from property taxes, fines/licenses/permits, miscellaneous, transfers, and other categories. General property taxes accounted for about 22 percent of this community's budget, a figure that is relatively low among rural communities in general. The community derived the remaining 30 percent of its budget from state-levied but locally shared taxes. These include estate taxes, motor vehicle license taxes, and state income, sales, and corporation taxes passed along to local governments. Federal sources made no contribution to this community's budget.

Most rural governments are funded by a combination of local, state, and federal revenues. In general, rural communities rely upon local sources of revenue for about 70 percent of their budget. Local governments typically rely on property taxes, often supplemented by local sales tax. Business taxes, user charges, and miscellaneous revenues such as fines and fees bring in lesser amounts. Very few rural counties or towns levy

TABLE 8.3 Sample General Fund Revenue

Description	FY 1989 Actual	FY 1990 Actual
Local Tax		
General property	$ 60,646.24	$ 65,408.23
Tangible personal property	13,059.92	8,326.37
Municipal income	0.00	0.00
Other local	0.00	0.00
Total Local	$ 73,706.16	$ 73,734.60
Intergovernmental-state		
Local government	$ 31,773.49	$ 35,765.78
Estate	17,068.69	51,486.72
Cigarette	111.37	341.13
Licenses	0.00	0.00
Liquor/beer permits	2,218.88	3,721.60
Gasoline	0.00	0.00
Other	0.00	0.00
Total State Shared	$ 51,172.43	$ 91,315.23
Federal grants/aid	$ 0.00	$ 0.00
Special assessment	0.00	0.00
Charge for services	0.00	0.00
Fines/licenses/permits	78,489.45	56,463.00
Miscellaneous	19,086.76	29,042.93
Other financing		
Proceeds/debt sales	$ 0.00	$ 0.00
Transfers	0.00	6,841.96
Advances	0.00	0.00
Other	85,000.00	40,000.00
Total Revenue	$307,454.80	$297,397.72

income taxes. The remaining 30 percent of local government revenues comes from federal and state assistance. Federal funds are generally derived from income taxes. State revenues are highly varied, sometimes involving sales taxes and other times relying chiefly upon income taxes.

Different types of taxes can be contrasted in terms of their relationship to the taxpayer's ability to pay. *Progressive taxes* place a disproportionate share of the tax burden on those able to pay, the wealthy. *Regressive taxes* do the reverse, placing a disproportionate part of the tax burden on middle- and lower-income taxpayers. Local taxes tend not to be progressive, with sales taxes being the most regressive of all. In contrast, real property taxes are more capricious than regressive. They are only slightly related to the ability to pay. For instance, elderly persons who own their own home or small farm and are on a limited fixed income will pay a higher proportion of their income or wealth on property taxes than will a prosperous tenant farmer or wealthy banker. Because they are derived from income taxes, federal funds are generally progressive. State funds come from a mixture of progressive and regressive tax sources.

Locally generated taxes depend on local economic activity. The 1980s were a particularly difficult period for rural governments: Farm values declined, the energy economy collapsed, timber and mining activity dwindled, and a nationwide recession with the attendant decline in retail trade occurred. Thus, the base for property taxes (real property values) and the base for sales taxes (retail trade) decreased sharply. Fiscal capacity of local governments declined at the same time that federal and state governments shifted the burden of particular services to local governments. Local governments suffered acute fiscal stress throughout the 1980s and into the 1990s.

Although property taxes have been the major source of local government revenue, they became increasingly unpopular in the 1970s and 1980s. Consequently, some rural areas have reduced their reliance on property tax significantly. Highly rural areas (counties with fewer than 2,500 urban residents) still collect almost 60 percent of local revenues from property taxes, however.

Efforts at raising additional local nonproperty tax revenues have proved difficult. Several factors hamper rural governments. These include a lack of staff and leadership to adopt and administer creative financing, the relatively low incomes in some rural areas, shrinking retail sectors in smaller communities, and state government restrictions on nonproperty tax sources (Reeder 1990).

In general, current mechanisms for funding local community needs have not proved effective, especially for rural communities faced with a declining economy. The tax burden on rural residents increases as the health of the local economy decreases. The inequity of such a system has become obvious in the financing of schools. Judges in recent court decisions in Kentucky and Texas invalidated state financing strategies, pointing to the tremendous gap between per-pupil expenditures in suburban and rural areas. Courts are insisting that states allocate state educational funds in such a way as to ensure that rural and suburban children alike have access to a quality education (see Box 8.1).

Federal Aid to Rural Governments

Historically, rural governments have depended upon federal aid to develop the services needed to create and maintain communities. As pointed out in Chapter 2, the federal government played a substantial role

BOX 8.1 RURAL SCHOOLS AND EDUCATIONAL REFORM: THE KENTUCKY CASE

The current educational reform movement is taking shape amid two changes. The first is the social and economic change that is occurring worldwide and that is resulting in pressure on schools to begin preparing young people for the more sophisticated jobs needed in the information age. The second is the increased fiscal stress being felt by local governments. Kentucky offers an interesting case study of the role each of these changes is playing in efforts at educational reform.

The first change relates to the role schools need to play in the new social and economic environment. Post–World War II schools are often described in terms of a "mass production" metaphor—schools designed to teach young people existing knowledge bases, punctuality, patience in performing rote operations, behaviors appropriate to hierarchical organizations, and so forth. Business and industry now talk of needing different skills. Increasingly, young people will need to know how to gather, organize, and communicate new information. They will need to be able to think critically and solve problems readily. The shrinking work force also means that a much larger proportion of young people need to finish high school and continue on to some form of postsecondary education.

The educational reform movement is also occurring within an economic context. In the 1960s, rural and urban schools alike began challenging how schools were financed. There was enormous disparity among schools in terms of how much money was spent per student. A series of court cases established that education was not a right under the U.S. Constitution and had to be challenged under state constitutions. Cases brought before state courts met with mixed results. Some state constitutions do define the state's responsibilities for education in such a way that the courts could order the state to develop a more equitable strategy for funding public schools.

In response, states began developing various strategies for ensuring that the amount of money spent on education per child was more equal across different school districts. This reform is complex, however, given that schools have been funded primarily through local property taxes. Two of the more common strategies were to (1) use state funds to supplement local funds raised in support of schools and (2) put a cap on per-student expenditures in an effort to control what the more wealthy districts could spend. As states began supplementing local funds, however, they also began imposing rules and regulations concerning how schools were run.

Kentucky has found itself caught up in these changes. Kentucky is a poor state—it ranks 42 in the nation for average personal income. High illiteracy rates and low high-school completion rates make it questionable whether the state will be able to take part in the new economy. Efforts to improve schools, however, have been hampered by tensions between local and state government. As of 1989, the state was contributing 50 percent of all funds spent on education. Yet the amount spent per student ranged from $1,471 to $3,347 among individual school districts. The state argued that it was contributing more than its share and that local districts were either not collecting property taxes or underassessing properties.

A group of sixty-six school districts, most of which were small rural districts in the Appalachian region of eastern Kentucky, filed suit against the state. They charged that the state's methods of financing public schools placed too much emphasis on local resources, with the result being that children in poorer school districts were receiving a less than adequate education. Their original suit was successful, but was appealed to the Kentucky Supreme Court. In a surprising turn of events, the court ruled that Kentucky's entire educational system, not just the finance formula, was unconstitutional. The state was given one year in which to restructure the entire school system.

continues

Box 8.1 *continued*

The Kentucky Educational Reform Act was passed by the Kentucky legislature in 1990. It outlined changes in three areas: (1) curriculum, (2) governance, and (3) finance. In exchange for a more equitable funding formula, rural Kentucky schools now find themselves faced with increased state involvement in both the curriculum and governance of schools.

Challenges to state funding formulas are being filed in many states. What schools seem to face is a choice between adequate fiscal resources or local control. Rural schools express concern that the state governments do not understand the differences across local communities and schools. Local differences do exist, but the state governments argue that schools must be held accountable in their expenditure of state funds. Whose side do you take?

---

in encouraging western expansion and settlement of rural lands. This section explores the different character federal aid has taken in the past, the focus on grants that occupied the 1960s and 1970s, and the "new federalism" likely to describe the future.

DEVELOPING LAND AND PEOPLE

One study (Lapping et al. 1989) points out that federal involvement in rural issues can be summarized by four broad themes: (1) settling the land, (2) developing the human resources and economic infrastructure needed to support communities, (3) supporting farmers, and (4) alleviating poverty. Each issue has dominated at one time or another, but all are woven through the development of rural communities.

Early federal involvement was directed almost solely toward the settlement of land. Under a variety of land grants, land owned by the federal government was eventually transferred to private ownership. Mineral laws and subsidies to the timber industry offered further inducement to settle new lands. Grants to railroads and to road, canal, and bridge systems encouraged the development of transportation networks capable of supporting a dispersed population.

This emphasis on land settlement eventually gave way to interest in the development of human resources and provision of roads, buildings, and services capable of supporting communities. The creation of land-grant universities in 1862 and the introduction of the cooperative extension service in 1914 put emphasis on the development of human resources. Programs introduced during the depression focused on the construction needs in rural areas. The federal Public Works Administration and the Civilian Conservation Corps built roads, bridges, hospitals, parks, and schools. The Rural Electrical Administration put electrical service in place throughout rural communities and farming areas. The interstate highway

Historically, the federal role in rural communities has focused on agriculture (photo courtesy of the Ohio University Telecommunications Center).

system added an important dimension to the transportation network and had substantial impact on rural communities.

In the 1960s, federal interest in rural support shifted to the war on poverty. President John F. Kennedy's visit to West Virginia placed the rural poor squarely before the public. President Lyndon Johnson continued this agenda, releasing studies that established the complexity of rural poverty if not the strategies for overcoming it. Farm subsidies introduced during the depression have remained as an instrument for increasing farm-sector income during times of overproduction and low prices. As the number of farmers continued to decline, those subsidies have had a decreasing impact on rural communities. Larger farmers tend to bypass the local community by purchasing inputs in bulk.

FEDERAL GRANTS-IN-AID

Categorical and block grant programs were created in the 1950s and had explosive growth in the 1960s and 1970s. Categorical programs provide funds to local governmental organizations to operate very specific programs, such as vocational-technical training or migrant healthcare centers. Block grants provide governments with funds to be used for special purposes such as community development. Although both types of aid can be helpful to rural governments, neither allowed the use of funds to be tailored to more specific local needs. Finally, in 1972, the federal government created general revenue sharing under which local governments received unrestricted funds for general operations and special programs.

The federal government funds some 828 programs that provide grants for economic development, agriculture and natural resources, infrastructure, human resources, general entitlement, and special programs. These programs spent $639 billion in 1987, with 17 percent of total funds going to rural areas (defined in this case as places of less than 20,000 population). More than 70 percent of federal spending in rural America, however, is actually a redistribution of income to individuals in the form of transfer payments (farm subsidies, social security, and welfare) rather than a grant of funds directly to rural governments or nonprofit organizations (U.S. GAO 1989).

Federal support of rural areas is substantial, but it remains highly focused on agriculture, to the exclusion of more broad-based support. The dollar share of federal funding that goes to rural areas is approximately equal to the proportion of rural people in the total U.S. population. However, farm programs receive nearly half of the nonentitlement funds going to rural areas. Although there is an increased emphasis on comprehensive rural development, agricultural support in the form of farm subsidies still dominates federal spending on rural development. In 1987, for example, $29 billion was spent on development programs for all of rural America; an additional $22.4 billion was spent on agricultural price and income support alone. Yet those engaged in farming number only 2 percent of the nation's population and less than 9 percent of the nonmetropolitan population.

If farm programs and entitlements are excluded, less than 10 percent of the remainder of federal funding goes to rural areas of less than 20,000 population. These areas are home to 16 percent of the population. Of particular importance is the fact that only 5 percent of federal spending on human resources goes to rural areas. Human capital is arguably the most important investment that can be made for economic development and certainly for the well-being of individuals who receive it. As agriculture continues to decline or disappear as the economic base of rural communities, the need to invest in human resources increases. The combination of the "brain drain" from rural areas, which was particularly notable in the 1980s, and the failure of the federal government to assist in upgrading rural human capacity does not bode well for the ability of rural areas of the United States to compete economically. In fact, many rural areas are coming to occupy in the world economy a position similar to that of Third World countries.

After a period of rapid expansion, federal aid to local governments declined during the 1980s, in both absolute and real dollars. This changed relationship is referred to as the "new federalism." Although a rural-federal partnership continues to exist, the character of that partnership has changed considerably.

MORE RESPONSIBILITY, LESS MONEY

President Ronald Reagan and his administration made large-scale reductions in federal assistance to state and local governments a major policy objective in 1981. Under this new federalism, federal support of local communities declined. With passage by Congress of the Omnibus Budget Reconciliation Act in 1981, President Reagan accelerated a trend to reduce the growth in federal aid to local governments started during the administration of Jimmy Carter. Federal aid as a proportion of total revenues, for example, declined 13 percent between 1981 and 1982 and again between 1986 and 1987. Using 1980 as a benchmark, researchers have shown that federal spending has decreased by 66 percent and loan guarantees by 41 percent (Working Group on Economic Development in Small Communities 1990). The Budget Reconciliation Act also converted seventy-seven categorical grants to nine new block grants. Sixty programs were eliminated.

Cuts in local services were dramatic, and the states were forced to adjust to declining federal support. In 1987, general revenue sharing was eliminated with equally dramatic results. Some rural governments depended on general revenue sharing for as much as 15 percent of their general fund budgets. In response, both state and local governments increased efforts to raise revenues. State aid has not compensated for the decline in federal assistance, however.

The decline in federal responsibility for rural development has led to increased state efforts to promote economic development. Today, most states have an economic development program, but unless such programs explicitly include a rural development component, rural communities generally receive much less than their share of state funds. Urban business interests often dominate state economic development programs. In addition, many state economic development programs focus on recruitment of industry, which is more appropriate for metropolitan cities and regional trade centers than for smaller rural communities.

With the cooperation of the National Governors Conference, the National Council of State Legislatures, the National Association of Towns and Townships, and other organizations, approximately ten of the fifty states initiated rural development policies between 1985 and 1990. These initiatives are important because of the diversity of rural areas in the

United States. States are better able than the federal government to deal with differences in communities resulting from differences in population growth and decline, in economic base (agriculture or retirement, for example), in rate of entrepreneurial development, and in education levels.

Yet state policy cannot substitute for an effective national rural policy. In particular, states are an inappropriate level for instituting policies pertaining to industry location, jobs, and income. When viewed from a national perspective, state recruitment policies tend to be a zero-sum game. One state can raid other states for industrial firms, but these efforts do not necessarily increase total industrial capacity or expand net employment opportunities in the nation. They simply move jobs from one state to another. Rather than taking the initiative by adopting policies that encourage the development of new jobs, the federal government is virtually abandoning economic development.

As the federal government withdraws from its rural partnership, rural governments continue to face substantial problems. To what extent states will step forward remains unclear. Thomas Stinson (1990, 72) has described the general situation this way:

> Most rural governments are likely to continue to be important providers of public services. Indeed, population decline may heighten the financial problems of small communities. Consolidation, inter-local cooperative agreements, contracting and shared service agreements are all ways for rural residents to retain access to minimally adequate levels of public services, but local resources may still be insufficient even after all management improvements have been utilized. Maintaining and improving the quality of public service in non-metropolitan communities is a key priority for the 1990s.

Resolution of these problems requires political will and power. It is questionable whether rural people have the political clout to obtain a funded comprehensive rural development program. The decline in rural voting power has resulted in large part from demographic shifts in U.S. society, as more people move to urban areas. Moreover, the way we turn population into votes has also changed. Every ten years, states reapportion congressional and state legislative districts based on the decennial census. States may gain or lose congressional seats, and areas within states can have legislative power eroded. In the 1960s, a series of U.S. Supreme Court decisions on apportionment of congressional and state legislative assemblies established the "one person, one vote" doctrine, which required that districts be drawn solely on the basis of population. Rural areas subsequently lost electoral (voting) power to urban and, later, to suburban areas.

As the relative power of rural areas continues to decline, rural officials may find it beneficial to look for an alliance with those in the inner city. Urban and rural areas alike face decaying roads and buildings, lack of economic growth, low-wage employment, inadequate social services, and poverty.

Government and the Economy

The lawsuit the Donovan family brought to oppose efforts to elect a Coker town council went all the way through the state court system, a federal district court, and finally the U.S. Supreme Court. Ultimately, the Donovans lost.

In 1991, the Coker local government celebrated its two-year anniversary. Malcolm Porter now serves on the town council. The town has access to surplus food and has set up a town-based nutritional program. Council members also discovered that they could apply for assistance in installing a water and sewer system. Children are doing better in school. The new water and sewer system has encouraged a few new businesses to move in. Progress is slow, but the people in Coker are encouraged. They now have the tool—a local government—with which to respond to local needs.

Local governments are important. They provide the vehicle for citizen participation and offer local communities access to state and federal funds. The need for these funds is obvious in communities such as Coker. It is the long-term impact of the funds, for the individuals who receive them as well as the communities who apply for them, that remains in question.

For sociologists, the larger issue is how the various levels of government can stimulate healthy local economies. No one questions the need for adequate food. Hungry, malnourished children cannot learn effectively and thus cannot develop the skills they will eventually need to support themselves and their families. It would be preferable, however, if the conditions that underlie the poverty in Coker were eliminated. Do federal programs stimulate local economic development, or do they simply increase rural dependence? Can states carve out a new role as they assume some of the responsibility?

In order to answer these questions, we need to understand just how governments actually shape the economy. No one has a complete picture of how powers are distributed across the three levels of government and the extent to which this distribution enables governments to stimulate new forms of economic organization (Eisinger 1988). Although the ability of government to tax is extremely important (O'Connor 1973), its ability to control land use and property may be equally important in sustaining and developing local economies (Campbell and Lindberg 1990). Sociologists and communities such as Coker share an interest in these issues.

Chapter Summary

In the United States, the system of government divides powers between the federal government and the states. States create local governments through either home-rule provisions (constitutional amendments) or general laws (state legislation). Most local governments are created by legislation.

Local governments are important to rural areas because they (1) offer a structure by which community members participate in local decisions, (2) provide services and community facilities, and (3) link local revenues to local needs. The many forms of local government found in rural areas can be sorted into two categories. General-purpose governments are those created to respond to the general needs of a county, city, or town. Special-purpose governments are created to respond to specific community needs, such as schools, water, or medical services. Governments in rural communities are often staffed by part-time officials and local citizens who serve as volunteers.

Because of their limited resources, most rural governments find it difficult to provide adequate levels of public services. By mandating certain services, state and federal governments can require that local resources be directed to services that are not needed. Multiple general-purpose and special-purpose governments can lead to conflict or fragmented responses to local community needs. Finally, most rural governments face fiscal stress that arises from a limited tax base but increased demand for local services.

The federal role in rural areas has changed substantially. Historically, federal involvement in rural areas focused on settling the land, developing human resources, constructing the roads and buildings needed by communities, supporting farmers, and alleviating poverty. Categorical and block grant programs during the 1960s and 1970s targeted federal funds to specific programs. The new federalism, initiated by President Reagan in 1981, eliminated general revenue sharing with local communities. Current federal involvement is characterized more by transfer payments to individuals than by support to community development efforts. States have responded by supporting local development efforts, but this may not be adequate.

Key Terms

Federalism is a system of government in which separate states are united by a central authority while retaining certain powers, such as the power to tax.

Fiscal stress in rural communities arises from a limited tax base but increased need for services.

General-purpose governments are governments created to respond to the general needs of a county, city, or town.

Progressive taxes place a disproportionate share of the tax burden on the more wealthy. The percent of income paid as income tax, for example, increases as a person's income increases.

Regressive taxes place a disproportionate share of the tax burden on those less able to pay. Consumer sales taxes become a decreasing share of people's income as their income increases. Wealthier people tend to save and invest a higher proportion of their incomes than do poor people.

Special-purpose governments are created to respond to specific community needs, such as schools or water.

References

Advisory Commission on Intergovernmental Relations (ACIR). 1991. *Rural Counties: The Challenges Ahead.* Washington, DC: U.S. Government Printing Office.

Beam, D. R. 1985. "New Federalism, Old Realities: The Reagan Administration and Intergovernmental Reform." Pp. 415–442 in Lester M. Salamon and Michael S. Lund (eds.), *The Reagan Presidency and the Governing of America.* Washington, DC: Urban Institute.

Berne, R., and R. Schramm. 1986. *The Financial Analysis of Governments.* Englewood Cliffs, NJ: Prentice-Hall.

Braaten, K. 1991. "Rural Counties: The Challenges Ahead." *Intergovernmental Perspective* 17 (Winter): 38–40.

Cahill, A. G., S. Rahman, and J. A. James. Undated. *Increasing the Governing Capacities of Small Local Governments in Pennsylvania: Policy Perspectives and Strategies.* University Park, PA: Department of Public Administration.

Campbell, J. L., and L. N. Lindberg. 1990. "Property Rights and the Organization of Economic Activity by the State." *American Sociological Review* 55:634–647.

Danbom, David B. 1979. *The Resisted Revolution: Urban America and the Industrialization of Agriculture, 1900–1930.* Ames: Iowa State University Press.

Eisinger, P. 1988. *The Rise of the Entrepreneurial State.* Madison: University of Wisconsin Press.

Lapping, Mark B., Thomas D. Daniels, and John W. Keller. 1989. *Rural Planning and Development in the United States.* New York: Guilford.

National Association of Towns and Townships. 1990. *Reporter.* Washington, DC: National Association of Towns and Townships.

O'Connor, J. 1973. *The Fiscal Crisis of the State.* New York: St. Martin's.

Office of Technology Assessment. 1991. *Rural America at the Crossroads: Networking for the Future.* Washington, DC: U.S. Government Printing Office.

Phifer, Bryan M. 1989. "An Overview of Community Development in America." Pp. 253–279 in James A. Christenson and Jerry W. Robinson, Jr. (eds.), *Community Development in Perspective.* Ames: Iowa State University Press.

Rasmussen, Wayne D. 1985. "90 Years of Rural Development Programs." *Rural Development Perspectives* 2 (October): 2–10.

Reeder, Robert J. 1990. "Introduction." Pp. 1–6 in Advisory Commission on Intergovernmental Relations, *Local Revenue Diversification, Rural Economies* March.

Snavely, K., and Alvin D. Sokolow. 1987. "Who Advises the Council? Sources of Advice in Smalltown Governments." *Rural Development Perspectives* 3 (February): 25–29.

Sokolow, Alvin D. 1982. "Local Governments: Capacity and Will." Ch. 19 in Amos H. Hawley and Sara Mills Mazie (eds.), *Nonmetropolitan America in Transition.* Chapel Hill: University of North Carolina Press.

———. 1987. "Introduction: Small Governments as Newcomers to American Federalism." *Publius: The Journal of Federalism* 17 (Fall): 1–14.

———. 1988. *Back Home: Grassroots Governments and the People They Serve.* Washington, DC: National Association of Towns and Townships.

Stinson, Thomas F. 1990. "Local Revenue Diversification: Implications for Nonmetropolitan Communities." Pp. 67–85 in Advisory Commission on Intergovernmental Relations, *Local Revenue Diversification, Rural Economies* March.

U.S. Census of Governments. 1987. *Government Finance.* Washington, DC: Government Printing Office.

U.S. Government Accounting Office (GAO). 1989. *Rural Development: Federal Programs That Focus on Rural America and Its Economic Development.* Washington, DC: Government Printing Office.

Valente, Maureen Godsey. 1985. "Volunteers Help Stretch Local Budgets." *Rural Development Perspectives* 1 (October): 45–48.

Waltzer, Herbert, Philip A. Russo, Jr., and W. Robert Gump. 1986. "Professional Networks and Local Officials: A Missing Link in Small Government Management." *Rural Development Perspectives* 1 (June): 35–39.

Working Group on Economic Development in Small Communities. 1990. *Take Charge: Economic Development in Small Communities.* Ames, IA: North Central Regional Center for Rural Development.

9

Economic Infrastructure

O

In Floyd County, Sara Johnson turns on the faucet. A mucky, grayish solution trickles from the spout. The county water system isn't working again. She'll have to go out and buy water. They'll need water to drink, wash dishes, even bathe in. Sara will have to take the family's laundry to the laundromat, a round trip of at least twenty miles. She hasn't the money for gasoline, let alone the time to spare for such a trip. Installed by the coal company, taken over by a private water company, and now owned by someone in another state, the local water system doesn't work half the time.

In Hebron, Carl Jones no longer takes the most direct route to Center City. In order to deliver his fresh vegetables to the farmers' market, Carl now drives an extra forty miles in his old pickup truck. The bridge over the creek has collapsed. Carl wonders when, and if, the county plans to replace it. The cost of the extra gasoline sure takes away from what he can make selling vegetables at the market.

Emily Bailey and her husband, Jim Smothers, recently moved to Wolf Point. They own a private consulting business that serves clients worldwide. Having grown tired of the hassles of city life, Emily and Jim were looking forward to a rural lifestyle. Much to their surprise, they found that digital switching is not available in the local telephone system. Emily and Jim can't hook up facsimile machines or computer modems, both of which are essential for communicating with clients. Their business founders as they consider moving again.

These people face problems—problems with access to clean water, safe bridges, and communications technology. The problems are not minor. Both Sara and Carl have limited incomes. The extra costs they bear in buying water or traveling an extra forty miles can mean the difference between remaining economically independent or having to turn to others for financial help. Emily and Jim enjoy living in the country, but if they cannot use standard business equipment they have little choice. They will have to move elsewhere.

These problems are equally serious to the communities. Floyd County finds it hard to attract business and industry. Basic services, such as clean water, are often not available. Hebron continues to decline as more and more of the small vegetable farmers find they cannot market their produce. Wolf Point cannot take advantage of the new opportunities created by technology. Many businesses no longer need to be located in large cities, but unless Wolf Point finds a way to install the proper switches and fiber-optic cables, it will be unable to attract people such as Emily and Jim.

Water services, bridges, and digital switches are all part of what social scientists call the economic infrastructure of a community. How we function in everyday life depends on the type, quality, and condition of the infrastructure available to us. How rural communities function in the new economy will depend on the infrastructure they can provide their residents. This chapter explores what economic infrastructure is, how it is provided, and how rural communities can organize to maintain it.

Defining Infrastructure

The term *infrastructure* refers to a foundation or a supporting framework. Used in relation to communities, infrastructure refers to the things that must be present to support the life of the community. This section defines what we mean by economic infrastructure and explores current issues rural communities face in providing that infrastructure.

THE ECONOMIC INFRASTRUCTURE

Economic infrastructure is the permanent physical installations and facilities supporting productive activities in a community. It includes roads; streets and bridges; airports and railroads; electric and natural gas utility systems; water supply systems; police and fire protection facilities; wastewater treatment and waste disposal facilities; schools, hospitals, and other public and commercial buildings; and telephone and fiber-optic networks and other communications facilities. As is obvious from the list, the economic infrastructure of a community refers to the equipment needed to support a series of networks. These networks enable people to get around, communicate with one another, and gain access to services and markets.

Of little utility in and of itself, economic infrastructure facilitates production. Buildings enable a factory to make products that can then be

Bridges are an important part of a community's economic infrastructure (photo courtesy of the Ohio University Telecommunications Center).

sold. Roads are used to take goods to market or bring raw materials to a production facility. Electricity provides light and energy for a variety of economic and domestic functions. These and other elements of a community's economic infrastructure enable individuals and businesses to be productive within the community. Although the economic infrastructure of a community is necessary, it is not sufficient to ensure the economic health and well-being of that community. People must be able to use the infrastructure in productive ways.

ACCESS AND CONSUMPTION

Two issues, access and consumption, are involved in people's use of the community's economic infrastructure. This section explores each of these dimensions. The next looks at the types of economic infrastructure that emerge from the interaction of these two issues.

Goods and services are considered *exclusive* when some people can be denied access to them. Elements of an economic infrastructure are *inclusive* when they are available to all users. Access to many utilities, such as water, electricity, or telephones, is exclusive because people must be hooked up to the utility in order to use it. Most streets and roads are available to anyone who wants to use them and are thus inclusive. Access to parks or recreational areas is often inclusive, whereas access to Disneyland is exclusive.

The decision as to whether a good or service is inclusive or exclusive depends on a number of factors. One factor is the extent to which access can be controlled. Radio stations, for example, might have a hard time making radio signals exclusive. A second factor is the decisions made about how a service is organized. Water, for example, can be treated as an inclusive or exclusive service—the category is determined by how the community chooses to organize delivery of the water.

A second feature of a good or service is the notion of joint consumption versus rival consumption. *Joint consumption* means that if one person uses a good or service, its use by another is not decreased. By contrast, *rival consumption* means that if a good or service is used by one person, it cannot be used by another. Roads, television and radio signals, and zoos are all capable of supporting joint consumption. Electricity is an example of a service subject to rival consumption; clean water is rapidly becoming so also.

The distinction between joint and rival consumption is obviously not a clear one. Goods or services can appear to support joint consumption in some circumstances and rival consumption in others. To some extent, the match between resources and needs affects how we characterize different forms of economic infrastructure.

TYPES OF ECONOMIC INFRASTRUCTURE

The two dimensions of access and consumption can be used to define different types of economic infrastructure. As shown in Table 9.1, crossing the two different forms of access with the two different types of consumption leads to four categories of economic infrastructure. Briefly explored here is the extent to which control by the private or public sector seems better suited for each category.

TABLE 9.1 Types of Goods and Services

Access	Consumption	
	Joint	Rival
Inclusive	Collective	Common-Pool
Exclusive	Toll	Private

In the lower right corner of the table are goods or services characterized by exclusive access and rival consumption; these are defined to be *private*. A landfill for which individuals must pay a fee in order to dispose of garbage is an example of a private form of infrastructure, regardless of whether it is publicly or privately owned.

Until recently, people did not think of waste disposal in terms of rival consumption. When people were free to dispose of garbage wherever they wanted, waste disposal was not even a form of infrastructure. Once it became clear that dumping garbage in road ditches, ravines, or old wells contaminated water supplies, disposal of garbage began to be characterized by rival consumption. Now most people are aware that the amount of garbage one household puts in the landfill limits the amount another household will be able to put in. Agreements to take in out-of-state garbage may limit a rural community's capacity to dispose of its own garbage, for example.

Toll goods or services are those subject to exclusive access and joint consumption. Access is limited, usually by the requirement that a fee be paid, but anyone who can afford the fee can use the facility. Toll roads, long-distance telephone lines, and fiber-optic communication systems are examples of economic infrastructure that are toll services. These are goods or services that can be jointly consumed by different people simultaneously. If one person uses a toll service, another person can use the same service without having to replenish it.

Goods or services for which inclusive access is matched with rival consumption are referred to as *common-pool*. Public school buildings are normally an example of this type of infrastructure. School buildings are available for use without a fee, but they can accommodate only a limited number of people. Use made of the school by one child might limit the opportunity for another child to use that same facility. Demands for use by a larger number of people require additional buildings or expansion of existing ones.

Finally, goods or services that link inclusive access with joint consumption are referred to as *collective*. Streets, roads, and public sidewalks are the most obvious examples of collective goods. Schools can be considered collective goods if the community decides to have the school run two shifts of children each day or increase class size rather than turn children away.

ISSUES FACING RURAL COMMUNITIES

Failure of the economic infrastructure of rural areas has become a pressing problem. Much of the existing infrastructure was built over fifty years ago, part of efforts to rebuild the country economically after the Great Depression. Community planners realized that rural people would prosper only if their communities had a well-developed foundation of streets, roads, public buildings, and utilities. Thus, a variety of public programs and private initiatives were established to assist rural communities in developing stronger infrastructures.

That infrastructure is now deteriorating. Nearly one out of every five rural communities reports that two-thirds of its water pipeline has been in use for more than fifty years. Among rural communities with bridges to support, one-third have had to defer maintenance on at least one bridge for more than a year (Reid and Sullivan 1984). A study of four midwestern states concluded that it would cost $2.5 billion to bring existing township roads and bridges back up to acceptable condition. That estimate includes the cost needed to repair or replace some 10,000 bridges, one-third of all bridges maintained by townships (Walzer et al. 1987).

Responsibility for maintaining and replacing water and sewer systems, roads and bridges, and public buildings has increasingly shifted from federal and state to local governments. Locally, infrastructure improvements are often financed through tax-exempt municipal bonds. These bonds can be either general obligation bonds or revenue bonds. General obligation bonds commit the community as a whole to repayment of the bonds. Consequently, funds are raised through increased taxes or a reallocation of existing tax revenue. Revenue bonds are repaid by the revenue collected as a result of the improvement.

Rural communities face a number of problems in financing infrastructure improvements. Rural communities often lack an economic base sufficient to support the large financial outlays required to solve their infrastructure problems. Because of the extent to which many communities now have a declining tax base, general obligation bonds are of limited use. Revenue bonds depend on a population large enough to make the increased costs manageable. In most cases, the per-capita costs of improving or even maintaining an economic infrastructure in rural communities tend to be rather high.

High per-capita costs in rural communities are a function of several factors. Because of the lower population densities there, rural areas must often function under unfavorable economies of scale (low number of users per investment). The greater distances to be served also make both the installation and maintenance of many forms of economic infrastructure more expensive. In some cases, the higher costs may be offset by simpler technology or individual solutions. Septic tanks and private water systems, for example, may substitute for expensive sewage treatment facilities and water distribution systems needed by more densely populated areas. Fewer streets are needed, and they need not be built to accommodate the heavy traffic common in urban areas. In general, however, economic infrastructure can cost considerably more per citizen to build and maintain in rural areas.

Some rural communities are turning to other alternatives, such as special districts or impact extractions. Kentucky, for example, went to a system of creating special districts to fund infrastructure improvements. Special districts allow the costs of improving the infrastructure to be borne only by those who will benefit directly. Impact extractions involve shifting the costs of development from the public to the developer. Bethel, Maine, gives developers two alternatives in connecting into the municipal sewer system: The developer can either construct a new replacement for existing lines or pay a sewer-system development charge. Both options provide the funds needed to upgrade and maintain the community's sewer system (Lynch 1991).

Public Versus Private Provision of Economic Infrastructure

Economic infrastructure can be provided and supported in a number of different ways. Public schools and roads, for example, are provided totally through public investment and control. Other forms, such as telephone companies, are developed through the private sector. Public or private control is not simply a dichotomy, however. It is a continuum, such that elements of public and private support can be combined in varying degrees. This section examines the four types of infrastructure in terms of how they are provided and proposes a framework from which to examine the choices a community makes.

PRIVATE AND TOLL FORMS

Private and toll goods or services can be supplied by either the private or the public sector. The choice of control, public or private, is typically a function of historical development, economic entrepreneurship, or fiscal prudence. Bridges, housing, water supplies, recreation facilities, and fire protection can all be offered directly to users by private suppliers for a fee that includes cost plus profit. On the other hand, some local governments provide goods usually classified as private, such as electricity or telephone service. Some economic infrastructure originally constructed at public expense may be converted to private and toll goods controlled by the private sector. Land in industrial parks or speculative buildings placed on that land are sometimes turned over to private firms as an incentive for them to come to the community. Thus, the three most common alternatives for providing private and toll forms of infrastructure seem to be private development and maintenance, public development and maintenance, and public development but private maintenance.

In many rural communities, natural monopolies maintain segments of the economic infrastructure. *Monopolies* are single companies that control the delivery of goods or services without competition. Monopolies can be either public or private. They are typically formed when exclusive services could be offered by different providers but for efficiency reasons are best organized as monopolies. Water services, electricity, telephone service, and fire protection tend to be offered by single providers. Although monopolies seem natural when only one delivery system exists, it is possible to provide service on a competitive basis. The recent restructuring of long-distance telephone service is an example. The owners of the infrastructure (telephone lines, cables, and switches) rent access to it to competitors.

Many of the goods and services that now come from monopolies were once provided on a competitive basis. In colonial Maryland, for example, fire protection was initially provided through insurance companies. Private companies sold insurance policies that included fire-fighting services from any number of competing companies. If a fire did break out, only the fire-fighting service identified by the insurance policy responded. One person might purchase such a policy; a neighbor might not carry any insurance at all. Such erratic access to fire protection was inefficient, to say nothing of dangerous to public welfare.

Many communities moved to provide more uniform fire protection through community-controlled and -purchased firehouses and fire-fighting equipment. In some communities, salaried fire fighters were hired. Other rural communities organized volunteer fire departments. No longer competitive, fire fighting has become a monopolized part of the economic infrastructure in communities.

As local resources become more scarce, some communities use their economic infrastructure to generate income. Bethel, Maine, provides fire protection to several surrounding towns. It charges each town an availability fee—a flat rate for making its fire department available—that is reminiscent of the old insurance policies sold in Maryland. When actually called to a fire, the Bethel Fire Department charges a rental fee for the trucks that show up at the fire scene, labor costs for the fire fighters involved, and overhead for providing the service. The fees have increased nontraditional sources of revenue available to Bethel and, presumably, made a higher level of fire protection available to the smaller communities (Lynch 1991).

Rural communities still face many issues pertaining to funding these services today. Decisions must be made as to whether fire protection should be supported through public or private means and whether it should be operated as a profit-generating or not-for-profit activity. Are volunteer fire fighters sufficient to meet the needs of the local area, or must there be full-time, paid staff? Should states intervene to mandate a certain level of training or commitment to fire fighting, or should communities be allowed to organize the service in response to local resources? If the community opts for public support, what proportion of funds should be derived from public moneys such as assessments of property taxes?

COMMON-POOL AND COLLECTIVE FORMS

Generally, collective goods or services can be provided only by the public sector. Common-pool goods or services are often also provided by the public sector. Because these include types of infrastructures that are available without a fee, the private sector has little incentive to provide them.

When collective goods and services are provided to an entire community, they are referred to as *public goods and services*. No one can claim an exclusive share; public goods and services are free to everyone. It is assumed that access to that good or service is a right of citizenship or residency.

Semipublic goods and services are those for which only part of the infrastructure cost comes from fees (a variant of private goods) or for which the full cost for a restricted facility comes from public funds (a variant of toll goods). Many municipal swimming pools, libraries, and landfills fall into this category. Generally, the public provides the costs of construction and maintenance, and fees cover the continued operating expenses of the facility.

In contrast to collective goods and services, common-pool goods and services can be made exclusive. Charging an access fee limits who can purchase the good or use the service. If the fee is relatively low, the common-pool good or service begins to resemble a collective good or service. If the fee is relatively high, however, access is effectively limited.

Other methods of exclusion involve limiting access to people of specific ages, ethnic groups, race, or gender. For example, there are two public institutions of higher education in the United States that continue to prohibit the entrance of women: the Virginia Military Institute (VMI) and

The Citadel in South Carolina. Although the VMI rule was challenged, the U.S. Supreme Court in 1991 enforced the right of VMI to deny women admission.

Well into the 1960s, blacks were denied access to community services such as schools, swimming pools, motels, rest rooms, and drinking fountains. This exclusion ended when blacks staged large-scale protests and initiated legal challenges, making clear that their rights of citizenship included access to economic infrastructure constructed at public expense. Further, citizenship rights also meant that certain goods previously defined as private, such as restaurants and bowling alleys, actually had a semipublic status.

COMMUNITY CHOICES

Deciding whether the public or private sector should be involved in organizing for a community's economic infrastructure ultimately relates back to the values of the community and its decisionmakers. Max Weber, a nineteenth-century German sociologist, argued that there were really two forms of logic involved in these types of decisions. The first, called *formal rationality*, is used when the provision of needs can be calculated in quantitative terms of profit and loss. *Substantive rationality* applies to situations in which goods or services are provided to people based on values rather than profit. Whether the enterprise is profitable is not important or is of secondary concern. Therefore, profit or loss will often not even be calculated. Values sought might involve a concern for maintaining status distinctions, being fair, or gaining and maintaining power.

Through their local governments, communities make decisions about what infrastructure to develop. These decisions are based on the perceived needs of the local people, often voiced by organized groups, as well as on the resources available. A community can decide to invest in a new landfill rather than a public swimming pool or in a new school rather than an industrial park. In many cases, investments in economic infrastructure generate insufficient profit or are too risky for the private sector to undertake. Thus, local communities must assume construction and maintenance costs if there is a belief that access to the service is a right of citizenship or residence in that community (substantive rationality). If that value is not held so strongly, then the community may choose to do without that particular service.

In the past, the federal government helped local areas with investments viewed as a right of citizenship—a clean water supply and sewage treatment, for example. These forms of a community's infrastructure were considered valid, regardless of whether a profit could be made. Substantive rationality based on concern for equity placed this form of infrastructure in the public sector. Federal involvement declined in the 1980s and 1990s, however. Access to a clean water supply and sewage treatment is now being approached through mandates. This strategy is less effective, but it is also less costly to the federal government. As discussed in Chapter 8, the costs are shifted to either the state or local level.

All of these decisions involve choices on the part of the community as well as for other levels of government. The examples that follow enable us to explore choices states and communities face in providing for the various types of infrastructure and the problems created by these choices.

Public Choices: Water Systems

When we think about water as a part of a community's infrastructure, we normally focus on the system established to deliver water to homes and businesses. Water, like air, is assumed to be available to all.

In parts of the rural West, however, this assumption is no longer valid. Urban growth increases the demand for water, threatening its availability for rural communities. The different legal systems governing access to water affect the extent to which water is viewed as inclusive or exclusive and its consumption as either joint or rival. Further, water services may be viewed as a source of profit; access is determined by formal rationality, or a right of every citizen, and thus a matter of substantive rationality. This section explores the larger political context that influences the availability of water as well as the local decisions communities face in providing and maintaining water systems.

ACCESS TO WATER

Communities must have a source of water. Los Angeles, for example, could not have grown to its present size had it not been able to divert water from the north down into the arid southern California lands (see Box 9.1). The land was initially so dry that land values were determined by the quantity and certainty of the water supply. "Sell the water and throw the land in free" became the slogan of real estate brokers subdividing the rolling hills of southern California. Recognizing the tremendous importance of water for all phases of residential and industrial development, public officials and private entrepreneurs struggled over whether it was to be in public or private hands. The classic movie *Chinatown* presents a somewhat fictionalized account of the intrigues involved in that fight.

There are legal doctrines that govern appropriate or fair use of surface water. The *riparian doctrine* governs water use in states in the East. Water rights are given to those whose lands are contiguous to streams. Landowners do not own the water, but can make reasonable use of the water

BOX 9.1 URBAN-RURAL CONNECTIONS?

Water! Who should have access to it? How much should it cost? Who should profit in delivering it to communities? How much should delivery cost? Which uses, residential or agricultural, are more important? These and other questions have connected Los Angeles with Owens Valley since the turn of the century.

Drought in the 1890s made Los Angeles aware of its vulnerability and the need to locate new sources of water. Two officials, Mayor Fred Eaton and water engineer Bill Mulholland, identified a potential source of water near Mammoth Lakes, California: the Owens River and Owens Lake. The river supported lush agriculture in the valleys on the eastern side of the Sierra Nevada. Farmers in those valleys controlled the river privately and were using the water to such an extent that the water level of Owens Lake was diminishing. The lake itself was becoming salty.

To gain access to the water, Los Angeles had to do two things. First, it had to buy the water rights from the local farmers, the right of way for an aqueduct, and land for a reservoir. Initial visits to Owens Valley by representatives of the city of Los Angeles were disguised as tourism. By disguising their true goals, city officials avoided skyrocketing land prices. Then officials had to change the uses approved for that water. That change involved a major public choice: Should water from Owens Lake be used to support residential use in Los Angeles or agricultural use in the Sierra Nevada?

The next step was figuring out how to get the water from Owens Lake down to Los Angeles. Eaton conferred with investors, who envisioned large profits in building the aqueduct and controlling the water rights. Mulholland sought public funds to develop the infrastructure as a public trust and pressured Eaton to give up a private role in the Owens Valley project, from which Eaton would have gained financially. Los Angeles was well on its way to gaining control of the Owens Valley aqueduct project.

Los Angeles quickly won the right to have the water system in public hands, in part because of the high construction costs. There was pressure from the privately held Pacific Light and Power Company to use the flow of the water to generate electricity. At this point, the city had to decide whether to become a public utility and provide energy. Officials decided to diversify into a related monopoly for electrical power generation and distribution.

Many utilities in communities across the nation are privately held. Others are local government monopolies. A number of communities, from the city of Los Angeles to the county seat of Harlan, Iowa, generate their own electricity and collect the revenues from it. The decision to function as a utility is based on assumptions of equity, efficiency, and the proper role of government in providing economic infrastructure.

Construction of the aqueduct led to the development of other economic infrastructure by Los Angeles. For example, a great deal of cement was required for construction of the aqueduct. Rather than buy it from private contractors, Los Angeles constructed its own cement plant at Monolith. The city invested public funds in an element of economic infrastructure that is private in most parts of the United States.

Once Owens Valley residents realized what Los Angeles planned to do with the water, the battle over who would control the water began—a battle that is still in the courts today. Owens Valley newspapers defended local water rights, while the Los Angeles newspapers declared that the well-being of Owens Valley communities must be sacrificed for the greater good and the greater profit of Los Angeles. To this day, decisions by the Los Angeles Department of Water and Power, the board members of which are nonpartisan but highly political, have a huge impact on communities all along the eastern side of the Sierra Nevada.

continues

Box 9.1 continued

The fight to stop construction of the aqueduct illustrates the role different levels of government play in providing economic infrastructure. The aqueduct, ultimately paid for by the taxpayers of Los Angeles, had to pass over public land. The people of Owens Valley tried to block the city's access to public land as one means of stopping the project. Not only was the aqueduct allowed to cross public lands, but the U.S. Forest Service, through presidential proclamation, claimed the entire Owens Valley as part of the Sierra Forest Reserve, thus eliminating private claims on the land.

Despite the city's investment and the diverse support for the project, Owens Valley residents continued to fight against it. In 1913, the first water from Owens Valley arrived in Los Angeles. The aqueduct went into operation in the late 1920s and was not fully completed until 1941. During this period, resistance to the aqueduct included physical attacks on it. Explosions would rock the valley as people attempted to blow holes in the aqueduct, angry as they watched lush vegetation and agricultural production wither for lack of water. The growth of Los Angeles was accompanied by the decline of the towns, ranches, and farms along the river valley. The communities and ranchers of Owens Valley had little chance to prevail when pitted against the financial and political power of the city of Los Angeles.

---

flowing over their lands as long as such use does not severely diminish the flow of streams or levels in lakes. The *appropriation doctrine* is used throughout the more arid states of the West. These policies allow users to divert water from its original channel, as long as the water is used for beneficial purposes and the amount of water withdrawn does not exceed what the user is entitled to under the permit. As originally implemented, the appropriation doctrine honored the rights of those who first used the water. Definitions of "beneficial use" have undergone changes; more recently, societal needs as well as individual uses of water are being recognized (Lapping et al. 1989).

Laws governing groundwater are even more complex. Early in this century, laws emphasized where the water was used. Landowners could use groundwater on their own lands even if it depleted the groundwater available to adjacent landowners, but these same landowners could not deplete groundwater resources by removing water from their land and using it elsewhere. More recently, some states have modified this doctrine to protect neighboring landowners and waterways supplied by the groundwater. Landowners are allowed to withdraw groundwater, but may not exceed their fair share of water resources or harm neighboring uses of groundwater.

Providing water to one community can mean lack of water for another. Thus, conflicts and public debates have emerged over who gets water from where and who pays for it. Although these issues are important throughout the country, they are gaining increasing attention in the Southwest and western plains. The people of Caliente, Nevada, for example, are becoming increasingly concerned about Las Vegas's efforts to buy up water rights. Under the appropriation doctrine, Las Vegas can purchase the rights to water and divert its use to support its rapidly growing population, even if this usage diminishes the water available to the people of Caliente. Denver is seeking access to the aquifer in the San Luis Valley in south-central Colorado, much to the dismay of rural communities and landowners.

Large-scale agricultural users have also been drawn into conflict with traditional dryland farmers. Water being withdrawn from the Ogallala aquifer to irrigate fields and support feedlots and packing plants in Garden City, Kansas, is lowering the water table. Dryland farmers and rural communities in the area are finding it necessary to dig deeper wells simply to continue to use water for livestock, residential, and commercial use. Because the Ogallala aquifer is essentially unreplenishable, residents fear that the future of any economic activity is being compromised.

WATER SERVICES

If water is available, communities can offer access in a number of ways. People can haul their own water or dig wells, assuming individual responsibility for getting water. Communities can organize a shared water system that can then be publicly or privately owned.

Water as a part of a community's infrastructure can theoretically be subject to both exclusive access and rival consumption. Water, especially clean water, is typically distributed throughout the community through pipes. Consequently, potential users can be excluded. Moreover, water resources are finite. Use by one member diminishes the use by another. Until recently, the characteristic of rival consumption of water seemed less noticeable on the local level. The "watering patrols" now used to control the use of public water on lawns or the rationing procedures used during periods of drought illustrate the extent to which water is now seen to involve rival consumption.

Because of these characteristics—exclusion and rivalry—the distribution of water at the local level is potentially suitable for private control. Rural areas are more likely to have private water supplies—wells sunk for individual homes. In urban areas, water is typically managed by the public sector. In general, the belief that all citizens have a right to clean water at a reasonable price has led to public control or regulation. In other words, substantive rationality has dominated over formal rationality.

WATER QUALITY

For people such as Sara Johnson, the problem is the quality of water, not its availability. The water that reaches residents of Floyd County is unusable. For years, rivers have been dumping grounds for industry. Sewer systems owned by cities often discharge into rivers or bays that are later used as sources of drinking water. Toxic chemicals from dumps, industry, and agriculture are seeping through soil to taint groundwater. Runoff of the chemicals used in fertilizers and pesticides is contaminating the water of lakes, streams, and reservoirs.

For the most part, rural communities are not prepared to deal with increased concerns about water quality. Among communities with public water systems, one in five unincorporated communities and one in ten cities of less than 2,500 population had not had their water tested for coliform bacteria in over a year (Reid and Sullivan 1984). A study conducted in the Adirondack region of upstate New York found that two-thirds of the municipal systems sampled had unacceptable concentrations of coliform bacteria (Rossi 1987). Coliform bacteria is a source of gastrointestinal diseases and is one of the most common problems found in rural water supplies. In 1980, almost a quarter of rural communities with wastewater treatment plants had wastewater flow that exceeded the designed capacity. Only 62 percent of incorporated places of fewer than 2,500 residents had water treatment plants at all (Reid and Sullivan 1984). If each household has its own well, testing and water quality are even more difficult to maintain.

Part of the solution is to treat wastewater and maintain water quality. Citizens in the small communities throughout Floyd County are insisting that the small, privately owned water companies make the investments needed to maintain water quality. These citizens rely on local and state governments to ensure that these investments in infrastructure are made.

Another part of the solution is to stop contamination of local water supplies. In some communities, citizen groups work together to see that clean-water laws are enforced. These groups trace contamination back to its source and then take public action to block the release of the contaminants. Citizen groups serve as watchdogs to ensure that private individuals and companies do not dispose of their waste at public expense. Private companies are encouraged to increase their investment in economic infrastructure for reasons of substantive rationality.

Clearly, public investment is also needed. The fiscal capacity of many rural communities, especially those lacking adequate wastewater treatment facilities and public water systems, is inadequate. State and federal governments have offered little help. The federal government cut its water and sewer grant/loan program in half between 1980 and 1983. In addition, federal revenue sharing was phased out in the early years of the Reagan administration. Changes in the tax structure at all levels and a reassessment of national priorities may be necessary in order to begin to solve these important infrastructural problems.

Private Choices: Solid Waste

Economic infrastructure includes the collection and disposal of solid wastes generated by households and industries. Urban areas are finding that they no longer have room for the volume of waste they produce and have arranged to transport it to rural areas for disposal. In many rural communities, waste disposal has become a source of revenue. Like water, waste disposal can be placed under either public or private control. As increased demand for disposal sites has been countered with environmental concerns, waste disposal has become an intriguing issue.

WASTE AS AN ECONOMIC VENTURE

Waste disposal involves exclusionary access and rival consumption. It is exclusionary in that most dumps and landfills restrict access, regardless of whether they are publicly or privately owned. Users must pay a fee in order to dump solid waste. Waste disposal involves rival consumption in the sense that land used to store solid wastes is land unavailable for other purposes. Urban areas are well aware of these rival uses—indeed, some have run out of land on which to dispose of their wastes. In rural areas, people sometimes simply leave waste where it is or toss it into the river. Even such casual disposal is ultimately a rival use of land or rivers because these areas fill up and no one else can use them.

By the late 1980s, the United States produced more than 1,200 pounds of municipal and solid waste per person each year, a statistic that does not include the hazardous and toxic wastes also produced in large quantities and even more difficult to dispose of. Because waste disposal is both exclusionary and rival as well as potentially very profitable, private interests have been drawn into providing this type of economic infrastructure. Rural communities themselves are looking toward waste disposal as an economic venture.

The Kim-Stan Landfill Company in Virginia was started by Jerry Wharton, an independent strip miner. His previous company specialized in quick profit: clearing ground, mining coal, and leaving the land exposed. Once the coal ran out, Wharton decided that waste disposal was one way to use the holes he had made in the earth. With little investment on the part of Wharton and his Chicago-based partners, the Kim-Stan Landfill Company was launched. The landfill did a booming out-of-state garbage business as cities and industries desperate for a place to dump their garbage took advantage of the Virginia mountains. This proved extremely profitable, and a great deal of waste was moved into the landfill site.

No one paid very much attention to what happened to the waste products once they reached the site. When an unusually high concentration of dangerous contaminants was noticed in the nearby Jackson River, however, an investigation was launched. In May 1990, the Commonwealth of Virginia closed the landfill. After first paying $250,000 to Wharton, the Kim-Stan Landfill Company declared bankruptcy. The public—the Commonwealth of Virginia—was left with the cleanup costs and remaining company debts.

Private landfills and waste disposal operations are now common. Certainly the notion of accepting solid waste from other areas is not especially new. In most rural areas, landfills have been developed regionally, or larger communities have simply charged neighboring towns for use of their facilities. What is new is the profit that can be made from accepting out-of-state garbage. Strip mines in northern Kentucky have been adapted for use as private landfills. A private firm has proposed a 6,000-acre landfill three miles from Welch, West Virginia. In return for permits to open the landfill, the developer has promised to build the city a sewer system that would clean up the Tug Fork River (Kilborn 1991).

Virginia's experience with the Kim-Stan Landfill, however, illustrates the issues involved. Solid waste disposal has implications for the environment shared with others as well as for the profits generated within a private enterprise. Even when the public would profit, as would Welch, West Virginia, decisions made today could compromise the use of land for other purposes in the future.

GOVERNMENT RESPONSES

Because of inadequate government oversight, disposal of solid waste, particularly toxic waste, has been more profitable to private waste management firms than valuable to society as a whole. The social costs often become apparent only years after the waste has been improperly disposed of. Consequently, waste management firms have found it easy to pass part of the true cost of waste disposal on to the government. Ultimately, taxpayers pay for the cleanup. Consequently, the public must assume a more active role in solid waste disposal. Governmental involvement may be of two types: regulation of private companies or direct public control of solid waste disposal.

If the first option is chosen, governments must find a way to retrieve the costs of cleanup or insist that those costs be integrated into the operation of the private landfills. As is illustrated by the actions taken by Kim-Stan Landfill Company, retrieving the costs of cleanup can be difficult. Alternately, governments can develop regulations designed to protect the environment. Firms would be required to take certain precautions designed to protect the groundwater, air, and appearance of the landscape. The cost of those precautions would then be integrated into the cost of the business and passed along to the customer through higher disposal fees. These costs would then be closer to the true cost to society and certainly cheaper for society as a whole than toxic waste cleanup would be after the fact.

If the second option is chosen, both government and the general public must acknowledge the need to deal with the social costs as well as the physical costs of disposal. This means greater use of recycling, careful selection of landfills, segregation of toxic from nontoxic wastes, and the selection of appropriate means for disposing of toxic wastes. If the local governments do not have the technical capacity to deal with these issues, state or federal governments may need to assume responsibility for developing appropriate procedures and regulations.

COMMUNITY RESPONSES

Solid waste is now recognized as a collective problem that communities can solve through organization. Solutions are not always arrived at easily, however. As occurs on most issues, opposing forces organize to protect their respective interests. NIMBY (not in my backyard) groups organized early as wealthy suburban communities sought to protect themselves from private landfills. Other community groups form coalitions to support recycling or to promote or oppose the choice of location for new landfills. In Greenup, Kentucky, an organization called GROWL (Greenup Residents Opposing Waste Landfill) organized to block the approval of a private landfill, based on fears that groundwater would be contaminated. Groups may protest the acceptance of waste from out of state or the proposed construction of toxic waste incinerators. They may also propose delaying a decision until the community can educate itself on both the benefits and risks; the people of Harlan, Iowa, sought a delay when faced with the possibility of a medical waste incinerator being built.

Recycling is a common response to the growing volume of trash. Participation in recycling programs is voluntary in some locales, mandatory in others. Community-organized programs have been successful in reducing the volume of solid waste needing disposal. Although some recycling enterprises can be profitable or at least break even, most incur costs for the community. Communities offer recycling programs to decrease the amount of solid waste to be processed rather than as a means to generate municipal revenue.

Because recycling programs cost money, the decision to recycle involves substantive rationality. Communities recycle because they are concerned about the environment, not because recycling generates a profit. As the costs of waste disposal increase and as regulations require that the true costs of solid waste disposal be passed on to the consumer, recycling may become more formally rational. Individuals may find it personally profitable to recycle much of their solid waste rather than pay the true costs of having it collected. Communities themselves may find it more profitable to recycle than open new landfills. As that occurs, private firms may find it possible to earn a profit, and recycling programs may shift to the private sector. Ultimately, recycling works only when the demand for recycled materials offsets the costs of recycling.

Federal Role: Making Linkages

By definition, rural residents are more isolated from markets and information than are urban residents. Two forms of economic infrastructure, transportation and communication technology, reduce that isolation. These infrastructures span larger distances and involve public-private partnerships to ensure rural access, however. Rural communities must provide the local infrastructure, but then hope that they are linked with other networks and that private companies provide the needed services. In the past, the federal government has played an important role in maintaining these forms of economic infrastructure.

TRANSPORTATION

Transportation continues to be crucial to rural areas. At the local level, rural transportation systems suffer from four major problems: inadequate new construction; deferred or otherwise inadequate maintenance of existing structures; inadequate fiscal infrastructure to serve economic needs; and financing problems.

Inadequate maintenance of roads and bridges is particularly acute. Seventy percent of the bridges in the north-central U.S. states, not atypical of other parts of the country, were constructed before 1935 and designed for a fifty-year life (Chicoine 1986). As a result, many are crumbling. No resources are available to reinforce or replace them. As this infrastructure deteriorates, people such as Carl Jones in Hebron are unable to transport goods to market.

The viability of a transportation network is a function not only of well-sited and safe bridges and roads but also of what means of transport are available. The federal government's decision to deregulate transportation has significantly decreased access in rural areas. Railroads abandoned a number of lines, isolating rural communities that produced low-value but high-volume products, such as wheat or timber. Communities such as Garden City, Kansas, invested in their own railroad spur in order to maintain regional linkages to their local infrastructure. Other towns were less able to step in where the private sector had withdrawn. The loss of those linkages meant the loss of a part of the community's economic base.

Public transportation, always deficient in rural areas, has become virtually nonexistent in many communities. Railroads abandoned most passenger service entirely. The interstate bus network has substantially reduced service, eliminating service to communities that do not lie along interstate highways and cutting service even to those that do.

Bus service illustrates the character of the public-private partnership involved in transportation. The public provides the roads, but private companies provide the means of transport. Decisions made to regulate bus service were based on substantive rationality. The goal was equity— to ensure that rural residents had access to public transportation. Regulations linked profit with service. In exchange for the right to serve profitable routes, bus lines were required to serve unprofitable ones. The expectation was that the profit generated along the better routes would exceed the loss generated along the more rural routes.

The Bus Regulatory Reform Act of 1982 reflected a shift from substantive to formal rationality. Communities no longer had the right to bus service. Routes are now selected strictly in terms of their profitability. During the first two years following passage of the act, the number of communities served by intercity buses declined by 20 percent. This equaled the decline that occurred during the seven years before the legislation. The routes abandoned were those to rural communities with few elderly residents and neither air nor rail service (Oster 1988).

Rural communities have also been affected by deregulation in the airline industry. Regulation of bus service was designed to ensure access. Regulation of the airline industry was designed to ensure equity in fares. When the airlines were deregulated in 1978, commuter airfares increased sharply. It now costs as much or more to fly the 225 miles from Roanoke, Virginia, to Washington, D.C., as it does to fly five times that distance from Kansas City, Missouri, to Washington, D.C. Although these charges reflect a difference in cost resulting from the lower passenger travel between Roanoke and Washington, they also reflect the little competition that exists along such routes. Deregulation initially reduced airfares, but the number of carriers has gradually decreased through economic failure. Fares and service have been left in the hands of fewer companies. Service to some rural communities has been abandoned altogether. Other service continues with the help of funds designated for essential air service (ESA), a federal program meant to bridge the transition from regulation to deregulation.

TELECOMMUNICATIONS

As the world economy becomes more integrated, information becomes more central to business operations. Information-age technologies can improve both the economic efficiency and the competitiveness of today's rural commercial enterprises. Rapid information flow is facilitated through modern electronics and telecommunications. These require not only investment by the individual (computers, modems, and facsimile machines) but also investment by the public (switching systems, underground cables, and satellite links).

Government involvement is crucial to the development of telecommunications infrastructure in rural areas. Rural communities often are not attractive to private companies, which prefer to lay cables in more densely populated areas. Local funds are often limited. Because information infrastructure links communities to one another and, therefore, crosses local government boundaries, both state and federal levels of government need to be involved. Such participation may involve direct public ownership, independent quasi-public or private collectively owned entities (such as the rural electric cooperatives organized to bring electricity to the nation's farmers), or subsidies to private firms. Regardless of the form of ownership chosen, the decision to subsidize telecommunications infrastructure in rural areas is a public choice.

A recent report by the Office of Technology Assessment (OTA) of the U.S. Congress (1991) suggests that relatively inexpensive telecommunications technologies appropriate to rural areas are available or in the process of being developed. The barriers to using these technologies are social rather than technical. The value of new communications technology for economic development is not as clear as when the telegraph and perhaps the telephone were introduced. More important, the context within which rural telecommunications policy is being developed is not very favorable. Returning to the old system of communications regulation is not desirable—and certainly not possible. The OTA study acknowledges that there is no consensus that communications technologies are a form of infrastructure, and that therefore government intervention in their provision would be appropriate: "Ironically, at the moment when communication and information technologies are beginning to play a critical role in business, the regulatory structure that once provided rural areas equal access to these technologies is coming unraveled" (U.S. Congress 1991, 5). However, if rural areas are to remain competitive with urban areas, government must play a role.

The Rural Economic Development Act of 1990 authorized but did not adequately fund a partnership among the U.S. Department of Agriculture, the Cooperative Extension Service, and the Rural Electrification Administration. The legislative base is in place, but whether there is a will to fund rural telecommunications infrastructure remains uncertain. Substantive rationality must replace formal rationality if rural areas are to be allowed to compete in the world economy.

Motivation to Act

To what degree and under what conditions do communities and governments provide the needed infrastructure? When will the communities in Floyd County insist on adequate water and sewer facilities? Can Hebron convince the county to repair its bridge? What will motivate the Wolf Point telephone company to convert to the digital switches now needed to support new technologies?

There are no simple answers to these questions, but research into local support of crime control raises some interesting questions. Sociologists have proposed two explanations for why communities differ in their willingness to support crime control. One explanation, called "public choice," assumes that the demand for police services by the community as a whole determines the extent to which funds are allocated in support of crime control. The second explanation, called the "conflict perspective," acknowledges that perceived need plays a role in the choices communities make. This perspective contends, however, that the felt needs of elites have much more weight than those of poor people (Jackson 1985; Jackson and Carroll 1981).

If we assume that a community has the capacity to raise funds in support of different forms of economic infrastructure, whose needs prevail? Are community choices a reflection of the community as a whole or do they respond to the elite?

Chapter Summary

Economic infrastructure includes the permanent physical installations and facilities supporting productive activities in a community. Examples include roads, bridges, telephone service, or water and sewage treatment and distribution facilities.

Access to various types of infrastructure can be exclusive (limited to some) or inclusive (available to all). Consumption of goods or services provided through the infrastructure can be either joint (simultaneous use) or rival (use by one diminishes the use by another). If we cross the two forms of access with the two forms of consumption, we can identify four types of economic infrastructure: private, toll, common-pool, and collective.

The form of economic infrastructure is a factor in whether it is provided and supported through private or public organizations. Private and toll goods or services can be supplied by either the public or private sector. Collective and common-pool forms of infrastructure are typically provided by the public sector. Selection of the provider, public or private, is ultimately a choice made by the community.

Two forms of logic govern such decisions. Formal rationality relies on a quantitative assessment of the choice—the choice must result in profit. Substantive rationality relies upon values other than profit. Federal or state support of local infrastructure is often based on substantive rationality.

Three categories of economic infrastructure—water distribution, solid waste disposal, and transportation/telecommunications—illustrate some of the concerns now faced by rural communities. Two issues, water availability and water quality, affect decisions related to the provision of water services. State and federal governments have become involved in issues related to water rights. Communities focus on the distribution and quality of water. For the most part, water is placed under public control.

Because solid waste disposal involves exclusionary access and rival consumption, private control is a possibility. Local, state, and federal governments have found it necessary to intervene, however, in order to protect the environment. Current interest is focused on strategies that ensure consideration of the social as well as physical costs when disposal occurs.

Finally, transportation and communication technologies all depend on some state and federal involvement. In an unregulated environment, access to services at a reasonable price ceases to exist for many rural communities.

Key Terms

Appropriation doctrine allows water rights to be established by the user even if the user does not own land adjacent to the streams. The user is limited to a specified amount of water that can be withdrawn.

Collective goods and services are forms of infrastructure that involve inclusive access and joint consumption. Roads and public sidewalks are the most common examples.

Common-pool goods and services are forms of infrastructure that involve inclusive access and rival consumption. An example is a public building with a defined capacity.

Economic infrastructure in a community includes the permanent physical facilities and services needed to support business and community life. Examples include roads, bridges, telephone service, and schools.

Exclusive access is a characteristic of economic infrastructure such that individuals can be denied access to the good or service. Utility companies are typically exclusive.

Formal rationality applies to decisions made on the basis of economic calculation of profit or loss.

Inclusive access is a characteristic of economic infrastructure such that there is unrestricted access to all who would use it. Roads are an example of inclusive infrastructure.

Infrastructure is the foundation or supporting framework needed for a structure or organization.

Joint consumption describes economic infrastructure such that the use of a good or service by one person does not diminish its availability to another.

Monopolies are single enterprises that have control over the sale and distribution of a particular class of goods or services in a particular geographic area.

Private goods and services are forms of infrastructure that involve exclusive access and rival consumption. In most communities, waste disposal in local landfills has become private.

Public goods and services involve forms of economic infrastructure that are provided to the entire community at no cost.

Riparian doctrine limits water rights to landowners whose lands are contiguous to streams. They can make reasonable use of the water, but cannot severely diminish its flow.

Rival consumption describes economic infrastructure such that the use of a good or service by one person diminishes or even eliminates its availability to another.

Semipublic goods and services include forms of economic infrastructure that are supported, in part, by fees collected from the user.

Substantive rationality applies to decisions made on the basis of values rather than economic calculation.

Toll goods and services are forms of infrastructure that involve exclusive access and joint consumption. Toll roads are the most common example.

References

Chicoine, David L. 1986. "Infrastructure and Agriculture: Interdependencies with a Focus on Local Roads in the North Central States." Pp. 141–163 in Peter F. Korsching and Judith Gildner (eds.), *Interdependencies of Agriculture and Rural Communities in the Twenty-first Century: The North Central Region. Conference Proceedings*. Ames, IA: North Central Regional Center for Rural Development.

Jackson, Pamela I. 1985. "Ethnicity, Region, and Public Fiscal Commitment to Policing." *Justice Quarterly* 2:167–195.

Jackson, Pamela I., and Leo Carroll. 1981. "Race and the War on Crime: The Sociopolitical Determinants of Municipal Expenditures in 90 Non-Southern Cities." *American Sociological Review* 46:290–305.

Kilborn, Peter T. 1991. "In Despair, W. Va. County Looks to Trash." *New York Times* October 16: A1–A2.

Lapping, Mark B., Thomas D. Daniels, and John W. Keller. 1989. *Rural Planning and Development in the United States.* New York: Guilford.

Lynch, Rodney C. 1991. "Nontraditional Revenues: Keeping the Property Tax Under Control in a Small Town." *Government Finance Review,* June: 38–39.

Oster, Clinton V., Jr. 1988. "Is Deregulation Cutting Small Communities' Transportation Links?" *Rural Development Perspectives* 4 (3): 13–16.

Reid, J. Norman, and Patrick J. Sullivan. 1984. "Rural Infrastructure: How Much? How Good?" *Rural Development Perspectives* 1 (1): 9–14.

Rossi, Clifford. 1987. "Improving Rural New York's Water Systems." *Rural Development Perspectives* 3 (2): 21–24.

U.S. Congress, Office of Technology Assessment. 1991. *Rural America at the Crossroads: Networking for the Future: Summary.* Washington, DC: U.S. Government Printing Office.

Walzer, Norman, David L. Chicoine, and Ruth T. McWilliams. 1987. "Rebuilding Rural Roads and Bridges." *Rural Development Perspectives* 3 (2): 15–20.

Weber, Max. 1968. *Economy and Society: An Outline of Interpretive Sociology.* Ed. Guenther Roth and Claus Wittich. Vol. 1. Berkeley: University of California Press.

10

Social Infrastructure

t he most important celebration in Decatur County, Kansas, is the 4-H fair held every year during the first week of August. In 1972, the contracted carnival notified fair officials that it would not come that year. Revenues had not been good enough. Many who attended the fair had not really liked the company, so the county was not necessarily sorry to see it go. But officials faced a dilemma. Where would they find replacements for the rides and games? Their fair was too small to attract any other company.

The problem is a familiar one in rural areas. Too small for the economies of scale needed by the carnival companies, Decatur County found itself with a fair but no rides or games. Unlike the people in many small communities, however, those in Decatur refused to do without.

In checking with other counties, the 4-H board learned of a community that had simply started its own carnival. The board talked with a local banker, who talked with others concerned about the fair. Within a short time, two carloads of people drove more than 400 miles from Decatur County to Hydro, Oklahoma, to see how a locally owned carnival functioned. When they returned, they formed the Decatur County Amusement Authority.

This marked the first formal step in the development of a homegrown carnival in Decatur County. To raise funds, those who had visited Hydro gave talks to civic clubs and churches, illustrating the presentations with slides from their trip. The carnival started the next year with a ferris wheel (purchased from a failed carnival with donated funds), a pony ride, and locally constructed kiddie rides and game

"Homegrown" carnival (photo by Jan L. Flora).

stands. That first year was so successful that the game stands ran out of prizes—organizers had to make a quick trip to Denver to buy enough prizes to last until the end of the fair.

The carnival has operated every year since for five days in August. A grandstand, a miniature train, and numerous other rides have been constructed over the years with local contributions of labor, supplies, and, occasionally, money. Booths are staffed by local organizations and individuals. All profits go to the Amusement Authority, which uses those funds for community projects, such as subsidizing the maintenance costs of the community-owned movie theater.

For every Decatur County, there are other rural communities unable to act collectively when faced with a problem. Other things being equal, the character of the people and their interactions with one another affect the capacity of the community to move forward. This chapter examines social infrastructure, the elements that contribute to it, and its role in helping communities develop. We start by taking a closer look at Decatur County.

Profile of an Entrepreneurial Community

Decatur County and its county seat, Oberlin, have a history of being entrepreneurial. These innovative efforts began with the formation of the Oberlin Industrial Development Company in 1962. With money raised through the sale of stock, fifteen acres of land were purchased for an industrial park. In turn, the land was sold to industries seeking local sites.

In 1969, the newly organized county planning commission became involved in regional hospital planning. The planning process included conducting a survey of hospital facilities to determine eligibility for funding that could improve the hospital and add a long-term nursing-care unit. Now this county of fewer than 5,000 inhabitants has a hospital with five doctors and two long-term care facilities. During the difficult economic times of the mid-1980s when hospitals in many other towns of comparable size were failing, Decatur County passed a bond to expand the hospital.

The Decatur County Area Chamber of Commerce (DCCC), formed in 1970, replaced the individual chambers of the three towns in the county. The first projects of the newly formed DCCC included establishing a countywide community-betterment committee; installing aluminum canopies over the sidewalks on the main street of Oberlin; commissioning and erecting a pioneer statue at the entrance of Oberlin; and organizing a community feedlot and a dairy, financed by selling shares of stock to local persons. The dairy later failed, but the feedlot still exists in the hands of an original investor and his son-in-law. Another project of the DCCC, not part of the initially planned activities, was the homegrown carnival. All of these projects came to fruition in the early 1970s.

In the mid-1980s, in response to the farm crisis, community investors put up seed money (a total of nearly a half million dollars) to establish factories to assemble bus coaches and boats. Although the two community firms failed in the difficult climate of the 1980s, their organization illustrates the diversity of leadership in the community.

The leadership of the bus coach firm included many people who had been involved in the feedlot and dairy; a younger group of leaders emerged to organize the boat-building company. The person who bridged the old and the new groups was Kent Reinhardt, who resigned his position as county extension agent to manage the faltering dairy. When the dairy failed, he became a partner in a local grain elevator and a feed, seed, and fertilizer store. Reinhardt stands as an example of an outsider who married into a local family and eventually attained a position of leadership in the community. His predecessor as county agent, Phil Finley, also played an important role in community leadership. Among other things, he was responsible for organizing the meeting that established the DCCC. His name is still mentioned with great respect.

The Human Dimension

Clearly, the success Decatur County has had in generating new sources of income and employment as well as in improving the quality of life depends on its people. The character of the individual and collective efforts to bring about improvements is as important as the economic resources available to a community. These individual and collective efforts form the social infrastructure of a community.

DEFINING SOCIAL INFRASTRUCTURE

Social infrastructure is both the social capacity and the collective will of local communities to provide for their social and economic well-being. Although both social capacity and collective will are subjective constructs, the latter is the more elusive and less visible of the two.

Economic infrastructure is easily identified. It often takes such physical forms as roads, bridges, factories, and even bank accounts. The contributions of these items to the local economy are obvious, and their value is easily calculated. The importance of these forms of economic infrastructure is self-evident.

The various forms of social infrastructure, however, are less visible, and thus some people think of them as less important to the community. More commonly, their importance to the social and economic well-being of a community simply is ignored. Research by rural sociologists has consistently shown, however, that a community's economic infrastructure alone cannot fully explain its well-being. Factors such as the quality of health and educational institutions, the presence of civic organizations and their viability, the prevailing culture and ethnicity, citizens' sense of community, the importance of entrepreneurship, and the extent of social stratification all greatly influence the effective use of resources or the persistent inability to improve social well-being.

KEY ROLE OF STRONG SOCIAL INFRASTRUCTURE

At the national level, evidence that social infrastructure is important is impressive. The remarkable economic and social recoveries of both Japan and West Germany from the social disorganization and destruction of their economic infrastructures incurred during World War II are a lasting testament to the high quality of their social infrastructure. Both of these countries were able to rebuild and reform their economies and societies within a generation. They are now said to have surpassed the United States as dominant global economic powers. These recoveries were not simply the result of building new factories and transportation facilities. Each country built upon a combination of local social capacity for economic development and upon a national collective will to achieve recovery.

Another example of the important role played by a community's social infrastructure can be found much closer to home. The plight of successive generations of inner-city ghetto dwellers reinforces the evidence that areas once characterized by high levels of poverty are very likely to remain poor if there is no concerted effort to develop social infrastructure. This perplexing and disappointing reality persists despite the investment of billions of dollars in welfare programs, housing, street maintenance, and urban development. Little of this money was invested directly in improving the social infrastructure of these areas.

The same is generally true for persistent rural poverty. Unfortunately, because rural poverty tends to be much less visible, it is less frequently addressed than urban poverty. An unsettling conclusion of contemporary social science research is that during the twentieth century, poverty levels in rural areas have been and continue to remain higher than those in the inner cities. Nevertheless, the political will to improve the social infrastructure of persistently poor rural communities is even weaker than it is in urban areas.

PEOPLE AS AGENTS FOR CHANGE

Social infrastructure is the human dimension of economic and social change. A viable social infrastructure, regardless of its ambiguous character, is a necessary but not a sufficient condition for community economic and social development. By the same token, however, a viable economic infrastructure is also a necessary but not sufficient condition for local development. The two frameworks, social infrastructure and economic infrastructure, collectively enable a community to address its problems and develop itself economically.

Too often, impersonal economic and social forces are seen as overwhelming human efforts. These forces are formidable, but they are not divorced from human activity. People, not bridges or buildings, make decisions. It is the actions of people—each of us and our neighbors—that transmit culture and legacy. It is people who must determine a community's development options, make decisions, and take action. Further, this action is often most effective through groups. Ultimately, it is the quality of social infrastructure that provides a measure of the degree to which people can act on their own behalf or, alternatively, give way to the interest of others.

Many believe that a community's social infrastructure cannot be easily altered or manipulated. Because social infrastructure can be improved through voluntary collective efforts that require little capital outlay, rural people probably have more opportunities to improve their social infrastructure than their economic infrastructure. However, such efforts often take a long time. This was the case in Decatur County, where efforts begun in the early 1960s did not reach maturity until a decade or two later.

Three Elements of Social Infrastructure

A community's social infrastructure consists of three elements: (1) local social institutions, (2) human resources, and (3) quality of social networks. Each of these shapes the capacity of a rural community to address its social and economic problems.

SOCIAL INSTITUTIONS

The most visible dimension of social infrastructure is those *social organizations* that provide services essential to the maintenance of physical, social, and cultural needs of a community. These include police and fire protection, churches and other cultural institutions, volunteer organizations, healthcare and educational institutions, public recreational facilities, public libraries, community kitchens and homeless shelters, centers for abused spouses, and other services.

Decatur County's excellent health facilities and good schools are examples of social institutions that not only contribute to the quality of life of local residents but also make it easier to attract industrial and service firms to the community. High-quality institutions do not just happen; they are the products of collective decisions to commit local resources to their development, maintenance, and improvement. Although those institutions are often formalized into bureaucracies with paid staff, their initiation and development frequently depend on concerned citizens voluntarily coming together to solve a mutual problem.

Obviously, many social institutions and the services they provide to the community are not the responsibility of the local government. They may be sponsored by the private sector or by state and federal agencies. Financial support comes from a wide variety of sources. Some are funded through taxes, others by voluntary donations of money and time, and still others by user fees. Most involve combinations of funding sources. However, two local sources of funding are particularly important indicators of success in the development of strong community social institutions: There must be a willingness to invest private capital locally and a willingness to support services through taxes.

Communities with relative equality but that also generate a budget surplus are more likely to pool resources and invest in potentially risky local enterprises than are communities with great inequalities or that are extremely poor. Over the years, Decatur County has been successful in raising substantial funds for the feedlot, the dairy, the boat factory, and the bus coach factory. In none of these cases was there a single major investor. Many community residents put up relatively equal amounts. None invested so much as to be faced with destitution if the venture failed.

The willingness to support local services through taxes is a particularly important aspect of social infrastructure. A low-tax ideology generally exists in rural communities. This is not surprising because rural people, particularly those in agriculture, are land-rich but cash-poor. Most of their financial resources are tied to the ownership of land and are not readily available or convertible.

Rural communities often avoid or delay raising taxes needed for maintenance or replacement of economic infrastructure or improvement of social infrastructure. They rely instead on the federal government to provide funds. This is frequently a gamble, but such behavior is particularly inappropriate now that federal funding for local social and economic infrastructures has declined so dramatically. In contrast, communities that are willing to raise local capital by taxing themselves have the independence and the means to recognize local needs and to act collectively to address them.

Most rural communities will have any number of social institutions; the existence of each type points to a need that the community has identified and organized itself to meet. The presence of social services reflects past decisions on resource priorities. Although programs increasingly are mandated at a state or national level, there are still opportunities for local areas to define and meet their particular needs. As funding from state and national governments declines, the obligation of local communities to prioritize their needs and mobilize the resources to meet them becomes more important.

Although the absence of some services may indicate the absence of a particular need, it is more likely that the need is being met elsewhere or not at all. Communities that are unable to provide the services their citizens require or that provide inadequate services face serious difficulties in achieving their development goals. Investments in schools, adult education programs, cultural activities, and recreational programs not only create individual capacity but also create opportunities for community members to learn how to work together. Investments in social institutions in turn foster the development of human resources and ensure the health and education of community members.

HUMAN RESOURCE BASE

No development factor is more important than a community's *human resource base*, the ability of community members to accomplish their individual goals and vocational tasks. A community may have a rich natural resource base but not have the people skilled and willing to nurture and harvest those resources. Average human intelligence does not vary greatly in any given population. What is actually more valuable in forming the foundation of a community's human resource base is what people know and their ability to learn (see Box 10.1).

The ability of people to participate in the labor force or in any other social endeavor is influenced by a number of factors, including their ability to learn and to cooperate with others, their technical skills and knowledge, their culture and socialization, and their socioeconomic position relative to others. So, too, the capacity of rural communities for socioeconomic development is influenced by the individual and collective capacities of members to organize and focus their talents and resources on their communities' welfare.

Social scientists measure human capacity in a variety of ways. Among these are educational attainment, vocational skills, state of health, and entrepreneurship (both individual and collective). Often communities with higher levels of each of these indicators have a higher quality of social services. More generally, communities do not fully use their human resource base.

The various expressions of entrepreneurship constitute one aspect of the human resource base. Like other components of social infrastructure, this is not a very visible attribute. Entrepreneurship can be identified in the way individuals or groups start new businesses or social services, but it is not an attribute that can be discovered through aptitude tests. Rather, it is a function of individual or group creativity and imagination. There are at least two general types of entrepreneurship: individual and collective.

Individual entrepreneurship is the type most widely recognized and acclaimed. Successful businesspeople, especially small-scale owner-operators, represent an American ideal. This type of entrepreneurship forms one dimension of our strongly held values of individualism and independence. These individuals are likely to be the first to realize personal gain by identifying particular niches in the business market for their services. However, for these entrepreneurs to act, they often need substantial supporting physical and social infrastructures. This support may be too

BOX 10.1 HUMAN RESOURCE BASE AND THE INFORMATION AGE

Although human capacity has always influenced a community's capacity to make or take advantage of economic opportunities, it grows ever more important as we enter the information age. The name for this new era refers to the many facets of computer and telecommunications technologies and their associated industries, all of which require more highly educated workers.

The telecommunications sector of the national economy is highly stratified by skill and opportunity. It includes the most sophisticated computer technology, highly skilled technicians, and highly educated professionals who not only are intimately familiar with the management of vast amounts of information but also know how to use that information in the creation of new knowledge and of wealth. Although these people and their technology often garner a great deal of publicity, the majority of people working in telecommunications are technicians and relatively low-skilled personnel. Nevertheless, even the low-level jobs require higher levels of education than needed for most manufacturing and service-sector work. Thus, the telecommunications industry, when compared with other sectors of the national or rural economies, requires a higher level of human resource capacity.

Speed and efficiency in processing information are the major commodities of the telecommunications industry. This information may be fast-breaking market changes or new software that may improve the efficiency of a dairy operation. It may also be timely communication between a rural manufacturer who provides parts to large auto manufacturers. Or it may be information about the local economy and society that can provide a better base for the community to assess its relative advantages and disadvantages in national and world markets. In brief, information has become a valuable commodity.

For rural people, the value of telecommunications technology is its capacity to reduce the time it takes information to travel from one point to another. Fiber-optics and satellite communications networks transmit information at the speed of light. Because distance has limited rural economic opportunity, many have hoped this industry would provide a means to bring rural economic opportunities more in line with those of metropolitan areas. Thus far, this hope has been realized only on a very limited basis. Not only is the physical infrastructure of fiber-optic networks unavailable for many rural areas, but also these areas lack the human capacity either to provide or consume the expanded base of information. Also, new urban-based markets may be opening up for rural telecommunications entrepreneurs, but so too are rural markets simultaneously opening up for urban entrepreneurs. Information can flow in both directions with equal ease. The human capacities of urban areas are in direct competition with rural areas.

What types of human capacities are playing important roles in rural efforts to participate in the information age? All of them. Foremost is education. The capacity to learn new technologies and to understand the value of new knowledge is critical. Telecommunications is a rapidly changing industry. The technologies are undergoing continuous change, as are the computer programs and the types of information being processed. The ability to stay abreast of this change and to take advantage of new opportunities is highly related to education. But supportive social services are important. If a highly educated and technologically sophisticated labor force is to be nurtured, there must be good health, education, protection, and other services available locally.

expensive for these individuals to provide for themselves. Consequently, local and even state agencies must underwrite investment in such infrastructures to assure that potential entrepreneurs can apply their skills locally.

Collective entrepreneurship is equally important but less often expressed in the business arena. Exceptions include employee- and community-owned businesses or cooperatives. The community-based businesses started in Decatur County are examples of collective entrepreneurship.

Historically, rural communities have been the home of many efforts embodying collective entrepreneurship. The formation of farmer-owned grain elevators at the turn of the century and the work of the Rural Electric Administration during the mid-1900s are two such cooperative efforts. A community may facilitate activity between the local private sector and a nearby community college or business-incubation center. A community may also develop its own businesses, employing local citizens and directing profits to a community revolving loan fund. The homegrown carnivals in Decatur County, Kansas, and Hydro, Oklahoma, are examples of not-for-profit community enterprises. The feedlot was initially a for-profit collectively owned enterprise, but later became a family enterprise. However it may be expressed, entrepreneurship is a valued human resource that requires nurturing at both the individual and community levels.

Observers of small communities have noticed that a combination of both individual and collective entrepreneurship can be a decisive factor in the success of economic development efforts. Individuals who demonstrate no entrepreneurial characteristics in some communities become successful entrepreneurs in others. This implies that there is a dynamic relationship between individuals and communities in enhancing this dimension of the human resource base.

QUALITY OF SOCIAL NETWORKS

A community may have strong human and natural resource bases and yet not effectively tap them because of weak or inappropriately organized social networks. In contrast, a community with a weak human resource base may effectively marshal its limited talents through a strong network of social relationships. *Social networks* are webs of relationships that link individuals within a community.

Several qualities of social networks allow communities to gain control of their social and economic development effectively. These are characteristics of what may be called entrepreneurial communities. They include depersonalization of politics; development of extracommunity linkages; diverse community leadership; and a broad definition of community. Each of these is discussed in turn.

Coffee shop in Sleepy Eye, Minnesota (photo by Tom Arndt).

Discussion of politics in many rural communities generally involves personalities, not issues. The quality of social networks is much higher in communities that accept and confront balanced disagreement and do not turn a public stand on a controversy into a symbol of either moral rectitude or degeneracy. Those who disagree on one issue may be allies on another in a coalition that facilitates collective resolution of a problem. Furthermore, disagreements can surface early and not be suppressed until they explode and divide the community. Political depersonalization requires the acceptance of controversy as a normal feature of community life.

Entrepreneurial communities foster extracommunity links and actively seek resources from other communities and from state and federal sources. They participate in regional planning groups, confer with the cooperative extension service, and apply for federal block grants. They also engage in lateral learning from other communities. Decatur County has developed the means to generate both vertical and horizontal linkages. There is rarely a state government program that county leaders do not know about and apply for. They have sent carloads and sometimes busloads of people to inspect carnivals, feedyards, dairies, and factories. They then adapt what they have learned to meet local needs and circumstances.

By emphasizing flexible, dispersed community leadership, communities avoid becoming dependent on a single broker who happens to have contacts or charisma. In entrepreneurial communities, members rotate through public offices and share informal leadership roles. Often newcomers to the community (those of less than ten years' residence) are active in leadership positions, as are women. Newcomers often bring with them a convert's appreciation of the community and an awareness of outside forces acting upon it. Over the years, Decatur County's development efforts have been characterized by collective decisionmaking and by different persons taking the lead on various projects. County leaders have been open to newcomers assuming leadership roles, although few women have achieved positions of real power.

The rural community has been a major source of identity and participation for its residents. However, as transportation has become more efficient and the population of many rural communities has declined, there has been a need to consolidate services. Those communities that have wide and relatively permeable boundaries—defining themselves as broadly as possible and embracing the residents of several discrete locales—are more likely to remain viable. Such mechanisms as a countywide chamber of commerce established two decades ago in Decatur County and the organization of multicommunity events such as the homegrown carnival are helpful in bringing about a broad definition of community. Thus, when enrollment decreased in two school districts within the county, school consolidation was accomplished with maximum participation and minimal sense of loss.

Choice and Information

Through the development of linkages with the outside, a community gains access to information it needs to make choices about its future. However, there is also an internal dimension to the effective use of information for community choices. Because of role homogeneity, rural communities tend to suppress controversy, as discussed in Chapter 3. However, some level of controversy is necessary in order to make informed and democratic choices. To enable people to weigh the advantages and disadvantages of alternatives, there must be debate in the community.

INTERNAL SOURCES OF INFORMATION

The local newspaper can play an important role in conveying or failing to convey the information needed to make informed decisions. It can also set the tone of community dialogue on an issue. If it seeks to provide information and to suggest that controversy is legitimate, it will help prevent the conversion of disagreements into rancorous conflict with the potential to split the community.

Unfortunately, in some small communities, the newspaper, often a weekly, tends to be long on ads and social announcements but short on news. The biggest zucchini of the season and the scores of the high school basketball games are highlighted, but there is seldom a reporter at the school board or town council meetings. Often, no hint of any bad news is allowed to appear in print. In only a minority of communities is the editor willing to take on controversial issues, address emerging community problems, and thereby risk offending people. It is communities where controversy is openly aired that are best able to process information from a variety of sources and make choices that have the potential to enhance community well-being.

EXTRALOCAL SOURCES OF INFORMATION

A community processes both locally generated information and information that comes from beyond local boundaries. Both types are mediated through the community's social infrastructure. An examination of two communities faced with a similar decision allows us to explore the way in which a community's social infrastructure affects its use of outside information.

As our consumption of toxic and nuclear material expands, we require new locations for disposal or storage. Isolated rural communities seem to be ideal locations, but find themselves the object of a national environmental debate. Both Caliente, Nevada, and the Kaibab Paiute Indian Reservation in Arizona have had to make decisions involving complex scientific, technological, and environmental toxic waste issues. What happens when powerful national interest groups present a community with credible competing versions of an issue—when the evidence seems to support each side? How does a community gather the necessary knowledge to make an informed decision?

Information is not value-neutral. The same technical issue can be presented from different perspectives that, in turn, suggest divergent community choices. Each of these communities sought information in different ways, ways influenced by their unique social infrastructures.

Caliente, a white community in eastern Nevada, used its ability to gain federal government grants to hire a consultant who could help interpret technical information on behalf of the residents. The decision to hire an outside expert was community-based, but Caliente residents were dependent upon the knowledge and value biases of that consultant. Other external organizations, one representing an international environmental interest group and the other representing a multinational toxic waste disposal firm, also provided enormous amounts of information. All of the information was embedded within arguments favorable to the particular interest group or consultant.

The Kaibab Nation faced a similar decision, but the decisionmaking process was quite different. Given their cultural tradition of honoring all requests of the tribe, the Kaibab entertained input from any member or group that petitioned the tribal council. As a result, the council heard testimony from the multinational firm seeking to locate a toxic waste incinerator on the reservation, from the same environmental group that visited Caliente, and from a university consultant solicited at the request of a neighboring Navajo tribe. The tribal council also depended upon a university anthropologist who had gained the trust of the tribe over a twenty-year period and a local tribal environmental group that was created by one of the reservation's most highly educated members. In the end, the council decided to accept the interpretation offered by those they knew rather than those they did not know; the incinerator was rejected. In acting on the recommendations of those they knew, the Kaibab trusted those who understood the tribe and its values, believing they would do a better job of processing and interpreting the technical information than those who did not.

Social Structure and Social Infrastructure

The quality of local social infrastructure may be analogous to a chain, with the weakest link greatly influencing its overall strength. For social infrastructure to work for a community, all three of its dimensions—social institutions, human resources, and social networks—require constant upgrading and maintenance.

These three dimensions of a community's social infrastructure can be either nurtured or blocked by other characteristics of a community, particularly by the local system of social stratification and the local power structure. Communities that have relative social equality and a significant middle class tend to have viable social services provided through sound institutions, competitive human resource bases, and active social networks. In contrast, communities with polarized social structures do not develop thriving social infrastructures.

A *polarized social structure* is characterized by great social distance between a small local elite of wealthy families and the poor of the community. This type of social stratification is associated with a sense of powerlessness by the majority of citizens in the lower-middle and lower classes. The result is a weakening of not only the quality of social networks but also of the community's ability to take advantage of existing human resources. Such stratification also has an impact on the development of those resources.

A community's social structure can influence its long-term capacity for economic and social development. It appears likely that communities that have low social inequality may have social infrastructures that aid in improving their collective well-being. However, places with great social distances (high social stratification) may have large proportions of their populations that are powerless to participate in key development decisions.

Social infrastructure includes the capacity of individuals within the rural community to act in both individual and collective ways. It includes the institutional infrastructure, the human resource base, and the quality of social networks. These in turn are mediated by a community's social stratification, power structure, and local leadership characteristics.

The social infrastructure of a community is particularly important because it can often be improved more easily than can many aspects of a community's economic infrastructure. Communities can work toward improving their system of social services, the capacity of their citizens to recognize and take advantage of economic and social opportunities, and the quality of their social networks. But such efforts are also often the very focus of social problems in rural communities.

The Secret of Success

Starting a carnival may seem trivial in the context of the enormous social and economic challenges now facing rural communities. The creation of the Decatur County Amusement Authority was significant, however, because it offered yet another opportunity for community members to work together. It demonstrated once again that the county could solve its own problems.

What makes some communities more successful than others? Why do some grow, but others decline? How important are organizations such as the Oberlin Industrial Development Company? Do individuals like Kent Reinhardt or Phil Finley make the real difference? If you wanted to help rural communities succeed, where would you focus your resources?

Sociologists differ in their explanations for why some rural communities are successful. Some point to the advantages created by location, natural resources, or economic base. Technical assistance directed toward helping communities capitalize on their advantages might be productive. Others emphasize the social institutions and networks needed for community development (Coleman 1988). Strengthening existing organizations or creating new ones more focused on economic development might be your strategy. Still other sociologists point to the social institutions, both formal and informal, that allow human development to take place (Flora and Flora 1990). Supporting schools, organizations like the Decatur County Amusement Authority, or self-help efforts might be useful strategies for helping communities survive. You be the judge—which explanation would guide your actions?

Chapter Summary

Social infrastructure is both the social capacity and the collective will of local communities to provide for their social and economic well-being. Because elements of social infrastructure are less tangible, many believe them to be less important to the community. However, social infrastructure helps explain the remarkable economic and social recovery of Japan and Germany after World War II. The lack of an effective social infrastructure also helps explain why economic efforts alone do not relieve poverty in the inner city or rural communities.

The social infrastructure of a community consists of three elements: (1) local social institutions, (2) human resources, and (3) quality of social networks. Social organizations, such as police protection, churches, or community kitchens, are the most visible element of social infrastructure. A community's human resource base can be described in terms of educational attainment, vocational skills, state of health, and entrepreneurship. Social networks describe the webs of human relationships that link community members. Characteristics of entrepreneurial communities include depersonalization of politics, development of extracommunity linkages, diverse community leadership, and a broad definition of community.

Ultimately, community choices are shaped by the information available to a community. The local newspaper plays an important role in making information available and encouraging debate on important issues. Resources from outside the community are becoming more important as communities face increasingly technical questions. How the community processes information is mediated by its culture and social infrastructure.

The quality of a community's social infrastructure depends, in part, on how the community is stratified. Communities that have relatively high social equality and a significant middle class tend to have strong social infrastructures. Polarized communities typically have weak social infrastructures.

Key Terms

Collective entrepreneurship describes a set of group processes, attitudes, and skills needed to organize, operate, and assume risk for a business or community venture.

Human resource base describes the ability of community members to accomplish their individual goals and vocational tasks.

Individual entrepreneurship describes a set of personal attitudes and skills needed to organize, operate, and assume risk for a business venture.

Polarized social structure describes a system of social stratification characterized by great social distance between a small local elite and other members of the community.

Social infrastructure is both the social capacity and collective will of local communities to provide for their social and economic well-being.

Social networks are webs of relationships that link individuals within a community.

Social organizations, an element of a community's social infrastructure, include either formal or volunteer groups that provide services essential to the maintenance of physical, social, and cultural needs of a community.

References

Coleman, James S. 1988. "Social Capital in the Creation of Human Capital." *American Journal of Sociology* 94:95–119.

Flora, Cornelia B., and Jan L. Flora. 1990. "Developing Entrepreneurial Rural Communities." *Sociological Practice* 8:197–207.

Part

Toward Community
Empowerment

11

Power in Communities

oe and Ellen McDougal had grown up in Small Lake and thought they knew the town well. Joe was employed in a small manufacturing plant. Ellen made crafts at home and worked part-time as a waitress in the Down Home Cafe, the central spot in town.

As their children grew older, Joe and Ellen found that there were not enough recreational facilities available for them. What was available was often not in good condition. In particular, they believed that lights were needed for the city park's baseball diamond. If lights were installed, more games could be scheduled for the children's softball leagues.

They went to the city council with signed petitions for several years with no result. Their elected officials explained there was no money for "recreational luxuries" and that nothing could be done. Finally, one of Ellen's regular customers at the cafe said, "Oh, if you want something done in this town, you really need to talk to Hank Jones, owner of the local feed and farm supply store." Ellen knew Hank because he drank coffee almost every day in the Down Home Cafe, but she had no idea he was that important in town politics. He seemed like just one of the boys. Hank had never been elected to public office.

The next day when Hank came in, Ellen poured his coffee and chatted with him about the need for lights at the city park and how important it was in keeping the youngsters out of trouble. Within a week, the item was brought before the city council again. It was easily passed and funded through a small assessment on property. Why had Ellen's casual conversation with Hank Jones been more productive than two years' work with the elected town officials?

In this chapter, we look at different theories of community power, different ways it is measured, different sources of power or vested interests, and the importance of outside linkages to community power. Finally, we examine some of the implications different power structures have for community development and change.

Identifying Power Structures

Previous chapters stressed the importance of the changing global economy on rural communities. Rural communities are greatly affected by outside forces. The smallest places feel the repercussions of national and international events. Yet as we saw in the discussions of the role and responsibilities of government, even quite small communities have the power to generate and distribute resources.

DEFINING AND EXERCISING POWER

Power is the ability to make something happen that otherwise would not happen or to prevent something from happening that others wish to make happen. Hence, the ability to affect the distribution of both public and private resources within the community is called *community power*. Who holds the power and how it is used can make a big difference in the quality of life for community residents and the future existence of the community itself.

An important dimension of power is the means by which it is exercised. These include physical force, institutionalized force or authority, and influence. In totalitarian regimes, power is often based on the threat of exercising physical force. Institutional power—power that derives from occupying a position of authority in an institution—requires subordinates to follow orders or regulations if they want to remain part of that institution. Only when superiors go beyond institutional rules is it acceptable for subordinates to refuse to carry out an order. Even then, refusal can jeopardize one's longevity with the organization. Influence refers to power derived from more informal relationships, such as friendship or social status.

Patterns in the exercise of community power are called *community power structure*. In the community, we can map local power to determine the degree to which it is widely participatory or more concentrated. For instance, in Small Lake there is a hidden power structure that has a great impact on what happens and when and how. The elected officials are not always the people running the town. In some communities, an important network of individuals who never face public election or accountability has a huge impact on what happens or does not happen.

COMPETING THEORIES

Social scientists are not in agreement about the way power is exercised in North American communities. Nor do they agree as to how one should go about determining how community power is structured. In part, the disagreements arise from the fact that different communities have different power structures. But researchers also bring different assumptions to their study of community power. This chapter describes four approaches to the study of community power: pluralism, elitism, class-based, and a variant of the class-based called the growth machine. Although most of the initial studies of community power were carried out in urban places, later elaboration and testing of the different theories occurred in rural communities. Consequently, we use these theories to explore power in rural communities.

Social scientists have devised a number of ways of determining who has power. Each of these measurement techniques is related to which theory of power is supported, and each tends to give somewhat different answers to the question "Who is running this town?" After we discuss each theory of power, we describe the method of measurement of community power most closely related to that theory.

Pluralism Versus Elitism

Early studies of community power were conducted from a pluralist perspective and focused mainly on who held formal positions in community government. In looking more deeply into how communities worked, sociologists began to notice patterns of inequality in the exercise of power and distribution of resources. In many cases, small groups of individuals controlled the community by virtue of their economic and social position. This led to a competing view of power—elitism. This section explores these two models and the strategies used by each in measuring power.

PLURALISM AND THE DECISIONAL TECHNIQUE

The pluralist approach to power—whether in the community or on the regional, state, or national level—is based on fundamental assumptions about the way democracies work. Adherents of the *pluralism* theory of power assume no dominant source of power. They assume that the capacity for acquiring power is widely distributed within the population unless analysis shows otherwise. That is, power is dispersed among competing interests. Although one particular group may prevail on one issue, its influence is not necessarily important to the next issue. Furthermore, one cannot determine without studying the situation what is the interest of any particular group (Polsby 1960).

Pluralists see citizens in a democracy deciding on political issues in the same way that they make decisions vis-à-vis the market—as unattached individuals. Thus, the individual is the basic building block of politics. Individual citizens exercise their political influence principally through voting. Essential for pluralism to work is the concept of one person, one vote. That vote may be exercised directly, as in the case of the New England town meeting. Much more frequently, it is cast for someone who represents a group of constituents. Under this system of representative democracy, citizens are not directly involved in making all public decisions; instead, the representatives they choose are periodically subjected to electoral validation. It is assumed that this periodic validation is a means by which representatives (be they school board members, town council-persons, county supervisors, state officials, or the president or prime minister of the nation) in a general sense reflect the desires of their constituents. Although individual voters may see their objectives deferred in the short term, particularly if they voted for the losing candidate, decisions should benefit the greatest number of people in the long term.

From the pluralist perspective, the U.S. democratic system is grounded in a legal system that prohibits power being used arbitrarily—the system of checks and balances among the different branches of government and the Bill of Rights and other laws guarantee to minorities freedom of expression and equality of opportunity. This equality includes the electoral system itself, in which those elected have only temporary power gained through periodic election and challengers have a reasonable opportunity of gaining office. All citizens share the civil right of participation in government through the election process, including the right to run for office themselves.

According to pluralists, representative democracy does not mean that all citizens exercise equal influence in politics. Some may choose not to participate—in voting, in party caucuses, or in contributing funds to a particular candidate. If they did participate and had the innate ability, they could have influence roughly equal to that of any other active citizen. Differences in influence among different classes or ethnic groups can be explained by the statistical tendency of certain groups or classes not to participate as actively in the political process as do others. It is the individual's decision to participate or not, and individuals who fail to participate have made the choice of noninvolvement.

The dispersion of economic, political, and social power that is assumed by pluralists also applies to the decisionmaking process. Pluralists believe the best way to assess how decisions are made and by whom is to look at overt activity—in other words, decisions are made by those in positions of formal power. Pluralists are suspicious of analyses based on assumptions of behind-the-scenes influence. In fact, they reject the idea that certain groups have certain a priori interests. They do not subscribe to the notion that different classes have different political interests. Whether they do or not is a matter for investigation. Hence, lack of controversy on a particular issue is, for the pluralists, an indicator that there is basic agreement among the citizenry on the publicly articulated position.

Those who study community power from a pluralist perspective use what is called the *decisional technique*. This research methodology involves identifying controversial public issues and using these issues to reveal the decisionmaking process. Newspaper coverage, observation, and interviews are used to determine which decisions were important and who made them. The information gathered through these sources generally shows a diversity of sources of inputs to public decisions; this diversity lends support to the pluralist perspective.

The classic pluralist study *Who Governs?* was conducted by Robert Dahl in New Haven, Connecticut. Dahl (1961) examined three issues—political nominations, urban renewal, and public education. He found that no single group dominated in all three decisions—different groups and individuals were active in each. Only the appointed bureaucracy and the elected mayor were common to more than one issue-area (see Box 11.1). Thus, Dahl concluded, his results supported the pluralistic perspective.

G. William Domhoff (1983) reexamined the urban renewal issue, exploring what went on behind the scenes as well as during the decisionmaking process itself. He found that urban renewal in New Haven was very much the product of economic interests that benefited handsomely from the program. The politicians were merely the implementors, not the decisionmakers. Dahl had looked at the decisionmaking process only after it became public, thus examining only the pluralist veneer. Thus, if one is using the decisional technique to determine who has power in the community, it is important to study the period that preceded public airing of the issue to see whose agenda the issue originally was on, the behind-the-scenes machinations that determined how the issue would be presented to the public, and which interests stood to gain when the decision was implemented.

ELITISM AND WHAT HAPPENS BEHIND THE SCENES

The elitist school of thought received its methodological orientation from Floyd Hunter (1953) in his study of Atlanta. However, the perspective obtained its name from the work of sociologist C. Wright Mills, who wrote *The Power Elite* (1956). Mills argued that a power elite—a coalition of government officials, business executives, and military leaders—controlled the nation and that the political and economic interests shared among individuals in the coalition were reinforced by their social similarities.

BOX 11.1   NEW HAVEN: SUPPORT FOR THE PLURALIST, ELITIST, OR GROWTH-MACHINE THEORIES?

New Haven, Connecticut, is a small metropolitan city. It had stopped growing by 1920, its port having declined with the advent of the railroads and its carriage-manufacturing enterprises having been put out of business by the automobile. Yale University began growing in the 1930s and soon became the city's primary engine of growth (Domhoff 1983, 188–189).

New Haven was first studied by Robert Dahl and a group of other political scientists from Yale University using decisional methodology. The city's population was approaching 170,000 in the late 1950s when Dahl studied it. Dahl selected three issue-areas "because they cut across a wide variety of interests and participants" (Dahl 1961, 333) and because they had prima facie importance to the community. They were (1) nominations to public office by each of the two main parties; (2) the New Haven Redevelopment Program, which received more federal funds per capita than any other urban renewal program in the country; and (3) public education, the largest item in the city's budget. Using newspaper accounts, documents, records, and extended interviews with participants, Dahl selected and analyzed eight major decisions taken over the decade of the 1950s in each of the areas of education and redevelopment. Decisions on who should be nominated by each party for mayor for the period 1941–1959 were also examined.

The "economic notables" included chief executive officers and chairmen of the boards of the major corporations operating in New Haven, major local property holders, all bank directors, and those sitting on the boards of directors of three or more firms operating in New Haven. Only 24 percent of those involved in exercising power—defined as successfully initiating or vetoing a policy proposal—were economic notables. (The percentage rises to nearly 40 percent if redevelopment issues are considered alone, excluding public educational issues and political nominations.) Only 16 percent of "social notables"—those whose families attended the annual debutante balls of the exclusive New Haven Lawn Club—were found to have exercised power in the three issue-areas. There was only about a 5 percent overlap between economic and social notables. Dahl concluded that the economic and social notables were no more involved in making important community decisions than were a half dozen other groups and that there was minimal involvement of the same people across issue-areas.

Urban renewal in New Haven was initiated by Mayor Lee, who took office in 1954, was reelected three times, and retired in 1970. During his tenure, the center of the city was transformed by replacing slums with high-rise student apartments and laboratories for Yale University and with commercial buildings in an expanded downtown. In fact, New Haven during that time received the highest per-capita federal funding for urban renewal of any city in the country. Dahl attributed this success to the extraordinary capacity and determination of the Democratic mayor and his aides. He pointed out that Lee's predecessor, a Republican, had been unable to galvanize the business community for such an effort and that Yale University played a passive role in the urban renewal process.

A decade and a half later, G. William Domhoff, a psychologist and sociologist who had chosen national power structure as his primary research activity, did a restudy of New Haven. Domhoff (1983) looked not only at Dahl's data, including transcripts of his interviews, but also at minutes of the chamber of commerce and in-house memos of key economic and governmental elites that had not been previously available. He came out with a quite different picture:

1. Using an interlocking-directorate approach for identification of the top economic elites and using membership in any of three elite social clubs in New Haven, Domhoff found a much greater overlap between the economic and social elites or notables.

continues

Box 11.1 continued

2. In reexamining the three issue-areas, Domhoff found good reason why the elites would not be heavily involved in school and nomination issues. Dahl had pointed out that because most of the social and economic notables sent their children to private schools, they would have little interest in public educational policy. Domhoff argued that they did have one interest with respect to public schools—keeping their taxes low. Indeed, he found that members of the Board of Finance, which makes recommendations on tax rates to the Board of Aldermen (city council), were overwhelmingly from the business community. With respect to political nominations, Domhoff argued that who gets elected is not of great concern to the elites unless they can be shown that it makes a difference to their interests. In fact, urban renewal—which was definitely of concern to the economic elites—was implemented by a Democratic mayor in cooperation with economic elites who were predominately Republican.

3. Urban renewal occurred through the close cooperation of Yale University, the economic notables, a powerful Republican senator, and the Democratic mayor. Critical to the success of the program were changes in federal laws beginning in 1954—the same year Mayor Lee took office—under the Eisenhower administration. These changes transformed the slum-clearance provisions of the 1937 Housing Act into a massive program to redevelop the central cities, with concern for the former residents of the "redeveloped" area occupying at best a secondary position. (Organized neighborhood opposition to urban renewal emerged in New Haven only after Dahl's study was completed, and it was not successful in stopping or ameliorating the effects of the program.)

Yale University began planning for expansion in the 1940s. In 1947, the Yale trustees appointed a committee to investigate the university's future needs. Headed by New York investment banker Prescott Bush, who also was a trustee, the committee produced a report released in 1950 that called for an $80 million development program over the next ten years with one-fourth of the funds going to a building program. Federal urban renewal laws required that after the local government had cleared the land, a private entity had to purchase the land. Yale became that entity. Yale's president appointed a close friend and graduate of Yale Law School, Morris Tyler, as the university's liaison to the New Haven Redevelopment Agency, and he effectively served as its legal counsel. Tyler was also a partner in the New Haven law firm that was most central in the city's business networks (as determined by Domhoff's interlocking-directorate study).

Yale's importance to the urban renewal effort was strengthened even more by the election of Prescott Bush to the U.S. Senate in 1952. (Bush was the father of President George Bush, also a Yale graduate.) He promptly obtained assignment to the committee that oversaw the urban renewal program. During his tenure in the Senate, not only did New Haven receive more per-capita funds for urban renewal than did any other city, but Connecticut also ranked top among states in its per-capita receipt of such funds. After the functions of Mayor Lee's redevelopment agency became routine, which was when Dahl did his study, urban renewal was largely controlled by the mayor, but in the crucial period of initiation, Yale University and the business elite were critical to the success of New Haven's urban renewal effort (Domhoff 1983).

The New Haven case studies demonstrate that a researcher's perspective and methodology can affect the results and interpretations. Which of the two approaches did you find more convincing?

Sources: Robert Dahl. 1961. *Who Governs? Democracy and Power in an American City.* New Haven: Yale University Press.

G. William Domhoff. 1983. *Who Rules America Now? A View for the '80s.* Englewood Cliffs, NJ: Prentice-Hall.

Members of the elite attended the same schools and universities, belonged to the same clubs, and relaxed at the same resorts. Also, the branches of the elite interlocked professionally. Business executives became politicians, politicians had business interests, and retired military leaders sat on corporate boards; all of these connections further ensured and strengthened mutual interests. G. William Domhoff in his *Who Rules America?* (1967) elaborated on and modified Mills's analysis at the national level, as did Domhoff's followers.

Elitism is a perspective based on the assumption that power conforms to the stratification system. Elitists argue that there is a hierarchical status system and that, in general terms, power is also distributed hierarchically. The premise is that sources of power (control over means of coercion, authoritative position, command of wealth or information, and prestige or other personal traits) can be cumulated. For instance, wealthy persons are often viewed as having exceptional talents; otherwise, it is commonly believed, they would not be wealthy. Possession of wealth can then lead to prestige, control over information, and authoritative position. The pluralistic theory of power sees within the community a series of factional coalitions—group boundaries are fairly fluid, members disagree on specific issues over time, and no coalition dominates for any extended period. The elitists, on the other hand, see a pyramidal structure of power—a few individuals representing key economic institutions with like interests have the largest influence in what happens in towns large and small.

Floyd Hunter (1953), in one of the most significant works on community power, *Community Power Structure* (a study of Atlanta, Georgia), developed the *reputational technique* for determining power in a community. Hunter collected lists of community leaders and activists from local newspapers and organizational membership rolls. He came up with a list of 175 names, then sought the aid of people knowledgeable about the community and who presumably knew about power and politics to cull the original list. They reduced the list to forty names; these people were then personally interviewed. Each individual was asked a number of questions including "If a project went before the community that required decisions by a group of leaders, leaders that nearly everyone would accept, which ten on this list of forty would you choose?" The responses gave him a list of top reputational leaders.

As a result of using this reputational technique, which has been modified by different researchers studying different cities, Hunter found an elitist power structure in the form of a pyramid. At the top was a small group of business leaders, an elite upper class. They dominated the city's economy through a web of interlocking directorships. They lived in the same exclusive neighborhoods, belonged to the same expensive clubs, and entertained each other in their homes. The elites rarely held office and were not visible to the general public. Only four of the forty top elites were public officials. The rest were bankers, manufacturers, and other business leaders. Their power was informal. Elected officials were subordinate to them—doing their bidding but not seeing them socially.

Hunter found this small policymaking group, largely from the business class, to be in overall agreement on most major issues. He noted that "controversy is avoided, partly by the policy-making group's not allowing a proposal to get too far along if it meets stiff criticism at any point in decision-making" (Hunter 1953, 111). Thus, Hunter did not conclude that this small group had absolute control over major issues, but he did propose that it played a major role in setting the public agenda.

Elitists criticize the decisional approach because it often focuses on controversial issues, defining power in terms of who makes decisions publicly. Elitists argue that most decisions are not controversial and are never debated publicly. Many of these decisions systematically support one set of interests in the community over another.

Viewed from this perspective, power lies with those who control the public agenda but who may not be visible players in the political process. It becomes important then to look at what issues in the community are never publicly decided—the nondecisions that appear just to happen. Crenson, in a study conducted when pollution became an issue in urban communities, concluded that the problem of dirty air became a "key political issue" in those communities where "industry's reputation for power was relatively puny," suggesting that the critical stage is not the point of public decision but when "a community sifts out subjects that will not be given political attention and so will never become key political issues" (Crenson 1971, 131, 90).

Power and Economic Interests

Class-based theories of community power focus attention on the economic roots of power. This theory and its variations assume that those who control the corporate economic system control the wider society. It is often in their economic interest to influence or to control political decisionmaking so as to achieve their economic goals. This section explores the class-based theory of community power and one of its more recent variations, the growth machine.

CLASS-BASED THEORY OF POWER

According to the *class-based analysis* of power, it makes little difference to the economic elites which person or group actually makes decisions as long as those policy and allocation decisions facilitate profit making. Those in official decisionmaking positions may not be the economic elites themselves, but the decisionmakers tend to represent the interests of the economic elites. This appeared to be the case in Small Lake, where Hank Jones, a local businessman, had a good deal of informal control over the city council.

The influential study undertaken in the 1930s by Helen and Robert Lynd (1937) found that economic institutions were key to understanding power and the distribution of resources in "Middletown," the name they gave to Muncie, Indiana. Now a metropolitan city, Muncie was a fast-growing nonmetropolitan community in the 1930s, increasing from a population of 39,000 in 1925 to over 47,000 ten years later.

The locally based Ball family owned and operated the Ball Jar Company, the largest producer of home-canning equipment in the world. The Lynds found that after the "bank holiday" in 1933, the family controlled or had a major interest in all surviving local financial institutions. The Balls were also heavily involved in local real estate and shaped the city's growth. Through philanthropy, they influenced the growth of the local college (now Ball State University), the hospital, the community fund, and the YMCA and YWCA. Although family members only occasionally held local public office, they controlled the Republican Party and had influence in the Democratic Party and were able to bring about or prevent change in many arenas. In short, they exercised political power in Muncie.

The Muncie studies questioned the independence of those holding political office. According to the Lynds, elected officials were of meager caliber—people the Ball family and the rest of the inner business group ignored economically and socially yet used politically. Those who controlled the economic institutions (the Balls were among these elites) did not want to bother with direct political involvement, but they did need to limit government interference in their concerns. Elected officials were thus considered a necessary evil.

A case study of business-class control and citizen mobilization in a small Kansas town by Hynes and Mauney (1990) offers insight into the reasons that the elites, particularly specific business interests, are concerned about city government and wish to control decisions.

Many rural communities own their own utilities; this was the case in the town studied by Hynes and Mauney. Utility pricing policies and rate structures in this Kansas town were such that domestic households paid higher rates than did commercial and industrial enterprises. These enterprises were almost invariably owned by the business group from which the town officials came. By charging high domestic utility rates, officials made it possible to keep property taxes low. This was to the advantage of those who owned a lot of property. Zoning decisions also were systematically made in favor of those with direct influence on the city council.

Special-interest groups also influenced the public financing of business projects that might otherwise have been funded through private sources. People with these vested interests had tangible reasons for controlling both community government and nongovernment institutions involved in distributing resources. Generally, they were quite accomplished at doing so.

Working-class people in rural communities have a set of interests different from the interest groups just described. Of primary importance are wage levels and benefits and actions that would increase the prevailing wage. Local governments influence wage levels by how much they pay their own employees, by whether they consciously recruit high- or low-wage firms, and by other such actions. Yet a number of structures in small communities prevent working-class citizens from influencing these decisions. They rarely sit on the public boards, and even when elected to office, they often find it difficult to attend the informal and sometimes the formal meetings called during daytime working hours. Hynes and Mauney document well the case of the working-class mayor in the town they studied. He was publicly ridiculed in the press because of his irregular attendance at city council meetings. His job kept him from the impromptu meetings called by city council, which was composed of small-business operators who had flexible schedules.

Hynes and Mauney also demonstrate very clearly the chilling nature of a local elite's tight control that keeps people from running for office or publicly bringing forward issues that they know are negatively affecting them. People are often reluctant to act because of their perceived vulnerability. For example, Hynes and Mauney report that one prominent member of the concerned citizens group became inactive when she came to fear that her cousin, a schoolteacher, would lose his job if her activities continued. When individual members of a power elite occupy economic, political, and civic roles almost interchangeably, one can expect little participation in decisionmaking. The more widely dispersed economic, political, and civic roles are within the community, the more likely that different citizen voices will be heard.

THE GROWTH MACHINE

With the publication of "The City as a Growth Machine" in 1976, Harvey Molotch introduced a variation of the class-based theory of community power. Studies in a number of urban areas had identified the importance of a group that later came to be called the growth machine. The *growth machine* is a coalition of groups that perceive economic gain in community growth. The growth machine is led by certain groups within the business class that set about to encourage growth and to capture its benefits. These groups tend to be a combination of interests of developers, construction companies, real estate agents, owners of commercial buildings and apartment rental units, banks, and other businesses dependent on "an increase of aggregate rent levels through the intensification of land use" (Logan and Molotch 1987, 13). Ability to increase aggregate rent levels (income from land or other real property) is heavily dependent on an increase in the community's population. These growth machines compete with growth machines in other communities to attract capital to generate jobs and increase return on land, buildings, merchandise, and services.

The most active elites in the local power structure are generally from the *rentier class*, those who receive their income from property. Members of this class promote population growth, usually in the name of increasing jobs. These modern rentiers have financial interests in the use of local land and buildings and include developers, commercial and residential landlords, and those who speculate in real property. The rentier class does not produce goods or services but rather makes money by preparing the ground for manufacturing or retail firms by providing them with desirable sites. Profits for the rentier class depend primarily on population growth but secondarily on friendly local governments. Local government, as we have seen, has unique powers to regulate land use, and it is land use that provides potential profit to this class of people.

The growth-machine ideology sees economic growth as being value-free—the creation of new jobs builds profits and simultaneously benefits the community. The growth machine and the rentier class are eager to attract industry because it generates commercial and residential construction and results in increased land values. Therefore, there is little discussion about what is produced, wage levels paid by new employers, and impact of new industrial or service firms on quality of life. In urban and larger nonmetropolitan communities, industry is often put in the low-income part of town. Thus, the profits are gained by people in the wealthy part of town, and the cost of development is borne by the poor, often in terms of decreased quality of life through polluted air, overcrowded schools, and traffic congestion. Similarly, as occurred in New Haven, urban renewal or downtown redevelopment occurs in the neighborhoods of the most powerless and vulnerable people.

Thus, the central conflict in many urban communities is between the growth machine and neighborhoods. This conflict can be understood in terms of a conflict between use value and exchange value. The two terms are almost self-explanatory. Something that has *use value* is valued by its owner because of its use without selling it. *Exchange value* is realized only when the commodity is sold.

For example, an apartment building has little use value to the owner. It has exchange value in terms of the income generated either from rental or from its sale. On the other hand, one's ancestral home has only use value because one has no intention of selling it. It may be sold when the individual dies, giving it exchange value, but the owner, now deceased, did not realize any exchange value from it—only use value. Some properties have values that lie in between these two extremes. For example, the home of a professional who expects to move several times has use value while the person lives in it, but maintaining its market value is of concern because of the expectation of selling it at some time in the not-too-distant future. Thus, any improvement the owner makes must be made with dual concerns: First, does it increase the owner's enjoyment of the house (use value)? Second, does it increase the salability of the house (exchange value)?

In the case of urban renewal, use value and exchange value come into direct conflict. Those who live in the affected neighborhoods embrace use values. They first seek to preserve their homes (the longer they have lived in them, the greater their use value compared with their exchange value). Second, neighborhood people have a vested interest in keeping the value of land low—it means lower property taxes. Those who are part of the growth machine emphasize exchange values. They thrive on profit derived from increasing land values and thus support efforts at urban renewal.

In rural communities, the growth machine has a similar composition to that in the cities. McGranahan (1990, 160) points out that "locally owned banks, utilities, law firms, and other firms operating largely within local trade areas," for which "income and wealth depend on the volume of business, especially to the extent that there are economies of scale," are likely to be part of the growth machine. The growth machine also includes those in construction, real estate sales, apartment and housing rentals, abstracting, and home insurance. The motto of the growth machine is "jobs and more jobs." Although the real goal is profits, the cry for jobs appears much more altruistic.

There are other groups in small towns that might be characterized as the no-growth coalition, though it differs somewhat from its urban counterpart. Unlike in the cities, the rural no-growth coalition tends to dominate, especially in the smaller non–trade center communities, though its precise nature depends on the principal source of the community's wealth.

The no-growth coalition in small communities includes manufacturers, processors, commercial farmers, and others who produce for an export market ("export" here means that the product is sold outside the community). Their interest is in having low-cost labor, not in generating a larger local market. Bringing in new employers, particularly branch plants that have paid higher wages in metropolitan areas, is not in the interest of this group. For instance, the peanut processors who dominated politics in Early County, Georgia, until the 1980s not only opposed higher wages but also were against spending on public schools because they feared that educating the largely black population in public schools would result in higher wages. In the 1970s, whites who could afford it often attended a white private academy, thus keeping down public school expenditures. Lower funding was doubly in the interest of the powerful group because (1) it helped keep wages down by keeping the bulk of the labor force unskilled and (2) it resulted in low taxes. Another example is in midwestern farm communities where (often retired) farmers usually dominate the board of county commissioners or supervisors. They favor a limited government, no-growth approach because they do not depend on the local population to buy their products and because they have an interest in low real estate taxes. The exception to their no-growth perspective is their interest in improved roads and bridges in order to get their products to market readily.

Retired persons, whose concern lies more with the use value of their homes than with their exchange value, also are part of the no-growth coalition. This group makes up a substantial part of the population of rural communities that are experiencing out-migration. Although retirees may not participate actively in community affairs, they tend to vote in large numbers and can sometimes defeat industrial revenue bonds as well as school and other infrastructure bonds.

The small village of Springdale in upstate New York studied by Arthur Vidich and Joseph Bensman (1968) is an example of a community where the no-growth mentality dominated at the time of their research. It was a community that after a long period of decline was fast becoming a low-rent bedroom community for industrial workers from nearby Binghamton. The business elite controlled village politics through an "invisible government" that consisted of the three members of the village Republican committee—a feed and seed dealer, the weekly newspaper editor, and a lawyer who was the clerk (counsel) to the village board. This group determined the nominees for village offices and manipulated voting behavior so that their candidates always won. (Because the Democrats who voted were a distinct minority in the village, nomination on the Republican ticket was tantamount to election.) The hours that the polls were open were not convenient for the industrial workers, and "safe" voters could be recruited as soon as it appeared that too many of the "wrong" kinds of people were voting.

Vidich and Bensman found the following informal requirements for being on the village board: (1) being a resident of the community for at least ten years, though preferable was lifelong residency; (2) being economically vulnerable and hence amenable to being manipulated by those holding real power, or having a kinship connection with one of the dominant figures of machine politics; (3) having little knowledge about the way government works; and (4) subscribing to a low-tax, low-expenditure ideology. The authors summed it up this way: "It thus happens that the incompetent, the economically vulnerable, and the appropriately kinship-connected individuals are elected with regularized consistency . . . to a village board on which they find they have nothing to do because, in their own perspective, the routine affairs of government are automatic" (Vidich and Bensman 1968, 116).

Vidich and Bensman indicated that another characteristic united the members of the village board as well as the invisible government: They all owned rental property. As owners of real estate, they should logically have been part of the growth machine. However, decline was so deeply imprinted in their experience that they had developed a low-tax approach to making money in real estate: keeping their expenses low and seeking to make money on rentals rather than on sale of real estate. The modest influx of commuter residents allowed them to reap some benefits of growth without having to spend their own or others' money to bring it about. All they had to do was to be sure that the right kind of people were elected to the village board. This was done by restricting the vote and ensuring that individuals believing in limited—very limited—government were elected to the village council.

In somewhat larger rural communities, influence over city government is more commonly exercised through semigovernmental units such as the chamber of commerce. (Chambers of commerce often channel government funds, but without much public accountability, for such things as tourism and economic development.) Both no-growth and growth-machine business interests choose to be active in the local chamber of commerce or similar civic organizations in order to seek to impose their view of local development.

Unlike urban communities, where the growth machine typically dominates, rural communities vary substantially in terms of whether they project a no-growth or pro-growth orientation. The ability of the no-growth group, as in Springdale, to make the routine affairs of government automatic is sufficient in some communities to defeat the growth machine and to keep new economic activity out. Other nonmetropolitan communities, often regional trade centers, are dominated by pro-growth groups. In other instances, as has occurred during times of crisis and population decline, the rentier class and those who benefit individually from low taxes may join together to save their rural community by seeking to attract or generate capital to increase employment in the community. Much more numerous are the rural communities that when faced with decline elect to do nothing.

LOCAL VERSUS ABSENTEE OWNERSHIP

Both the San Jose study discussed later (Trounstine and Christensen 1982) and the growth-machine literature suggest that the increasing international ownership of firms will result in less involvement in day-to-day community issues by industry and business and more involvement of an increasingly diverse group of players. Further, the awareness citizens have of nonlocal ownership encourages them to mobilize collectively as insiders against outsiders to address serious issues such as environmental pollution. At the other extreme, a major employer may threaten to quit the community if it does not win concessions on issues that directly affect its profitability.

Increased nonlocal ownership could lead to bias favoring the growth machine. Nonlocal firms tend to have managers who are geographically mobile and who thus exert less long-term influence in the community. Managers of absentee companies generally invest neither their personal capital nor their energy in community affairs or charitable activities. In contrast, local industrialists or civic leaders are active in all civic realms and are often linked to the rentier group through coownership of speculative property. Local industrialists are often philanthropists providing a trickle-down of local wealth.

Further, nonlocal firms are usually linked to national or international supply networks; local entrepreneurs do not benefit from such commercial links. There are smaller multiplier effects from absentee-owned firms than from those locally owned. When local businesses are aligned with the growth machine, these benefits, both tangible and symbolic, can be exploited to foster the growth mentality and to generate support for policies that benefit local firms.

The concentration that is occurring in manufacturing firms is also occurring in the media. Daily newspapers are less likely to be locally owned than they used to be. Chain newspapers with limited links to individual communities are less likely than locally owned newspapers to be active promoters of the local growth machine and, therefore, are more likely to take an independent editorial stand. Domhoff (1983) points out that local newspaper publishers are not committed to a particular faction of the growth machine but to the growth machine in general: The newspaper's interest is in selling more newspapers and, in particular, more advertising. Thus, the local publisher often serves as an arbiter among different groups within the growth machine, acting as a spokesperson for the growth machine as a whole. Hence, when the newspaper is no longer locally owned, the growth machine loses an important integrative element.

Similarly, banking is becoming more concentrated in fewer interstate firms with less interest in controlling the uniquely local resources of tax rates and land use. Unlike its locally owned predecessor, the consolidated bank is unlikely to be allied with the local growth machine. It may also be less interested in investing in the local community.

Absentee-owned enterprises have a contradictory impact on the community. They may create space for greater community pluralism through their lack of interest in local politics. That lack of interest will mean less commitment to the interests of the dominant community elites. This lack of political coordination among economic elites provides a greater opportunity for nonelites to organize in their own interest. Alternatively, when an issue arises that affects the absentee-owned firm directly, it may threaten to leave the community if the issue is not resolved favorably for it. That threat may carry considerable weight if the firm makes a large contribution to the economy of the community.

Power Structure and Community Change

With the decline of branch manufacturing plants in rural areas in the early 1980s and the expanded growth of service-sector activities, the growth machine—whether local or national—has found it more difficult to manage community symbols to its own benefit. Because industrialization was generally seen as the solution to all communities' problems, the local growth machine could convince local governments to offer tax breaks to new industries. Such offers were made, even though people on fixed incomes found that they lost more than they gained from the presence of such plants, and although unemployed persons often did not benefit because more educated commuters took the new jobs. Now the service sector has replaced manufacturing as the growth sector. This has created new problems for nonelites and for some elites in rural communities. In larger nonmetropolitan communities, downtown malls built through urban renewal have uprooted people from poorer neighborhoods, or suburban malls have replaced locally owned stores with chains and franchises within the mall. Merchants in small communities have been "Wal-Marted" by the general merchandise chain store in the nearby larger community.

Environmental awareness has increased as people have become more concerned about urban garbage filling rural landfills or about nuclear waste dumps and missile sites replacing farm and ranch land. In some cases, the interests of the entire community coalesce if such facilities do little to generate wealth for local elites. Just as frequently, such issues split communities desperate for jobs and income.

In rapid-growth communities, the new in-migrants are often professionals with a strong commitment to the residential value of the community, organizational skills, and a willingness to participate in community affairs. Their commitment includes concern for the environment often coupled with an unwillingness to pay the fiscal and social costs of development. In short, national economic groups are being challenged locally for their growth-machine mentality.

In response, national economic elites are mobilizing anew to have impacts at the local level. Management-level personnel in branch firms are required to become active in local organizations and to form their own associations that lobby local governments, support political candidates, and publicize their views on zoning, land use, and the free enterprise system. As the interests of national and local elites diverge, the national elites and power structure seek to convince local elites that the ideology of the national growth machine should be their ideology also. Thus, local chambers of commerce may come up with programs that seem antithetical to local development needs but that match the U.S. Chamber of Commerce's political and ideological agenda—that of the national growth machine.

Communities vary enormously in the degree to which power is concentrated and in the degree to which it is wielded by local or absentee individuals, firms, and institutions. It is important to assess the structure of local power in analyzing how change takes place within a community and what kinds of tactics are needed in order to institute grassroots change. Challenging the power elite is an empowering experience because disenfranchised groups can learn to be successful through their mobilization. However, it is also risky because of the ability power elites often have to control information and symbols and, thus, totally discredit people who are in opposition to them—not by systematically attacking their position on issues, but by casting doubt on their personality and character.

Seeing the Complete Power Structure

Decisional and reputational approaches for measuring community power emerged with pluralist and elitist perspectives of power. Selecting one technique for use in a community study would bias the results in favor of that perspective. More recent studies have introduced new measurement techniques and combined research methodologies in order to create a more complete picture of community power structures.

Another way to measure who holds power is by doing network analysis of the key positions in major institutions in a community. This approach is used by both the elitists and the class-based theorists of community power. Class theorists use it to determine the corporate structure and to identify the top corporate leaders. Domhoff used this method to determine who were the top economic elites or notables in New Haven.

Network analysis involves obtaining the names of the members of the boards of directors or officers of all the important firms and/or organizations in town, determining linkages between organizations or individuals, and assessing patterns of linkages. Network analysis in various circumstances shows a single power elite or different power factions (see Box 11.2). The people are then ranked according to their number of connections and their centrality in the networks. Networks of interlocking firms can be examined to determine the kind of resources they bring together and whether they represent a growth machine or other type of resource network.

Balanced studies of power structure often combine a number of these mechanisms to limit the theoretical bias of the studies. An example of a study that combines methods is *Movers and Shakers*, a study of community power in San Jose, California, by Philip J. Trounstine and Terry Christensen (1982). They did a reputational study, conducted a network analysis, and, finally, looked at actual decisions using a historicojournalistic approach. (One of the authors is a journalist.) The historical analysis helped identify which issues were important. The most important ones included annexation and land use policies, urban renewal, and district versus at-large elections. Research on how decisions were made went beyond the formal decisionmaking to include examination of agenda setting and manipulation of symbols. The authors found that there was indeed a pro-growth power structure. However, the power structure changed over time. Mechanisms evolved to increase democratic participation and flow of information and, hence, the degree of pluralism. These included changes in ownership of the newspaper from local to absentee and the change from at-large to district election of public officials. As pluralism increased, the strength of the pro-growth faction declined.

Further, Trounstine and Christensen found that as ownership of major firms in the area shifted from local to multinational firms, pluralism in fact increased. The multinational firms were very interested in specific decisions directly affecting their operations but less interested in other decisions within the community. Thus, their strategy was to decrease the range of their power but to keep it relatively strong in areas directly affecting their immediate financial interests.

In summary, there are a number of ways to identify which groups and individuals have power. Important vested interests in local communities need to be identified and linked to the exercise of community power. The specific arenas in which power is sought and exercised will mainly be defined by the participating groups.

Who Gains?

Joe and Ellen McDougal were able to enlist Hank Jones's influence in getting lights for the city park baseball diamond. Had the issue been more

270

BOX 11.2   MEASURING THE GROWTH MACHINE

Community power structure can be measured by networks of communication. An important means of communication among corporations is through a common member of their boards of directors. If two corporations are willing to have one or more individuals know the inner workings of both firms, that suggests a certain level of trust if not commonality of goals between the two companies. Thus, one approach to analysis of community power is to discover resource networks of corporations with interlocking directorates. By looking at the functions of the component corporations, the researcher can determine the purpose of those resource networks. This approach was used in a study of interlocking corporate directorates in Manhattan, Kansas. That study showed the existence of a tightly interlocked growth machine.

The two most important industries in Manhattan, Kansas, are Kansas State University and Fort Riley. Fort Riley, a U.S. Army base and home of the First Infantry Division, is located fifteen miles to the west of the city. Manhattan had a population of about 30,000 permanent residents and 15,000 students at the time of the study. The steady growth of the university and expansion of Fort Riley during the two decades preceding the study resulted in a 45 percent growth in the city's population between 1950 and 1970. Thus, the principal private economic activity within the community during that period centered around land development and construction, both residential and commercial.

Annual corporate reports from the Kansas Secretary of State's office provided names of the members of boards of directors of all Manhattan-based corporations with over $100,000 in assets. The names were computerized, and a computer program was developed that identified the most tightly interlocked corporate clusters or cliques. Three large cliques emerged; each was based on one of the three major banks in the community. The Union National Bank clique was the largest and the most densely interlocked of the three:

Union National Bank Clique

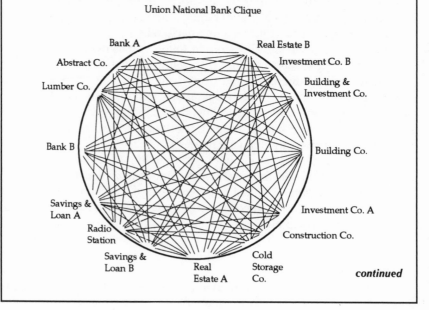

continued

Box 11.2 continued

As can be seen from the figure, nearly all the core corporations in the Union National Bank network were related directly or indirectly to the growth machine. Of the fifteen core companies in the Union National Bank clique, eight were involved in construction, construction supplies, land investment, and real estate. Four were financial institutions, providers of capital for residential and commercial development. The abstract company—the only one in the city—was important in providing members of the growth machine with knowledge of real estate movement because all property transactions within the city and county must be registered with the company. The principal partner in the abstract company was on the boards of five of the development companies and of the Union National Bank. The clique also contained the only radio station in town; it was linked to the only newspaper through common ownership. Among the core firms, the only one that was not part of the growth machine was the ice company, which was started in another era by the two brothers who had historically dominated the Union National Bank and were the preeminent leaders in the community for a couple of decades.

The cliques centered on the other two banks showed a growth-machine orientation also, but were less complete in their control of resources. (The only important growth-machine industry absent from the UNB clique was the city's structural steel and pipe supply firm; it was part of the second-largest clique, that of the First National Bank.) The three major cliques were linked with one another principally through members of local law firms, several of whom were present or past elected officials at the local and state level. Thus, lawyers served not only as gatekeepers to the larger political system but also as the glue that held the various cliques together.

A similar network analysis was conducted for the voluntary-organization sector of the community, and the impact of the corporate sector on the voluntary sector was determined. Persons employed by the firms that were in the corporate cliques were overrepresented (compared with their proportion of the adult population of the city) in the largest and most densely interlocked voluntary clique, which centered on the chamber of commerce, by a factor of twenty-five to one. Other businesspeople were overrepresented by a factor of nine to one. Independent professionals and university and government officials were represented at approximately the same rate as they were in the community as a whole. Finally, the 59 percent of the population that was lower-middle class (clerical and sales workers), working class, and service workers had no representatives on the boards of directors of those voluntary organizations.

This study illustrates how network analysis can be used to assess the presence of a growth machine and to determine the extent to which economic notables are involved in a community's key voluntary organizations.

Source: Jan L. Flora and C. James Killacky. 1975. "The Structure of Economic Resource Networks and Their Influence in the Voluntary Sector of a Small Midwestern City." Unpublished paper. Manhattan: Kansas State University.

272 Power in Communities

sensitive, however, they might not have been so successful. Issues that directly affected Hank's feed and supply store might have had a different outcome. Sociology has long been concerned about power in modern society. A major sociological problem has been which segments of the population gain from what kind of activities.

Studies of community power structure have shown that in different circumstances, different power actors were important. For example, upper-middle-class environmentalists were able to confront the growth machine in certain U.S. cities (Molotch 1970). Other sociological studies show different winners. For example, a study by Clarence Lo suggests that the tax revolt in California began in working-class communities because they were hard-pressed financially and citizens felt that taxes were the reason they had little discretionary income (money to spend once basic expenses were paid). Further, they felt that government was inefficient and uncaring. However, to have an impact, that group was joined by business interests. Ultimately, the tax revolt favored real estate developers (Lo 1990).

From early studies that concentrated on a power elite that exercised monolithic control (Mills 1956), the focus has shifted to particular issues to reveal diversity in who controls what and profits from it. Even rural communities like Small Lake can have complex power structures.

Chapter Summary

Community power is the ability to affect the distribution of both public and private resources within the community. Power can be exercised in three ways—physical force, institutionalized force, and influence. Patterns in the exercise of community power are called community power structure. That structure affects communities and how they function.

Social scientists do not agree about how power is exercised, nor do they agree about how to measure it. Pluralism assumes that the capacity for acquiring power is widely distributed within the population. This model relies on the decisional technique to detect and measure power. Researchers identify controversial public issues and then use the decisionmaking process employed to resolve those issues as a device with which to measure power. The elitist perspective of power assumes that power conforms to the way in which a community is stratified. Power is not widely dispersed but instead held by just a few. Researchers who use an elitist model of power rely on the reputational technique to measure power. Knowledgeable persons in the community are asked to identify those with the greatest reputation for power.

The class-based theory of community power assumes that those who control the economic system control the community. A more recent variation of this model is the growth-machine model. The growth machine is a coalition of groups that perceive economic gain in community growth. This coalition exercises power in order to promote economic growth. The model has been applied successfully to urban areas. Rural communities differ more in terms of whether they project a growth or no-growth orientation.

In order to make power structures more pluralistic, broad participation in setting the community agenda is important. Once the issues are made public, they need to be discussed and debated adequately. However, without the first two steps of community empowerment and broad participation in agenda setting, the final decisionmaking process of discussion, debate, and compromise is relatively meaningless.

Key Terms

Class-based analysis as a theory of power assumes that those who control the economic system control the community.

Community power is the ability to affect the distribution of both public and private resources within the community.

Community power structure is the patterns identified in the exercise of community power.

Decisional technique is the pluralists' preferred strategy for measuring power. Researchers identify controversial public issues and then look at the decision-making process used to resolve those issues. Those who make the decisions are deemed to have power in that issue-area. Frequently, different issues are examined to determine if the same or different people exercise power across issues.

Elitism as a perspective of power assumes that power generally conforms to the system of stratification, and that wealth, prestige, and power tend to be associated with one another.

Exchange value describes the fact that objects such as a house have value to the owner insofar as they can be exchanged for something else.

Growth machine is a coalition of groups that set about to use power to encourage growth and capture its benefits.

Network analysis is a way to measure power by looking at the patterns of linkages between organizations and individuals considered to be important in the community.

Pluralism as a theory of power assumes power is an attribute of individuals and that the capacity for acquiring power is widely distributed within the population.

Power is the ability to make something happen that otherwise would not happen or to prevent something from happening that others wish to make happen.

Rentier class includes those whose principal income derives from rent from or the increase in value of property. It includes landlords of residential, commercial, and industrial establishments and of agricultural land, as well as speculators in land and buildings, including developers.

Reputational technique measures power by asking knowledgeable members of a community to identify those they think have power.

Use value describes the fact that objects such as a house have value to the owner insofar as they can be used or consumed.

References

Crenson, Matthew A. 1971. *The Un-Politics of Air Pollution: A Study of Non-Decisionmaking in the Cities*. Baltimore: Johns Hopkins University Press.

Dahl, Robert. 1961. *Who Governs? Democracy and Power in an American City*. New Haven: Yale University Press.

Domhoff, G. William. 1983. *Who Rules America Now? A View for the '80s*. Englewood Cliffs, NJ: Prentice-Hall.

———. 1967. *Who Rules America?* Englewood Cliffs, NJ: Prentice-Hall.

Hunter, Floyd. 1953. *Community Power Structure.*Chapel Hill, NC: University of North Carolina Press.

Hynes, Eugene, and Verna Mauney. 1990. "Elite Control and Citizen Mobilization in a Small Midwestern Town." *Critical Sociology* 17 (Spring): 81–98.

Lo, Clarence. 1990. *Small Property Versus Big Government: Social Origins of the Property Tax Revolt*. Berkeley: University of California Press.

Logan, John R., and Harvey L. Molotch. 1987. *Urban Fortunes: The Political Economy of Place*. Berkeley: University of California Press.

Lynd, Robert S., and Helen Merrell Lynd. 1937. *Middletown in Transition: A Study in Cultural Conflicts*. New York: Harcourt, Brace, and World.

McGranahan, David A. 1990. "Entrepreneurial Climate in Small Towns." *Regional Science Review* 17:53–64.

Mills, C. Wright. 1956. *The Power Elite*. New York: Oxford University Press.

Molotch, Harvey. 1976. "The City as a Growth Machine." *American Journal of Sociology* 82 (2): 309–330.

———. 1970. "Oil in Santa Barbara and Power in America." *Sociological Inquiry* 40:131–141.

Polsby, Nelson W. 1970. "How to Study Community Power: The Pluralist Alternative." Pp. 297–304 in Michael Aiken and Paul E. Mott (eds.), *The Structure of Community Power*. New York: Random House. Reprinted from *Journal of Politics* 22 (August 1960): 474–484.

Trounstine, Philip J., and Terry Christensen. 1982. *Movers and Shakers: The Study of Community Power*. New York: St. Martin's.

Vidich, Arthur, and Joseph Bensman. 1968. *Small Town in Mass Society*. Princeton, NJ: Princeton University Press.

12

Special Needs

hen Mary and David McTarnahan moved with daughter Amy, who has
mental retardation, to a small town in the Pacific Northwest from Los
Angeles, they were extremely excited. They felt that the small-town
atmosphere would be much better for Amy than the large polluted city
they had left. Yet once they got to Smith City, they found that instead of
becoming easier and more comfortable, life had suddenly become very
difficult for Amy. The local schools did not provide special classes
because there were so few students with mental retardation in the
district. Amy's parents tried to work with the teachers to develop a
special curriculum for her. This proved to be difficult, and several of the
teachers suggested that she stay home or that the McTarnahans look
into putting her in the state institution that could provide classes
designed to respond better to Amy's needs. Suddenly Amy's condition
became a problem.

In this chapter, we examine five populations with special needs: people
with physical or mental impairments, the elderly, the poor, substance
abusers, and illiterates. These are very different types of people with
different types of problems. The problems of each group are often defined
by the community (and at times even by group members) as idiosyncratic
personal problems. Some are seen as inevitable, as in the case of the
impaired and the elderly, and others the fault of the individual, as with
the poor, illiterates, and substance abusers. But in each case, the community can define the problems as ones that have an impact on the whole
community and that therefore require a community response. That response can be paternalistic or participatory. This chapter discusses how
problems initially defined as personal can be redefined as social problems

in ways that allow rural communities to address them more effectively—and in ways that empower the special population.

The Problems of Meeting Special Needs

In urban areas, a number of formal structures have been set up to provide for portions of the population who are disadvantaged and have special needs. These include formal programs in the school for students with mental retardation, formal literacy programs sponsored by school districts, organized daily activity for the elderly, and rehabilitation programs for substance abusers. These programs may be inadequate to the growing need, but both governmental structures and civic organizations have recognized their collective responsibility to provide for those with special needs. In urban areas, these have been defined as social problems requiring citizens to work together through governmental as well as civic organizations to solve them.

THE DENIAL SYNDROME

Providing for such special needs is more often defined as an individual problem in rural areas. Such a reaction is characteristic of the *denial syndrome*. Residents of rural communities have said "We take care of our own" and yet have, in fact, ignored the special needs of special populations. Sometimes denial of a problem is expressed the way it was in Amy McTarnahan's case—an adolescent with mental retardation enters the community and is treated as a disruptive outsider. With other special-need populations, such as the poor, substance abusers, and even illiterates, communities often blame the individual. Local residents feel that if such individuals would just straighten up and take care of themselves, there would not be a problem.

Denying the problem leads to two characteristics of community response to special needs. The first, known by sociologists as *blaming the victim*, is the tendency to treat special populations as people who could change and become like everyone else if they were just motivated to do so. Thus, very often when a community solution is sought, it tends to be in the form of punishment rather than treatment. Children with handicaps are isolated until they become less disruptive. The poor are not given any help unless they convince the community of their willingness to work, and people with problems of substance abuse are ostracized until they make up their minds to give up their bad habits. Blaming the victim absolves the community of any responsibility for having helped cause the problem.

Second, the denial syndrome also allows communities to rely on individual or family rather than community solutions. This, too, can be seen as part of a culture of independence and respect for the family. It is believed that the family should take care of the older person, the person with mental retardation, the poor person, or the individual who abuses chemical substances. Thus, even if such individuals are not punished, they are often ignored, because it is assumed that their families will motivate them to act in a more acceptable fashion.

Problem de. il occurs in both rural and urban areas, but it is more dominant in rural areas for reasons discussed in the chapter on culture (Chapter 3). Residents of a community simply say there is no problem: "We take care of our elderly; the elderly have no problems." "Children who have mental retardation are treated like everyone else. There is no need for special education." "We have no poor here; we are all just folks." "Of course people can read as much as they need to." And finally, "We do not really have a drug problem here, just a couple of troublemaking kids." However, the larger and more heterogeneous population in urban areas makes it easier for advocates of special populations there to organize to provide services. Thus, many of the models for services delivery to special populations are urban ones. They may respond to needs of special populations in rural areas, but the delivery systems often are entirely inappropriate.

ISSUES OF SIZE AND CAPACITY

Cultural aspects of rural communities often make it more difficult to respond to special needs. But lack of response also stems from spatial and economic aspects of rural communities. Because rural areas often consist of small, dispersed, and relatively homogeneous populations with large distances between communities, it is more difficult to find the "critical mass" of users of specific services. State and federa v funded programs require a certain number of users in order to be cos. effective and thus are rarely available in rural areas. Further, the great distances between places makes it very time-consuming for individuals to obtain the specialized services that are offered. Finally, even if there is a critical mass—a large enough number of any kind of special population that would in fact require special services—rural areas are often poorer than urban ones (the poverty rate in nonmetropolitan areas is equal to that in the central city). Communities are unable to fund the programs needed to meet these special needs. Thus, rural areas face the same kinds of problems in serving the needs of special populations as do urban areas. Yet problems are more difficult to solve because of the disadvantages of low population density, distance, and inadequate resources.

Nevertheless, rural communities have some advantages in serving the needs of certain special populations. In many rural areas, people have known each other for a long time and know they can count on one another when times get tough. Informal social ties can mean that formal organizations are not needed. Thus, a handicapped child who has grown up in the community can be integrated into the school system from the beginning. Each teacher knows along the way that special accommodation will be made, and all the children in the classroom help in making sure that this exceptional child is part of the entire school community. This practice of mainstreaming, natural in some rural settings, is now being used in urban areas.

Traditional social networks can be used to help special populations access services. Community members can drive the person needing special treatment to the specialist. These informal networks are often more available in rural areas and can be seen as more responsive to individual needs. Further, their utilization means avoiding costly and sometimes rigid bureaucracies to serve special needs.

Community solutions, when they do occur, are often the task of voluntary associations rather than a responsibility of local government. This puts a heavy burden on rural churches, for example, to organize meals-on-wheels programs and care for the elderly or to provide the kinds of food, clothing, and shelter for the poor, both those who live in the community and those who pass through. Thus, some of the community-level solutions place a huge burden in both time and money on a small proportion of the total community population.

Although few rural communities develop programs that are completely tax-supported, there are some excellent examples of partnerships. Voluntary organizations often provide the labor while tax dollars from the community, the county, and even state and federal sources provide the cash to run the programs. Although not numerous, these programs offer models for responding to special populations when tax dollars are limited. Features of a rural culture, strong social networks, are combined with the sense of collective responsibility often found in urban settings to result in humane and effective responses to the needs of special populations. However, rigid federal and state legislation may hamper the implementation of such innovative solutions.

Categories of Special Needs

Who are those with special needs in rural areas? We briefly examine here five different special-needs populations, particularly with an eye to how some rural communities have responded to their needs and the kinds of locally based solutions that can be provided. These groups are the elderly, the handicapped, the poor, substance abusers, and functional illiterates.

THE ELDERLY

There are increasing numbers of elderly in rural areas, both because of out-migration from resource-based communities of persons in the middle age groups and because of in-migration of retirees to destination-retirement communities (see Figure 2.8 in Chapter 2). There are numerous rural counties with nearly 20 percent of their population above age 65, compared with a national average of 12 percent elderly.

Increasing at an even more rapid rate than elderly people in general are the frail elderly, roughly defined as those individuals 85 and over. These elderly are poorer than the average population and are overwhelmingly female. They tend to live alone, have low incomes, and are often isolated from relatives, who in previous generations would have lived in the same community, providing the basic support to allow a mother or grandmother to maintain her personal independence. Basic domestic activities, such as cooking and cleaning, become more difficult for them to carry out, and there is often an effective shortage of persons available to perform these services, either because many elderly persons cannot afford to pay for them or because of rapid out-migration of young people. Ready access to quality healthcare is also a major problem for this group.

On the whole, older rural Americans tend to have lower incomes, less access to services, less access to transportation, less adequate housing, and poorer health than their urban counterparts (Lapping et al. 1989). Despite these problems, various studies indicate that rural people are happier and just as satisfied with housing and certain other services as their urban counterparts. For instance, although the evidence is to the contrary, rural elderly consider themselves to be in better health than the urban elderly. The relatively high level of satisfaction is probably the result of stronger ties to neighbors and family and of greater community involvement (Lassey et al. 1980).

When extended-family members are present and able to provide daily services to their relatives, rural areas provide an ideal place for the elderly to remain independent. Housing is cheap, and the level of crime is low. The degree of neighborliness in communities means that there are a number of people upon whom one can depend for everything from going to the store to taking one to the hospital in case of emergency. The neighbors will notice if one's newspaper is picked up later in the day than usual and will investigate to find out why. Thus, there is not the need for moving too soon to a group-care facility.

Yet the increasing out-migration of young people from rural communities means that many elderly are left without family support and only

The elderly make up a growing part of rural communities (photo courtesy of The Permanent Art Collection, Kansas State University).

moderate neighbor support. As wage rates have dropped in rural areas, more and more women are entering the formal labor force both for the money and the benefits. This has resulted in lower participation in community organizations, particularly those women's organizations that traditionally provided for the less fortunate, as well as fewer women who devote time to neighboring care. Thus, there has been an increasing need to develop formal mechanisms to provide basic necessities to the elderly.

There are a number of special problems that the rural elderly have, whether they live in declining resource-based communities, growing recreation communities, or other rural areas. Getting to where they need to go becomes problematic because many cannot drive, and public transportation is often limited or nonexistent. Property tax increases that often accompany local efforts at economic development can be a problem for the nonaffluent elderly because they rely heavily on pensions and other sources of fixed income.

Communities that have successfully dealt with the problems of the elderly have acknowledged that (1) elderly people do have special problems and (2) we cannot depend on family or neighbors to solve them. Programs to address these problems are often "nested" because solving one problem reveals another that must also be solved if the first solution is to be effective. Communities have established daycare centers for elderly people who wish to maintain independence and communal dining centers to provide meals for elderly persons unable to cook or too poor to buy food. However, centers for the elderly are only effective if elderly people can get to them. Special transportation systems for the elderly have been put in place in some rural areas to take elderly to the center, to the store, and to the homes of friends and relatives for visits. In many communities, this is the only remaining form of public transportation.

As with other populations with special needs, the elderly are not simply a burden on the community but also a resource. Many communities now try to develop themselves as retirement communities, attracting location-neutral income from the pensions and medical insurance programs of retired individuals. It is also recognized that as this population ages, the burden on the community increases as the provision of services becomes more costly and transfer payments cover a decreasing proportion of those costs.

Elderly people contribute not only their money to the community but also their minds. The elderly can be a tremendous resource for the community through their participation in community affairs. For instance, combining elder care with daycare for children allows for important intergenerational interaction and growth and can be a benefit for both ends of the population continuum (which are often referred to as the dependent population). Further, the experience and wisdom of retired people (elderly and nonelderly alike) can be extremely important in finding alternative solutions to the other problems communities face. In rural communities, people who participated in the past continue to participate once they retire if there is an organizational mechanism available for them to do so. The elderly represent an important resource that can be integrated into provision of community services for a wide variety of groups.

It is important to make sure that when the elderly participate, they not only provide services to other elderly people through senior centers and similar activities but that they also participate in community-wide organizations. Some rural communities that have been retirement-destination communities have found that older in-migrants are less likely than younger in-migrants to support tax increases for social services (Glasgow 1985). If community participation by the elderly is limited to helping only other elderly, large differences in generational values may develop. The elderly need to be part of the entire community to enable them to recognize the importance of investment in future generations as well as the importance of retaining a viable community in the near term.

THE HANDICAPPED

Any population has a wide variety of developmental differences. These differences, as shown in the case of Amy McTarnahan, often mean that if individuals on the disabled end of this continuum do not have special services, they cannot begin to function as other members of the society do. In the case of individuals with disabilities, as well as all special populations, the desire of the community to treat them the same as everybody else conflicts with the need to provide them the kinds of services and mechanisms necessary for them to function as near to their potential as possible.

Service provision is easier in urban communities because their substantial resources and locational advantages enable them to develop facilities and programs for relatively large numbers of handicapped individuals. In rural areas, there will be fewer people with any particular developmental disability, and they will be less likely to be identified because of the moral connotations that often go with such disabilities. For example, in some settings, mental retardation is attributed to sins of the parent rather than normal genetic variations. Thus, these problems are less likely to be identified as social problems and, when identified, less likely to be dealt with.

Very often children and adults with disabilities have special educational needs. In the past, funding for these educational needs has come from the federal government. But in rural communities, in particular, there is still much discussion about whether such students should attend public schools and to what degree they should be integrated into regular classes. For example, should a child with visual impairments be taught braille in the school system (perhaps requiring hiring a special teacher), sent to a special school that is designed specifically to meet his or her needs, or be kept at home to be cared for and taught by parents? Many schools in rural areas with reduced tax bases and reduced federal funding for their programs are facing real dilemmas in how to serve the educational needs of children and young people who have disabilities.

Individuals who have developmental disabilities often have special healthcare needs requiring consistent treatment or therapy. Rural hospitals and mental health centers are currently facing decreased availability of funding and reducing staffs. Further, the ability of rural residents to pay for these healthcare needs is decreasing—they are less likely than urban residents to have health insurance because they are less likely to be employed by the large organizations that offer it. Local hospitals and medical clinics are staffed by generalists rather than the specialists often required by physically handicapped individuals. Specialists are not readily recruited to rural areas. Thus, to serve the healthcare needs of handicapped individuals, it is necessary to provide good referral services as well as transportation services to get mentally and physically impaired people to appropriate therapy and treatment for their particular problems.

Traditionally, rural communities have always accepted the handicapped—those with developmental disabilities are clearly a part of the community. What differs are the attitudes that underlie this acceptance. In traditional societies, individuals who had disabilities were thought to have mystical powers. They were respected and sometimes feared. Some rural communities simply tolerate the handicapped—loving but also patronizing them. Other communities seek to integrate the handicapped into the community by meeting their special needs. Group homes for adults who have developmental disabilities, the provision of access for individuals in wheelchairs, and classroom mainstreaming of children who have developmental disabilities offer a few examples. These programs operate out of a sense of respect for those who are handicapped—respect for their ability to overcome a handicap as well as interest in integrating the handicapped into the community. Communities that learn to recognize, appreciate, and respond to differences in abilities find themselves able to be more flexible in responding to other communitywide problems as well.

THE POOR

In 1989, 15.7 percent of persons living in rural areas had an income below the poverty level, a rate 30 percent higher than in urban areas (U.S. Bureau of the Census 1990). After a steady decline in the post–World War II era, poverty—both rural and urban—leveled off in the 1970s and grew noticeably in the 1980s. After 1979, the gap between rural and urban poverty, which into the early 1970s had steadily narrowed, began to widen once again. In 1986, the rural poverty rate was equal to that in central cities. The gap began to narrow again in 1987, as rural areas belatedly pulled out of the 1982–1983 recession (Table 12.1). However, the rural-urban gap remains greater than it was in the late 1970s.

Poverty grew in rural areas in the 1980s for a variety of reasons. Most important is the fact that in that decade, the quality of industrial jobs in rural areas declined even faster than in urban areas. In the 1970s, rural industrialization grew substantially; urban industrial employment stagnated. Employment of educated and skilled persons grew in rural areas, as did unskilled employment. In contrast, there was unusually high out-migration of skilled and educated persons from rural areas in the 1980s, which reflected the increasingly peripheral nature of the rural economy in

TABLE 12.1 Persons in Poverty, 1986–1989

Type of Residence	Poverty Rates (percent)			
	1986	1987	1988	1989
Metropolitan	12.3	12.5	12.2	12.0
Inside central cities	18.0	18.6	18.3	18.1
Outside central cities	8.4	8.5	8.3	8.0
Nonmetropolitan	18.1	16.9	16.0	15.7

Source: U.S. Bureau of the Census. 1990. *Current Population Reports.* Series P-60, Nos. 160, 161, 166, 168. Washington, DC: U.S. Department of Commerce.

that decade (see Chapter 2 for discussion of peripheral and core industries). This is reflected in lower wage rates and lower benefits.

Although the rural poor are more likely than the urban poor to be in the labor force (Jensen 1988), many of the employment opportunities in rural areas are with companies so small, or in jobs so marginal, that minimum wage and benefit legislation does not cover them. The service sector, which tends to be a low-wage sector, especially in rural areas, has replaced manufacturing as the rural growth sector. Further, there is a strong low-wage ideology in rural areas, which discourages unionization.

Rural communities are noted for their ability to respond to extraordinary tragedies that lead to temporary poverty, such as a fire or more recently, at least in some communities, the farm crisis. As discussed in Chapter 3, rural people tend to feel that proper attitudes lead to hard work. And hard work should lead to material success. Thus, lack of material success—such as an inadequate income or the lack of a decent place to live (preferably owned)—is viewed as a moral failing. Community members often see assistance to those who are out of work or poor as "handouts" that reward such moral failings.

Culture plays an important role in defining how community members distinguish between the "worthy" poor and the "unworthy" poor. The worthy poor are usually seen as those in poverty because of a catastrophe or inexorable processes, such as aging. The unworthy poor are defined as able-bodied individuals without a job.

Rural people are quicker than urban people to categorize poor people as the unworthy poor. An indirect indicator of this is the fact that in a national survey a significantly greater proportion of rural people than urban people (55 percent to 49 percent) responded positively to the question of whether too much is being spent on welfare (based on analysis of National Opinion Research Center (NORC) data, integrated surveys from 1980 to 1990).

However, O'Hare (1988) makes a strong case that according to dominant rural values, a higher proportion of the rural than urban poor are worthy

TABLE 12.2 Welfare Receipt Among Poor Nonmetropolitan and Metropolitan Families, 1987

	Nonmetropolitan	Metropolitan Total	Central City
Families with income below poverty line	15.2%	10.1%	15.4%
Families with income below 0.75 of poverty	10.3%	6.9%	11.2%
Poor families that received welfare income[a]	29.9%	42.1%	50.5%
Mean welfare income[a] among recipient families	$2,928	$3,652	$3,911

[a]Welfare income includes AFDC (aid to families with dependent children) and general assistance. The former is a federal program, the latter a state and local program.

Source: Adapted from Leif Jensen. 1988. "Rural-Urban Differences in the Utilization and Ameliorative Effects of Welfare Programs." *Policy Studies Review* 7 (4): 782–794.

poor. For instance, 62 percent of poor rural adults in 1986 held a job at least part of the year (the comparable figure for the urban poor was 54 percent). The greatest growth in rural poor between 1979 and 1986 was among young adults ages 18 to 44, among whom poverty increased by 55 percent. Does this mean young rural people lack the work ethic? That is hardly the case. A high percentage of these poor young adults—higher than for their urban counterparts—were in the labor force. One quarter of rural poor young adults held two or more jobs. Seventy-two percent of the children of young rural poor came from families having at least one adult working (the comparable urban figure was 59 percent). Also, a higher proportion of rural than urban poor were in married-couple families, were homeowners, and paid taxes, other indicators of solid citizenship that thus place these people among the deserving poor (O'Hare 1988).

The collective view that able-bodied persons in poverty are undeserving has an impact on the behavior of the poor. Because of the shame involved in admitting that one needs help, many rural poor do not seek the assistance that is available to them. The rural poor are less likely than the urban poor to take advantage of the state and federal assistance programs available to them (Table 12.2).

Although they form a lower proportion of the population than their urban counterparts, single parents in rural areas face particularly severe problems. Daycare is generally not available at an affordable price. Single

TABLE 12.3 Poverty Status in Nonmetropolitan Areas by Type of Family, 1989

	Number of Families Below Poverty (in thousands)	Poverty Rate (percent)
All families	1,934	12.5
Families with children under 18	1,394	17.7
Married-couple families	1,053	8.2
Married-couple families with children under 18	626	10.3
All female-headed households	794	37.9
Female-headed households with children under 18	721	47.8

Source: U.S. Bureau of the Census. 1990. *Current Population Reports.* Series P-60, No. 168. Table 23. Washington, DC: U.S. Department of Commerce.

parents who are in a family network often use female relatives to care for children, but increasingly those female relatives have had to join the labor force and are no longer available as babysitters. Thus, the single parent is faced with low wages and lack of daycare. There are some communities, such as Harlan, Iowa, that have instituted a community-supported daycare system with a sliding fee scale that enables single parents and two-parent families in which both spouses work to find reasonable, reliable, quality childcare. However, this kind of activity is the exception rather than the rule.

Growing poverty among young parents means growing poverty among children, who are part of the so-called worthy poor. Increasing poverty among rural children is one of the best-kept secrets in this country. As in urban areas, rural children are now the age group most likely to be in poverty. In 1986, one in four rural children was in poverty. Between 1979 and 1986, the poverty rate among young adults and children grew twice as fast in rural areas as in urban areas. In 1989, the poverty rate among rural families with children under 18 was 41 percent higher than for all rural or nonmetropolitan families. As in U.S. central cities, nearly half of the female-headed families in rural areas with children under 18 were in poverty (U.S. Bureau of the Census 1990). Shown in Table 12.3 are poverty rates in nonmetropolitan areas by family structure.

Another problem of poverty in rural areas is the fact that to gain better-paying jobs, workers need to travel great distances. The cost of transportation and lack of public transportation often force families to depend on old, unreliable automobiles. Not only is getting to work difficult, but it is challenging and costly to get to places to purchase groceries and other necessities at a reasonable price. The declining availability of intercity public transportation as bus and train routes have vanished makes the rural poor even more vulnerable.

The one comparative advantage of living in rural areas for the rural poor is cheap housing. But the high inflation in urban housing prices means that the rural poor who have housing basically are trapped. They are unlikely to be able to move to a place that pays better wages, because they cannot afford the housing costs involved. One of the strategies poor people have developed in rural areas is to send one member of the family to live temporarily in a higher-wage area, often with relatives, while the rest of the family remains at home. Often remaining at home means not having a vehicle and having very little money. Lack of transportation and money in turn limits the family members' ability to participate in community activities. That further isolates the rural poor.

Because of the moral connotations associated with poverty, integrating people who are poor into the rural community is often more difficult than integrating people who are elderly or who have developmental disabilities. Enabling the poor to participate involves providing basic necessities such as healthcare that often must be underwritten, at least partially, on a local basis. Local governments are increasingly pushed to provide healthcare and other welfare programs because of the sharp curtailment of federal funding of social programs in the 1980s and 1990s.

The farm crisis in some communities helped reduce the stigma of poverty and made the needs it represents more legitimate. Many communities responded to the consumption needs of the hardworking poor by such poverty-reducing mechanisms as winter coat trades—members of the community assembled the clothing their children had outgrown, sorted it by size, and then made it available to everyone. Other mechanisms involve such seemingly trivial matters as exchanges of prom dresses; such solutions allow individuals to acquire some of the symbols of normal community participation at minimal investment and therefore participate in mainstream community activities. These kinds of activities do not solve the economic problems of poverty, but they do reduce social isolation of the rural poor and can eventually lead to the inclusion of similar efforts as part of community-level programs.

The able-bodied poor constitute about one-third of all poor people, both rural and urban. The central cause of poverty among the able-bodied rural poor is a lack of employment and low wages. Unemployment is higher in rural than in urban areas, but the rural poor are more likely to work than the urban poor (O'Hare 1988). Economic development efforts that seek to expand quality employment in both urban and rural areas will be the most effective long term antipoverty program. Such an effort must be coupled with educational reform involving substantial investment in upgrading the capabilities of young people, particularly in areas of persistent poverty.

Short-term alleviation of poverty will have to include income transfers and will require political support to increase appropriations for such "welfare" programs. Given the present antiwelfare mood, political support can be gained only for the worthy poor. Children are the most obvious target group. Expansion of aid to families with dependent children (AFDC), the WIC (women, infants, and children) program, and other programs benefiting children (and the families of which they are a part) is likely to be much more effective than the current spate of "workfare" programs. Such an effort has greater chance of success if coalitions are formed among advocate organizations serving the urban and rural poor. Only if the welfare of children becomes defined as a strategic interest of the United States is there a chance of making substantial inroads against poverty.

SUBSTANCE ABUSERS

Another special population in rural areas includes those who abuse chemical substances. Substance abuse is often viewed as an urban problem. Particularly in the 1970s, middle-class families moved to rural areas because they believed smaller communities offered a safer environment in which to raise children. That included the feeling that, among other things, their children could avoid the pressures of drugs and alcohol.

Indeed, earlier studies showed higher rates of drug and alcohol abuse in urban areas. Recent research, however, shows that such differences have largely disappeared. A national study (Lowman 1981) found that heavy weekly drinking among high school students in rural areas exceeds the overall rate for urban areas. Another study shows that rural youths drink less frequently than urban youngsters, but they drink in larger quantities (Newcomb and Sarvela 1988). A recent study of junior and senior high school students in a rural county in northeastern Ohio shows that by the time students are seniors, nearly half of them have driven drunk and over half have ridden with a drunk school-age driver (Sarvela et al. 1990). It is not surprising that alcohol-related deaths in motor vehicle accidents are higher among rural adolescent males than for their urban counterparts.

One of the constraints to identifying alcohol abuse as a social problem requiring a collective response in rural areas is that such activity is viewed as normal. Having "one too many" is viewed as an individual problem rather than an indication of major social dysfunctions that should be collectively addressed by the community. Rural ministers report that attempts to have prevention programs through the churches are met with resistance by the congregations. In some areas, church members feel that people should not drink at all. Drinking is viewed as an individual moral problem rather than a response to societal pressures. Thus, there are no societal solutions, only individual ones.

Drugs are increasingly a problem in rural areas. A recent study of New York State (Treaster 1991) indicated that more upstate New York students were abusing drugs than were their counterparts in New York City. Similar results were obtained in a study of three rural communities in a Rocky Mountain state (Swaim et al. 1986). In the New York study, white students showed higher rates of abuse than black or Hispanic students. These results are consistent with nationwide results on alcohol abuse; black students are much less likely to abuse alcohol than are white students (Lowman 1981). Of course, the problem with these studies is that only students are included. The school dropout rates in New York City are much higher than in the rest of the state, and drug abuse among school dropouts is much higher than among students (Treaster 1991). Still, regardless of whether usage is higher in the cities, it is clear that there is a drug problem in rural America—with alcohol, tobacco, and marijuana being the substances most frequently used by students.

Yet it is difficult for residents of rural areas to admit that these problems amount to anything more than that a few "bad eggs" have brought drugs in from urban areas. Substance abuse treatment and referral services are as underfunded in rural areas as in urban areas, but rural areas face the added difficulties of identifying abusers as people with problems that need to be treated. The tendency is to categorize them as people with moral defects who need to be punished so that they will conform to the community's behavioral standards.

As equally important as treatment is education. Studies of drug and alcohol use indicate that students are experimenting with these substances at an earlier and earlier age. Thus, drug and alcohol education programs— with emphasis placed most heavily on alcohol and tobacco—should be instituted in elementary school (Newcomb and Sarvela 1988; Sarvela et al. 1990). Effective drug education programs are dependent on community recognition of drug usage as a social problem, not simply a moral problem.

ILLITERATES

Conventional wisdom has it that illiteracy is a more serious problem in rural areas. Any discussion of rural illiteracy is difficult, however; it is complicated as much by the diversity found in rural communities as by the changing definitions of literacy. Considered illiterate are those whose skills were once more than adequate for the demands made upon them,

TABLE 12.4 Rural Illiteracy Rates (in percent) Based on Grade-Level Equivalents
(Adults Aged 20 and Older), 1980

	4th Grade	8th Grade	12th Grade
National average	3.8	20.8	37.5
Range of state averages	0.7–8.9	7.8–36.6	19.8–52.6

Source: U.S. Bureau of the Census. 1980. *Part C: General Social and Economic Characteristics.* Washington, DC: U.S. Department of Commerce.

those who have immigrated to rural areas from other countries and who lack skills in English, and those who completed school but did not master the skills needed in today's economy. In addition to the diverse population found in rural areas, the definitions of literacy have changed over time. Most of us grew up thinking of literacy as simply the ability to read and write. This definition guided early strategies for measuring literacy, but it has been replaced by more sophisticated measures and changing societal needs. Around 1930, efforts to define and measure literacy shifted to grade-level equivalents of formal schooling. Early definitions used a third-grade education as the benchmark, but by the 1950s the Census Bureau was using a sixth-grade level. Some states are now looking at definitions of illiteracy based on completion of high school (twelfth-grade equivalency). During the 1970s, literacy was defined in functional terms that explored how well adults applied reading and writing skills to everyday situations. More recent efforts to measure literacy have focused on an adult's ability to process information and apply logical/mathematical reasoning in a variety of everyday tasks.

Despite these different definitions, grade-level equivalents still offer the most detailed description of the number of rural adults who lack needed literacy skills. Adult illiteracy levels in rural areas, based on definitions for fourth-, eighth-, and twelfth-grade equivalencies respectively, are summarized in Table 12.4. Data presented include the national average illiteracy rate as well as the range of state averages for each of the three educational levels selected. Averaged over the nation as a whole, adult illiteracy rates in rural areas increase from 3.8 percent at fourth-grade equivalency to 20.8 percent at eighth-grade equivalency to 37.5 percent at twelfth-grade equivalency.

Regardless of which definition of illiteracy is selected, regional patterns exist. Illiteracy rates are highest across the southern part of the country; this area extends northward to include Kentucky and West Virginia in the East and, to a lesser extent, California in the West. Rates are lowest in New England and across much of the Great Plains, the Rocky Mountain

TABLE 12.5 Rural Illiteracy Rates (in percent) Based on Grade-Level Equivalents (Adults Aged 20-24), 1980

	4th Grade	8th Grade	12th Grade
National average	0.9	5.3	21.7
Range of state averages	0.3–2.1	1.4–11.2	9.5–33.2

Source: U.S. Bureau of the Census. 1980. *Part C: General Social and Economic Characteristics.* Washington, DC: U.S. Department of Commerce.

states, and the Pacific Northwest. The patterns seem independent of the extent to which a state's population lives in rural areas. Vermont, with more than 65 percent of its population classified as rural, has illiteracy rates lower than Oregon, with 37 percent of its population considered rural. Much of the Southeast is extremely rural, but states such as Idaho, Maine, and Iowa have significantly lower rates of adult illiteracy despite equally sizable portions of rural populations. Thus, ruralness by itself does not seem to explain the different rates of rural adult illiteracy found across the fifty states.

Historically, educational levels have been lower in rural areas. Until the middle part of this century, poorer quality schools in many rural areas, coupled with relatively lucrative job opportunities in natural-resource–based activities, meant that rural youth often left school at an earlier age than did urban youth. Throughout much of the Great Plains, however, rural schools now report some of the lowest dropout rates nationwide. As machines have replaced workers in natural-resource–based economies, rural youth have been drawn into the same economy as urban youth. Thus, it seems relevant to ask how adequately this picture predicts the future.

Table 12.5 presents the illiteracy data for the youngest cohort (those aged 20–24 in 1980) of the population described in Table 12.4. Rural rates of illiteracy are less than 1 percent at the fourth-grade level and increase to more than 20 percent at the twelfth-grade level. For the young adult, the most sizable increase in rural illiteracy occurs when the definition shifts from an eighth-grade equivalent to a twelfth-grade equivalent. This contrasts with the adult sample as a whole, for which the two increases (fourth-grade to eighth-grade equivalent and eighth-grade to twelfth-grade equivalent) are about the same.

Regardless of the segment of the rural population examined, rural illiteracy rates remain a serious problem. The character of the problem is not uniform across the fifty states, however. Nor is the problem among younger rural adults as serious as it was for those a generation ago. As rural economies change and increased literacy skills become a necessity, however, rural illiteracy will remain a barrier to statewide and local development efforts. The most serious and persistent problems occur across the South, Southwest, and Appalachia.

Given the size of this special population, how can rural communities respond? Illiteracy is a problem that has gained national attention. Federal and state funds have been directed to a vast array of programs, some relevant to rural settings and others not so relevant. In general, educational programs designed to respond to those with limited literacy skills are quite diverse. In a survey of rural literacy programs, more than 3,000 programs were found to be affiliated with some fifteen different agencies. Most programs are linked to schools, libraries, or local literacy councils. These programs face the common problems of reaching a dispersed population with limited funds. Although several projects are experimenting with technology, principally television and videotapes, to reach rural populations, these strategies are not yet widespread. Some projects have found the local newspaper to be an effective vehicle for literacy instruction.

Perhaps the most challenging aspect of rural literacy practice is to develop strategies that reach those least willing to participate in programs. Communities that have integrated literacy into some other community activity, such as community development efforts, have found themselves more successful at serving hard-to-reach populations. Programs that use former clients as integral parts of program planning and client recruitment also experience greater levels of success. In general, however, most rural literacy programs are extremely fragile—dependent on the stamina of one or two very dedicated individuals.

Paternalism Versus Participation

The traditional way of dealing with special populations or special problems has been an individualistic, paternalistic one. Paternalism involves the person with power giving to the individual certain goods and resources in expectation that the recipient will be properly grateful and subservient. Paternalism includes particularism: Whether a person receives help is determined by the degree to which the donor controlling the resources views the potential donee as worthy. Worthiness is related more to being properly grateful than being in actual need. Further, paternalistic approaches tend not to have widespread community support. Instead such aid depends on particular individuals and how they feel when approached by the person wanting a favor. And the aid given is indeed a favor received—it involves personal obligation on the part of the receiver to the giver.

An alternative model to paternalism in addressing the needs of special populations is participation. Participation means that the community as a whole takes collective responsibility for the problem and its solution. Further, to the degree possible, the special population itself will be part of the community solution to the problem. Thus, a participatory model involves the community taking responsibility by providing services to the special population through voluntary organizations and local governments. Special populations also work together to meet the problems. Elderly people form senior centers and senior groups to deal with their own problems and those affecting the community as a whole. Individuals who have disabilities form support groups that enable them to participate in larger community activities and decisionmaking. As the special population participates in decisions on how to deal with their own problems, they begin to understand how they can contribute to solutions to other community problems as well.

Substance abusers can form support groups such as Alcoholics Anonymous to provide support to people attempting to change their use of addictive substances. These groups participate in educating the community as a whole about the problems of drug and alcohol abuse. Drug and alcohol education in the schools would include peer education.

People who are illiterate can participate in programs to increase the educational level of all people in the community. For example, in Ivanhoe, Virginia, graduates of basic literacy courses went on to a GED (general equivalency diploma) program that they helped organize, then began to set up college classes. These classes were qualitatively different from those traditionally offered because they were designed by the students themselves to meet their collective needs.

People who are poor can organize to set up cooperative mechanisms to meet mutual needs. They can also work with local communities to determine objective ways of defining cases in the community in which basic requirements for food, shelter, and clothing are not met. When services must be provided, such as housing or daycare, those in need can organize to determine how these services can best be provided. These solutions involve local commitment to providing resources to enable people in poverty to live as integrated a life as possible within the community and thus contribute to its betterment. Provision of transportation services, school lunch and breakfast programs, clothing exchanges, and public housing all contribute to a better quality of life within the community and a broader range of talent participating in solving a spectrum of communitywide problems.

Access Versus Choice

Although the McTarnahans still face problems in getting Amy some of the special services she needs, they no longer face a reluctant school system. Federal regulations require schools to provide programs that integrate children who have mental or physical handicaps into the life of the school. Amy attends some regular classes and then spends the rest of her day working on an individualized educational plan designed to respond to her special needs.

In many respects, Amy and her friends at school both benefit. Amy learns to function in a normal social environment, and her friends learn to broaden that environment to include those who have physical or mental handicaps. Access to education has been extended to a special population in ways that enrich the experience of the community as a whole. The only problem is the cost. Smith City's school budget was extremely tight, so the special education programs simply increased pressure on local taxes.

Few question the appropriateness of special education programs, but many rural communities struggle with the increased costs created by federal and state mandates. As the mandates increase, communities find themselves in a paradoxical situation. The very institutions, such as schools, for which the mandates sought increased access become too expensive for the community to maintain.

This tension between access and choice has remained a recurring theme in responding to the needs of special populations. Federal and state governments assume responsibility for ensuring access by introducing mandates that require an array of services to be made available to special populations. Faced with the responsibility for raising funds to provide these services, local governments call for increased choice about which services are appropriate to the needs of the community and about how those services should be provided. What seems most necessary are policies that ensure access but encourage diversity, based on the needs and resources of local communities.

Chapter Summary

Providing for special needs of special populations is more difficult in rural areas because of distance, cost, lack of critical mass, and labeling that attributes such special needs to individual moral deficiencies. Yet rural areas can provide alternative solutions through participation more easily than urban areas can because of the existing social networks and the smaller scale involved. Rural areas thus have the potential (and in a few cases, have demonstrated such leadership) for addressing problems that face all communities, rural or urban, with viable solutions that involve participation of both the special populations and the community as a whole.

Key Terms

Blaming the victim describes explanations that assume deviant behavior is entirely the fault of the individual. These explanations assume that the community or society did not contribute either directly or indirectly to the problems faced by special populations.

Denial syndrome describes the tendency of some rural communities to deny that a special population exists. Community members see any problem as being one for which individuals are responsible.

References

Glasgow, Nina. 1985. "Newcomers from Cities Support Rural Growth and Development." *Rural Development Perspectives* 1 (2): 7–9.

Jensen, Lief. 1988. "Rural-Urban Differences in the Utilization and Ameliorative Effects of Welfare Programs." *Policy Studies Review* 7 (4): 782–794.

Lapping, Mark B., Thomas L. Daniels, and John W. Keller. 1989. "Special Populations: The Poor, the Elderly, and Native People." Pp. 299–312 in Lapping, Daniels, and Keller, *Rural Planning and Development in the United States*. New York: Guilford.

Lassey, Marie L., William R. Lassey, and Gary R. Lee. 1980. "Elderly People in Rural America." Pp. 21–37 in William R. Lassey, Marie L. Lassey, Gary R. Lee, and Naomi Lee (eds.), *Research and Public Services with the Rural Elderly*. WRDC Publication #5. Corvallis, WA: Western Rural Development Center.

Lowman, Cherry. 1981. "Facts for Planning: Prevalency of Drinking Among Senior High School Students." *Alcohol Health and Research World* 6 (1): 29–38.

Mead, Lawrence M. 1986. *Beyond Entitlement: The Social Obligations of Citizenship*. New York: Free Press.

Newcomb, Paul R., and Paul D. Sarvela. 1988. "Familial Factors Related to Rural Youth Drinking Practices." *Human Services in the Rural Environment* 12 (1): 6–10.

O'Hare, William P. 1988. "The Rise of Poverty in Rural America." *Population Trends and Public Policy #15*. Washington, DC: Population Reference Bureau.

Sanders, Jimmy M. 1991. "'New' Structural Poverty." *Sociological Quarterly* 32(2): 179–199.

Sarvela, Paul D., Deborah Jenkins Pape, and Srijana M. Bajracharya. 1990. "Age of First Use of Drugs Among Rural Midwestern Youth." *Human Services in the Rural Environment* 13 (3): 9–15.

Swaim, Randall, Fred Beauvias, R. W. Edwards, and E. R. Oetting. 1986. "Adolescent Drug Use in Three Small Rural Communities in the Rocky Mountain Region." *Journal of Drug Education* 16(1): 57–73.

Treaster, Joseph B. 1991. "Study Finds Drug Use Isn't Just Urban Problem." *New York Times* October 1:A16.

U.S. Bureau of the Census. 1990. *Current Population Reports*. Series P-60, Nos. 160, 161, 166, 168. Washington, DC: U.S. Department of Commerce.

Wilson, William Julius, and Robert Aponte. 1985. "Urban Poverty." *Annual Review of Sociology* 11:231–258.

13

Generating Community Change

When Sue James and her husband Bart moved to New Richland, a service-center town in the upper Midwest, they were excited about the clean air and the neighborliness that made it different from their previous residence in St. Louis. But they soon found that there were some advantages of a larger setting that they really missed, particularly in terms of recreation. Further, there were few summer jobs for teenagers.

Bart, the new superintendent of schools, often met for coffee with a group of local farmers and businesspeople and found that several of them shared his interest in golf. All would appreciate a chance to play locally. After they discussed it further with friends who shared their enthusiasm, they decided to open the project up for town consideration.

Bart and Sue placed a notice in the local paper announcing an open meeting to discuss construction of a community golf course. Forty people appeared. Committees were set up to consider possible sites and organizational structures. At the next meeting over a hundred people were present. All of the meetings were reported in detail in the local paper.

The site committee presented four potential sites that in the following weeks were visited by most of the members of the town, even those who did not play golf. At the next community meeting, which was attended by several hundred, the pros and cons of each site were presented. The assembly voted on which site to choose, and the farmer who owned it agreed to sell it at the market price for agricultural land. The local community development corporation established in the early 1970s was used to raise money for the project, and in just two months the purchase price was raised through donations and selling local shares in the golf course.

The golf course was laid out, and local farmers donated time and equipment to help the city do the construction necessary, including drilling two wells, one for the clubhouse and one for the fairways and greens. A separate community golf course corporation was established, a manager/golf professional was hired, and the club was off and running! A local couple established a concession stand at the course, and the pro set up a pro shop. Students found work in the summers as grounds keepers and caddies, local people were now able to play (and many learned the game), and the course proved an attraction for out-of-town players who found its riverside location attractive and the well-kept nine holes a pleasure to play.

Sue and Bart feel even more a part of the community because of their participation in the creation of the golf course. The community has an additional asset in terms of residents making an investment in themselves, and the economic benefits to the community through creation of new jobs and the attraction of outsiders to the community have proved to be unanticipated benefits of the project.

Community development occurred in New Richland because of its social infrastructure. Local people invested in themselves. They were able to mobilize many sectors of the community to work together to make things happen. In New Richland, with its history of self-investment and community participation, such activities were relatively easy to undertake. Economic development was a result of but not the major motivation for the golf course project.

In other communities, community change seems almost hopeless. New people move to town with great dreams for community improvement. Or local residents concerned about a declining economic base seek to attract industry, with ever-decreasing likelihood of success. What makes the difference between towns that develop and change in response to felt needs and those that seem unable to respond effectively to the current climate of economic deterioration in most rural areas? What are the components of community development, and what makes it happen?

This chapter examines three models of community development. The assumptions behind them are followed by illustrations of how they can be and have been implemented. The three models are then compared in terms of their linkages to the outside and their approaches to the planning process. Then two approaches to *economic development* are introduced and related to the three models of community development.

Community and Economic Development

Central to the concept of community development is the idea of *collective agency*. Collective agency is the ability of a group of people—in this case those living in the same community—to solve common problems together. For community development—and collective agency—to occur, people in a community must (1) believe that working together can make a difference and (2) organize to address their shared needs collectively.

Community development is much broader than economic development. Indeed, one could argue that economic development could be antithetical to community development for two reasons: Economic development (1) does not necessarily involve collective agency and (2) may not result in an improvement of the quality of life. For instance, the high rates of economic growth in the boomtowns we have previously examined negatively affect community development. Incomes at least of some members of the community may increase, but as negative factors appear—crime rates increase, schools become overcrowded, housing prices soar, neighborliness declines—quality of life for the majority of the residents may deteriorate. This is particularly true when the economic growth is triggered by an absentee firm in the community, whether it be an oil or coal company, a national meat packer, a recreational conglomerate, or a transnational manufacturing company.

When we look at *community development*, we focus on what local people do to improve the overall quality of life of the community. In the difficult economic times of the 1990s, economic development is seen as the dominant means for community betterment. But bringing jobs is not enough. And bringing the wrong type of jobs may decrease the community quality of life. Discussed next are approaches taken by community members and leaders to improve their collective well-being and how these approaches relate to collective agency.

Models of Community Development

Community problem-solving does not take place automatically, even in a community like New Richland. Problems must be identified, potential solutions considered, organizational means put in place, and resources mobilized. There are a number of models of community development that can facilitate these steps. Explored here are the alternative models and how they might serve in different types of communities.

Three major approaches to community development have been laid out by Christenson (1989): self-help, technical assistance, and conflict. Each of the approaches involves several differences: role for the change agent, orientation (task versus process), clientele, image of the individual, con-

His future depends on communities as well as a livelihood (photo courtesy of the U.S. Department of Agriculture).

TABLE 13.1 Comparison of Three Models for Community Development

	Self–Help Model	*Technical-Assistance Model*	*Conflict Model*
Change agent	Facilitator, educator	Adviser, consultant	Organizer, advocate
Task/process orientation	Process	Task	Process and task
Typical clientele	Middle class	Leaders, administrators	Poor, minorities
Image of individual	Inherently good, but goodness is suppressed	System-defined player of roles	Oppressed
Basis of change	People can identify and solve problems collectively	Science provides a means to solve problems	Power is the most basic of all resources
Core problems addressed	Capacity of people to take collective action	Capacity to harness science to solve human problems	Concentration of power in the hands of a few persons
Action goal	Community capacity	Technical problem	Redistribution of power

Source: Adapted from James A. Christenson. 1989. "Themes of Community Development." In James A. Christenson and Jerry W. Robinson, Jr. (eds.), *Community Development in Perspective.* Ames: Iowa State University Press.

ception of the basis of change, core problem to be addressed, and action goal (see Table 13.1).

SELF-HELP MODEL

The *self-help model* emphasizes process: people within the community working together to arrive at group decisions and taking actions to improve their community. The process is more important than any particular task or goal. In this model of community development, the aim is to institutionalize a process of change based on building community institutions and strengthening community relationships rather than to achieve any particular development objective.

The New Richland golf course contains major elements of self-help community development because putting it into place involved reinforcing patterns of community interaction, cooperation, and decisionmaking. The change agents, the school superintendent and his wife, acted as facilitators

Generating Community Change

for community input rather than as the source of all knowledge about golf courses. People viewed the project as something they decided together rather than the result of the best technical advice.

The golf course project took a while to get off the ground because of the large number of meetings required to get everyone's input, form the appropriate committees, and respond to each committee's reports and suggestions. Yet once the golf course was established, it was easy to make it part of the public agenda in terms of both local participation in running it and in convincing city government to participate in its maintenance.

The self-help model is a whole-community approach and is usually led by members of the middle class. The decision to build a golf course in New Richland before obtaining communitywide input was related to the fact that Sue and Bart James were definitely middle class. Those who play golf as well as those who have the means to contribute equipment or invest in shares in a community corporation tend to be relatively secure financially. However, if the New Richland project had been a purely self-help effort and had involved persons from various classes and social groups, the initiators would probably have begun with a more diffuse goal, such as increasing recreational opportunities in the community. The decision to build a golf course—or an alternative recreational facility, such as a lighted softball diamond—would have been part of the process rather than the reason for devising the process.

As discussed by Littrell and Hobbs (1989), the self-help model makes a number of assumptions about the structure of the community. When these assumptions do not apply to a community, self-help as a strategy will be difficult to implement. These assumptions include (1) that community members have a similarity of interest and that community development involves building consensus; (2) that generalized participation and democratic decisionmaking within the community are necessary and possible; and (3) that the community has a degree of autonomy such that community actors can in fact influence the community's destiny.

A central assumption in the self-help model of community development is that communities are homogeneous and consensus-based. In fact, despite the norm of "we're all just folks" in many rural communities, most communities have increasing disparities in income and access to other resources. Thus, development efforts that depend on existing local leaders for community organizing may systematically bias development efforts away from the problems of the least advantaged citizens. That, in turn, can give rise to increased inequalities and increasing poverty or to conflict-based community development activities. In fact, interests within communities can conflict, as we saw in the case of power structure (Chapter 11).

Education can be an important part of the self-help process. Women in Ivanhoe, Virginia, successfully integrated personal and community goals (photo courtesy of the Ivanhoe Civic League).

Participation and democratic decisionmaking are essential to the self-help model of development. The self-help approach assumes that it is indeed possible to motivate a broad-based band of community members to participate in community affairs. However, if community residents are uninterested or unmotivated and do not want to become involved, participation will not take place. Some groups of local residents will not see the community as relevant to their welfare, as happens, for example, with some farmers who feel their well-being depends almost entirely on government programs. Thus, farmers may simply bypass the community and be actively involved only in their commodity organizations that focus on the national and not on the community level. If in a particular community no farmers are active participants in efforts to solve community problems, broad-based community participation cannot be said to exist—one important segment of the community is uninvolved.

Because the self-help model focuses on the process rather than the outcome, wide participation is important. Even if the stated objectives of the specific project were met, the success of the effort is judged in terms of the extent of community involvement. If the quality of community interactions was not enhanced, the process cannot be used to solve another community problem. In a word, the process was not institutionalized; from the self-help point of view, the effort was not successful.

One obstacle to effective use of the self-help approach in small towns is the fact that people know each other in too many roles. Thus, the risk of taking a public stance, which is sometimes necessary for effective discussion, is worrisome because it may result in public disagreement with a boss, a customer, or a colleague. This risk is seen as too great in many small towns (see Chapter 3 for a discussion of role homogeneity).

Further, different segments of the community have different levels of participatory skills. Higher education and professional employment give a disproportionate voice to the more privileged segments of any community, in part because they have practice in participation. As mentioned in the discussion about legacy (Chapter 4), middle-class youth are raised with verbal and discussion skills, whereas obedience—until a confrontation situation arises—is part of working-class socialization patterns.

Finally, self-help models of development assume a significant degree of community autonomy. Yet as shown in earlier chapters, rural communities are highly involved in regional, national, and even international networks that have enormous impacts on them. Being dependent on the global economy, however, does not mean that it is useless for communities to undertake self-help activities. But it does make it important that the global economic trends be understood. For example, self-help efforts at attracting branch industrial plants to rural communities were often successful in the 1970s. They will only infrequently be effective in the 1990s because of restructuring of the global economy. Part of the process of the self-help model therefore includes community education about the community's place in the global economy and the current trends within it.

TECHNICAL-ASSISTANCE MODEL

In contrast to the self-help model, the *technical-assistance model* stresses the task to be performed. A few local leaders might decide that the community needs a golf course. After talking among themselves in private, they call in technical experts to assess the local situation and to find the most efficient way to build and run it. Golf course construction might require obtaining government grants or finding a private investor. The method of funding would be determined by the consultant and the local leaders. The site would be chosen based on objective criteria determined by experts in golf course construction. The success of the project would be based on the presence or absence of a golf course at the end of a prescribed period. The combination administrator–golf pro would be chosen on technical criteria. If a capable administrator were found, the project would continue. However, if the club pro proved inefficient or dishonest, it would be up to the town leaders (if the course is publicly owned) or the board of directors (if it is privately owned), not users of the golf course or its employees, to correct the situation. Limited oversight could then lead to limited success.

It is assumed in this approach that answers to community problems can be arrived at scientifically. The problems themselves are phrased in technical terms that call for expert advice regarding choices among a variety of technically feasible options. In this approach, local residents desiring to participate in decisions must assimilate and absorb a great deal of information concerning complex legal and scientific issues. This greatly decreases motivation to participate. A common response is to assume that there is only one technically appropriate choice and, thus, the experts should be left alone to make it.

Another assumption of the technical-assistance approach is that development should be evaluated based on the achievement of predetermined measurable goals. Not only is the achievement of the goal important, but equally so is the efficiency with which it is achieved. Cost-benefit analysis, a technical tool developed by economists to determine the ratio of costs to benefits to the public of projects, is a particularly appropriate tool for this approach. Local citizens are defined as consumers of development— not participants in it.

Government bureaucracies are the most frequent employers of the technical-assistance approach. This approach often works to the advantage of the power structure, which typically is able to set the agenda (see Chapter 11). The power structure is frequently able to prevent a particular problem from reaching the level of public discussion or, in other cases, to prevent certain technically feasible solutions to a publicly defined problem from being considered as realistic options.

The extent to which rural communities often focus on the recruitment of industry as the most feasible strategy for local economic development illustrates how politics interacts with the technical-assistance model. Successful growth machines are able to define such recruitment as an essential economic development objective, especially in communities experiencing a loss of services or population. This is done by identifying recruitment of industry as the only technically feasible alternative for generating new employment; the message is carried by influential organizations such as the chamber of commerce or the community development office of the city. In fact, other economic development options may be better. In a declining community where the elderly are a high proportion of the population, for example, transfer payments (social security, Medicare and Medicaid, private pensions, health insurance) are a large portion of community income. A program for development of locally owned services used by retirees would keep that money circulating in the community and could perhaps generate more employment and greater employment stability and income than would a potential new factory. But in most cases, recruitment of industry wins out because the elderly-income multiplier does not even reach the agenda. Furthermore, companies considering a move do not want it publicized until the decision is final. Also, they prefer to deal with a single person who represents the entire community. Both of these facts militate against broad community participation in efforts to recruit industry.

THE CONFLICT MODEL

The *conflict model* is similar to the self-help model in that it brings people together to articulate their needs and problems, to develop indigenous leadership, and to help organize viable action groups (Christenson 1989, 37). It is different from self-help in that it seeks to redistribute power. A major organizing tool is to confront those forces seen as blocking efforts to solve problems. Using a conflict approach, a group of local people outside the local power structure would come together to discuss their problems and needs. Those could include recreation and job creation. As the golf course project was put forward by the elite of the town, the group seeking empowerment would mount a counterproposal—a local swimming pool—that would also create jobs and provide recreation for the young people and poorer members of the community who could not afford golf clubs or lessons.

Instead of either calling in outside experts or working in an informal fashion with local elites to mobilize local resources, the conflict-oriented group would identify a potential site and then approach the city council and the local landowner with the demand that the land be donated or purchased. The organizers would focus on building strong groups to make these demands, stressing the lack of recreational facilities, particularly for the less well-to-do members of the community who cannot drive to other communities. Emphasis would be on the obligation of those with power within the community—the city council and local landowners—to act responsibly in response to the needs of the community.

Another conflict-model scenario would be that once the golf course was established, the group would demand access to the course for youth, minorities, and the elderly and call for subsidized transportation and public equipment for these users. In this way, the principle of community-wide access to collective resources would be enforced.

The conflict approach to community development has urban origins. The approach was codified by Saul Alinsky (1969), who began as a community organizer in Chicago in the 1930s in a Polish neighborhood known as Back of the Yards. By working with the residents in the working-class community to identify their grievances, the organizers helped them make specific demands of the city government. This methodology has been expanded to black organizing in Chicago; Rochester, New York; Boston; and Kansas City. It has been the basis of organization of the United Farm Workers; Caesar Chavez trained with Alinsky's group. ACORN (Association of Community Organizations for Reform Now), founded by Wade Rathke in 1970 based on Alinsky's organizing principles, has worked hard to implement and refine conflict methodology. Many community organizers around the country continue to use and modify the approach, including the Land Stewardship Project that organizes farmers in Minnesota.

Alinsky says that the world and, hence, any community is "an arena of power politics moved primarily by perceived immediate self-interests" (1971, 12). Although the technical-assistance approach views the existing power structure as having the interests of the community at heart, the conflict approach is deeply suspicious of those who have formal community power.

The conflict approach assumes that power is never given away—it always has to be taken. The goal of the conflict approach is to build a people's organization to allow those without power to gain it through direct action. Because organizations of the powerless do not have access to significant monetary resources, they must rely on their numbers. Their numerical strength is only realized through organizational strength.

Such organizations must be democratic and participatory. Alinsky believed that downtrodden people (whom he called the Have Nots, as opposed to the wealthy Haves and the Have-Some, Want-More middle class) acquire dignity through participation. Their experience is that of being denied participation, treatment central to their being Have Nots. He saw democracy and participation instrumentally—as means, not ends. The overall ends of community organizing should be such things as equality, justice, or freedom. But in an open society such as the United States, undemocratic organization by the Have Nots can negate those ends.

Alinsky also placed emphasis on the learning process. Organizing should be accompanied with a conscious effort to broaden horizons. Such education then helps prevent the Have Nots, once they become Have Some, Want Mores, from acting in their immediate narrow self-interest. Learning of this type, he felt, rarely takes place in schools, which serve to immobilize or disarm those without power. Indeed, Alinsky studied sociology in college and quit in disgust.

Learning what carries one beyond the narrow interests of one's class is not that common even among those who were once Have Nots—hence the duality of reality. An institution that originally served the interests of the downtrodden may come to serve the needs of the rich. For instance, the Tennessee Valley Authority brought electricity to the people of the "hollers" in the Cumberland Mountains, then later encouraged the strip mining of those same mountains and hollows. By the 1960s, the people Alinsky organized in Back of the Yards in the 1930s had become opposed to the empowerment of blacks who sought to use the same tactics they had used a quarter century earlier.

The Three Models in Operation

Now that the basic assumptions and characteristics of each approach have been discussed, we turn to how the three approaches are implemented.

SELF-HELP APPROACH

The self-help approach can be implemented in many ways. One of the most common set of steps of implementation, stressed by such existing community development entities as cooperative extension services, is the social-action process. The stages of this approach are described through the use of the acronym SOCIAL, which stands for study, organize, commit, incorporate, act, and look back ("The Social Action Process" 1987). The study phase (problem identification) is usually carried out by members of an existing organization in the community who are alerted to the existence of the problem by one or more persons in or outside that organization.

The steps of the SOCIAL phases are as follows:

S Study
  1. Recognize the social system by clearly identifying the system in which the action will take place.
  2. Consider previous social-action situations: What have been the community's past experiences with organized change?
  3. Identify the problem or opportunity.

O Organize
  4. Initiate the idea and bring together a small group of people who believe something should be done about it. This group becomes the *initiating set*, the "idea people."
  5. Legitimize the idea by getting respected members of the community to support it. The legitimizers may be formal or informal leaders and "may have power because of money, prestige, a key position, knowledge, or correct judgment in the past."
  6. Diffuse the idea. At this point, the idea becomes public and a new group of people become involved in convincing the others in the community that a problem or opportunity exists. It is at this point that a town meeting may be held.

C Commit
7. Establish the need by using one or more of these techniques: providing basic education through information-gathering groups, program development committees, or study groups; competing with other communities ("If they did it, why can't we?"); conducting a trial project; building on past experience; channeling gripes; or carrying out a needs survey or questionnaire.
8. Get commitment in public that individuals will give time or money to the enterprise.
9. Set goals with specific time periods and task assignments with objectives written down and communicated to all concerned.

I Incorporate
10. Determine means through discussion of the alternatives possible to meet the goals.
11. Develop a plan, which should identify a time schedule, committee organization, types of personnel needed, buildings required, visual aids needed, methods and techniques to be used, needs for meetings, and means of publicity. All participants must know their part and have a "job description."
12. Organize resources, including time, people, information, money, in-kind contributions, and physical facilities. In this step, it is crucial to fit the person to the job. Those doing the work should be recognized publicly and often.

A Act
13. Launch the program, usually through a major event such as a fund drive, a kickoff dinner, a full-page newspaper ad, or a big publicity campaign.
14. Follow through. Make sure that all complete their assigned tasks and keep others informed about progress of the project.

L Look back
15. Evaluate progress at the end of each step and at the end of the process.

This approach places heavy reliance on agenda setting by the existing power structure. Recognizing the cozy relationship with traditional community leaders that this approach represents, and seeing the need for more rapid change as resource-based communities experience serious problems of out-migration, unemployment, and decline of services, advocates of the approach developed by cooperative extension services have modified it so as to incorporate broad community participation in the problem-identification phase rather than wait until the organize-to-sell phase. Involving a broad spectrum of organizations and occupations in strategic planning and holding open town meetings offer approaches that draw the wider community into identifying problems.

TECHNICAL-ASSISTANCE APPROACH

In the pure technical-assistance approach, a local entity, either a local government or a private entity such as a chamber of commerce, calls upon an outside expert either to (1) develop and assess the effectiveness and efficiency of alternative solutions to a particular problem or (2) design the most efficient way to perform a certain task (that is, develop a predetermined solution to a predetermined problem). In the latter instance, which represents the vast majority of technical-assistance consultancies, the expert does not question the task assigned or how it was determined that this particular problem was important. The expert merely develops a plan for how the solution can be implemented.

At times technical assistance can be delivered by local experts such as planners. They generally receive their orders from local or regional government officials. They usually define how to perform a particular task efficiently; defining what the task should be is reserved for the politicians.

Mark Lapping and his colleagues (1989) outline the steps planners should undertake for effective economic development. In the technical-assistance approach, an individual with technical competence is called upon to complete each step in the process. Clearly these steps can also contribute to the self-help approach; the degree to which such integration is feasible depends on who decides what and who carries out each step.

1. Gather information and data
2. Identify the problem
3. Analyze the problem
4. Develop goals and objectives
5. Identify alternative solutions
6. Select a solution
7. Implement the solution
8. Enforce the plan
9. Monitor the effort and give feedback
10. Readjust the solution

CONFLICT APPROACH

Because of the control exercised by the existing power structure, the conflict approach is generally catalyzed by an outside organizer going into the community. These are the steps generally followed to build a permanent, multiple-issue community organization for achieving local members' interests and to link with other like-minded groups across the state and nation:

A. An outside organizer enters the community, usually at the request of a local group wanting change. The organizer

1. Appraises the local leadership, looking at both formal and informal institutions in the community.
2. Analyzes the community power structure. Who has power and what are their vulnerabilities and strengths?
3. Analyzes the situation and the territory. In particular, what seem to be the major problems, what conflicts would different attempted solutions lead to, and which of those conflicts are winnable?

B. The organizer and her or his new allies build a people's organization by

4. Stimulating those outside the power structure to voice their grievances. The organizing process must provide opportunities for people to express anger and overcome fear. Creating an organizing committee of community leaders and canvassing residents in their homes are both effective strategies.
5. Synthesizing the grievances into a statement of the problem. An effective strategy for this has been neighborhood house meetings. For the conflict approach to be effective, it must concentrate on a single issue at a time, although the organization cannot be a single-issue organization. The issue selected should be winnable.
6. Giving the problem organizational form by developing alliances with existing organizations of the disenfranchised, by bringing them together in new organizations where necessary, and by forming alliances with groups of potential sympathizers.

C. The coalition engages in direct action by

7. Demonstrating the value of the power of a large number of people working together to make gains from the traditional power structure through direct action. In particular, to retain legitimacy, people's organizations need to produce a stable supply of what public administration expert Sherry Arnstein (1972) terms "deliverables"—wins that are quickly achieved and yield visible benefits wrested from those controlling political and economic institutions.

D. The people's organization is then formalized by

8. Developing a permanent organizational structure. It should require payment of dues and have a structure that involves members in policy, financing, and achievement of group goals and community improvements.

In rural areas, particularly in the Midwest, where conflict with one's neighbors is viewed as disruptive and bad manners, the most effective use of conflict organizations appears to be in mobilizing against the outside. In particular, efforts have been directed toward stopping nuclear waste dumps, power lines, school consolidation, and polluting industries.

An example of such an organization is Save Our Cumberland Mountains (SOCM, pronounced "sock 'em"). SOCM was established in 1972 as a dues-paying, membership-based group that employs professional organizers. The organization is centered in the Cumberland Plateau region of eastern Tennessee and currently has a membership of 1,400 families in chapters that are county- or community-based. Operations are described this way (Davis and Gaventa 1991, 19):

> The SOCM chapter is the primary political unit of the organization. . . . The various chapter groups send representatives to the larger SOCM Board or to various issue-driven steering committees such as the "legislative" committee, which largely lobbies state legislators in Nashville. . . . The SOCM Board and the various committees hold a great deal of power in the SOCM organization and plan many of the group's political activities. In order to qualify for staff assistance, the chapter groups must have been actively working on an issue that they have identified themselves, in response to some problem originating in their local community. In theory, the staff organizer is not permitted to direct political strategy or to overtly influence the decision-making process of the local chapter.

Recent successes of SOCM include preventing the establishment of a National Guard training center and thereby saving hundreds of homes and farms; getting portions of Rock Creek Gorge in Bledsoe County, Tennessee, declared unsuitable for mining; and preventing the building of a proposed medical waste incinerator in Roane County, Tennessee. In Kentucky, Kentuckians for the Commonwealth (KFTC), an organization with similar organizational structure, succeeded after many battles in stopping the strip mining of land that was being done legally without the surface owner having any rights in the matter. This practice is based on a type of land deed called the "broadform deed." KFTC led the campaign in a referendum for a state constitutional amendment to eliminate the broadform deed and won with an 82 percent majority in 1988 (Davis and Gaventa 1991, 20–21).

All of these instances involved a group confronting an outside public or private entity in order to stop a project or policy deemed detrimental to the inhabitants of the local community. Organizers from outside the local community and support from the parent organization are important elements in the local chapter's success against such outside forces.

Factors in Effective Change

We now examine two important factors in all three models of community development—outside linkages and the planning process—to see differences and similarities among the models.

LINKAGES FOR COMMUNITY CHANGE

None of the models of community development presented here denies the need to obtain outside resources in order for community development to take place. In the technical-assistance and the conflict approaches, an outside person or persons are central to the process. In both cases, an objective of the effort is often to obtain resources from the outside. The self-help approach appears to emphasize reliance on local resources. However, as will be seen, the ability to mobilize local resources is often a proof to those who control outside resources that the self-help effort is serious. Thus, there is a complementarity between mobilizing local resources and being able to obtain resources from outside the community. This is particularly true under conditions of quite limited outside resources because those who control such resources are especially keen that their funds be well spent. What better place to spend them than on a project that leaders have shown can generate resources?

Outside resources are becoming increasingly scarce as both federal and state governments deal with mammoth deficits by cutting funding for social programs, including those that benefit rural communities. The need remains for outside resources, including capital and information. Possibilities of grants from both private and public sources have declined, but communities still need to forge links to access those funds that exist. There are a variety of state and regional venture-capital funds being started by both private- and public-sector groups that can be an important input into community development.

However, these linkages to the outside through investment can be risky in terms of the collective agency of a community. There is an old saying, "He who pays the piper calls the tune." This means that the source of funding, whether the federal government or a multinational corporation, can impose a large number of conditions on delivery of capital resources. Sometimes those conditions actually cost the community more than it gains. For example, some studies have shown that the tax abatements, infrastructure construction, and other financial incentives poured into attracting industry in the 1980s did not even pay back the local public investment, much less create wealth in the local community (Rosenfeld et al. 1985).

Another important type of outside linkage is less hierarchical and, therefore, less risky in terms of loss of collective agency. Communities increasingly are forming horizontal linkages with other communities that have faced and dealt with similar problems of their own. This type of "lateral learning" by community groups tends to foster rather than retard collective agency. Community groups analyze their situation and consider alternative ways to confront it. Often a community member knows of another community that has faced a similar problem. Citizen-to-citizen exchanges take place as the group that has tried a solution explains the process as well as the outcome to the other community. For example, when Lexington, Nebraska, became the site of a large IBP meat-packing plant, community leaders met with their counterparts from Denison, Iowa (IBP headquarters), and from Garden City, Kansas (location of IBP's largest processing plant), to learn of the problems and discuss potential solutions.

PLANNING AS PART
OF THE CHANGE PROCESS

Increasingly communities are recognizing that planning is a key part of development. Planning may serve any of the types of community development, but the approach to planning differs significantly according to the model of community development being pursued.

Planning is an integral part of the technical-assistance model of community development. Under this model, the primary concern is with the final product, the plan, which can then be used as a map that displays the explicit tasks that must be performed. Professional planners charged with developing community planning documents may consult with the community when necessary either by talking to designated leaders, conducting surveys, or presenting results to community meetings. Community members are involved in the process not as active participants in the decision-making process but as passive providers of information on which such decisions are made. For example, if the plan calls for a golf course, there is little need under the technical-assistance model to get wide community input into the series of decisions entailed in construction and operation.

The increasing complexity of the decisions communities are forced to make gives a great deal of power to the city engineer or administrator who is closest to the source of technical information. Their clear expertise in understanding the arcane language of zoning and taxing alternatives aids in this process. Just as the city or county attorney in the past was able to dismiss a call for change by saying it was not legal (and thus forcing the person or group who wanted change to hire a lawyer to get an alternative opinion that then had to be taken to a higher authority), now the city engineer can dismiss any change in community resource management by saying the proposed change does not fit the plan. At this point, the conflict model of community development becomes appropriate because a group may mobilize to seek alternative experts to support an alternative action. But most often, the first "technical" judgment goes unquestioned.

A version of the planning process is favored by practitioners of self-help community development. When conducted in a highly participatory way, planning not only allows for development of a collective vision of community but provides mutually agreed-upon signposts to help achieve it. For example, the commitment and incorporation phases of the social-action approach are, respectively, the goal-setting and implementation-design phases of that planning process. But unlike in the technical-assistance model, they are embedded within a participatory approach. Community members who participate in the social-action approach or similar processes have some role in shaping the goals and means of implementing those goals (although as was discussed earlier, community opinion leaders may have already channeled the social-action process toward certain problems and away from others). In the most participatory approaches that use the self-help model, there is broad participation in determining the basic questions to be asked. The downside of the self-help approach to planning is that it is clearly more time-consuming than is the technical-assistance approach.

The conflict model of community development involves a quite different view of planning. By definition, the conflict model is used by those who do not have power, and thus the relationship between goals and means is less obvious than in either of the other two models. The tactical plan for implementation of goals is heavily dependent on the response of the powerful opposition to the earlier actions of the group practicing the conflict approach. Tactics may change from day to day. Alinsky (1971) emphasizes the importance of the element of surprise in responding to those who are in power. Several factors—this need for flexibility, quick response, and surprise, coupled with the fact that initially the community organizer (who is usually from the outside) must be a catalyst for building an organization—are tendencies that militate toward a narrowing of decisionmaking to a small group of people or sometimes to a single leader. However, the long-term survival and effectiveness of the organization in achieving its goals depend on broad and deep support from among the disadvantaged group. That support is best maintained through broad and active participation. So long as the organization commands few resources, participation, if not democratic decisionmaking, is central to maintaining support for the organization. Numbers are a substitute for financial resources. Thus, there is a permanent tension in the organization or movement between democracy and centralization of control. As the organization becomes more successful in gaining resources, participation and democracy may decline unless democratic decisionmaking processes were explicitly attended to in the organizational phase. Thus, in addition to goal setting, the strategy for organizing is a central part of the planning process for a group using the conflict approach.

Models of Economic Development

Economic development is defined differently by different people. Some see economic development as synonymous with an increase in community income. Others view it in terms of an expansion in the number of jobs. Still others would say that economic development involves an increase in population. The relationship between community and economic development depends on the kind of economic development that is pursued. There are a number of models for how economic development takes place. The model that members of a community adhere to influences the kind of action they undertake to bring about change. In short, there is a relationship between the kind of economic development model pursued and the kind of community development model pursued.

THE FIRM-RECRUITMENT MODEL

One model of economic development is that of recruitment of firms. The *firm-recruitment model* assumes that there is considerable geographic mobility of private-sector firms as they seek more favorable locations. Early tactics aimed at firm recruitment during the growth years of the 1950s through the 1970s were quite straightforward and involved such things as the construction of industrial sites and proactive recruiting of industry by more sophisticated cities. It was assumed that any particular locality had a series of advantages to offer and that firms would somehow find them, although by the 1970s it became clear that despite the favorable climate for domestic industrial growth, a community had to develop a sophisticated approach to firm recruitment if it were to be successful. Planners and social scientists carried out studies to see where firms located and what they looked for when they chose new sites.

By the economic downturn of the 1980s, states and localities began to realize that only a few firms moved each year, and those that did usually went overseas for cheaper labor and more lax pollution controls. Competition for the few firms serious about relocating in the United States became intense. States began instituting a wide variety of inducements for firms, including grants, loans, loan guarantees, tax incentives, targeted industrial revenue bond financing, tax-increment financing, and state enterprise zones. When one state or locality offered an incentive, others felt obliged to do so. Less publicized but also prevalent during the 1980s were changes on the state and federal levels that weakened organized labor. Communities used low wages as a bargaining chip in attracting firms. In fact, in a number of high-growth areas where public infrastructural investments and favorable tax structures attracted industries, the jobs that were generated paid so poorly and the working conditions were so bad that immigrant workers had to be recruited to fill them. Packing plants in Kansas and Nebraska are examples of this kind of industrial recruitment. Political scientist Peter Eisenger (1988) refers to these attempts to reduce the cost of local land, labor, capital, infrastructure, and taxes as "supply-side development."

The firm-recruitment model is most compatible with the technical-assistance approach to community development. Local governments would hire economic development professionals to obtain grants for infrastructural development, to develop local tax-incentive packages, and to recruit new firms. These activities required little grassroots participation. In fact, they were antithetical to broad-based community involvement. Obtaining grants requires technical knowledge of bureaucracies and procedures. Negotiations with firms that might move to the community are said by some to be best carried out in secret. Firms insist on such secrecy so that communities competing for their branch plants can be played off against each other. Also, a company may not want its present work force to know about the potential move. Firms considering a move prefer to deal with only one person who can speak for the entire community. Such approaches discourage broad community participation.

THE SELF-DEVELOPMENT MODEL

In contrast to recruitment as a model of economic development is what Eisenger refers to as demand-oriented approaches to economic development. These include the search for new markets and new products to fit those markets. Instead of simply offering incentives to any firm willing to move, public-private partnerships are formed that help determine what firms will be underwritten by the public as those with the most potential for success—and positive community impact.

One type of demand-side development that has been effective in rural communities is the *self-development model*. This involves public-sector groups, usually a city or county government, working with private groups of individuals within a community to establish a locally controlled enterprise. A national inventory of self-development projects (Green et al. 1990) identified a number of different types of self-development efforts and mechanisms through which they worked. Key to each of them was local investment of time and capital, coupled with a sound management structure and good links to outside resources of both capital and information. Although the short-term impact on number of jobs created may not be as great as when a branch plant of a major multinational corporation relocates to the area, communities involved in self-development have found that the risk is lower and the gains more consistent than found even in successful recruitment of industry. Further, self-development communities were more successful in attracting branch plants than were areas not using this approach. The choice of an emphasis on self-development did not preclude firm recruitment, although it did make the communities less likely to offer extreme tax benefits or public investments in infrastructure.

Self-development involves sustained local economic development activities. It encourages broad-based participation—involving newcomers, women, and minorities. It depends on and encourages the development of community organizations. Self-development contributes to community development. By encouraging participation, it gives community members a feeling of control over the economic life of their communities. In short, it promotes collective agency. It is most consistent with the self-help form of community development, although it also can be compatible with the conflict approach.

Do Communities Act?

Sociologists have long asked "Do communities act?" (Tilly 1973). Did the people of New Richland act, or did Sue and Bart James simply push forward a pet project? Will the golf course actually improve the quality of life in New Richland? Can it generate economic activity helpful to maintaining the community? The answers to these and other questions depend on how community development is defined—geographically as well as in terms of what measures of development are valued. Both are changing.

The territorial community no longer serves as the place where people live, work, and consume goods and services. Improvements in automobiles, the development of the interstate highway system, and the extent to which capital replaced labor in agriculture, mining, forestry, and manufacturing all changed where jobs were located. People were freed from the need to live, work, and shop in the same place.

Various indicators of community development are no longer interchangeable. The indicator of success one chooses—population retention (residence), employment creation (work), or vitality of retail trade and service activities (consumption)—influences the strategy chosen for economic development. Efforts to influence one variable, such as employment, may not result in concomitant improvement in other variables, such as population, retail trade, or even something as broad as quality of life (Flora and Flora 1991).

Sociological research has begun to identify which communities act under what circumstances. Davis (1991) and Logan and Molotch (1987) argue that more and more action for social change is increasingly occurring not where people work but where they live. Logan and Molotch suggest that within a particular geographic community, coalitions develop around enhancing exchange value (pro-growth coalitions), and in response others develop around enhancing use value (neighborhood coalitions); the suggestion is that subcommunities rather than whole communities may act.

Chapter Summary

Community development describes what people do to improve the overall quality of life in the community. Although community development often involves economic development, it implies far more. Central to the concept of community development is the concept of collective agency. Collective agency is the ability of a group of people to solve common problems together.

There are three models of community development. The self-help model focuses on the process by which people work together to arrive at group decisions and take action. It assumes that communities are homogenous and consensus-based. The technical-assistance model focuses on the task to be accomplished and uses outside expertise to help community leaders accomplish that task. This model assumes that answers can be arrived at objectively by using the scientific method. The conflict model focuses on the redistribution of power among community members. It assumes that power is never given but must be taken. Each model gives rise to a different community development strategy.

Two factors are important to all three models of community development. Communities need linkages to outside sources of information and capital. These linkages, which can be with external agencies or with other similar communities, enable lateral learning to occur. The second factor is planning. Planning is a key part of development, but the approach will differ depending on the model of community development being followed.

Economic development is one part of community development. Consequently, the type of economic development strategy pursued should match the community development model used. Two of the more common approaches are the firm-recruitment model and the self-development model.

Key Terms

Collective agency is the ability of a group of people to solve common problems together.

Community development describes what people do to improve the overall quality of the community.

Conflict model of community development focuses on the redistribution of power among community members.

Firm-recruitment model of economic development assumes that there is considerable geographic mobility of private-sector firms. In this model, community leaders seek to engage community resources to attract those industries.

Self-development model of economic development uses public-sector groups working with private-sector groups to establish locally owned enterprises.

Self-help model of community development focuses on the process by which people work together to arrive at group decisions and take action.

Technical-assistance model of community development focuses on the task to be accomplished and uses outside expertise to help community leaders accomplish that task.

References

Alinsky, Saul D. 1971. Rules for Radicals: A Programmatic Primer for Realistic Radicals. New York: Random House.

————. 1969. Reveille for Radicals. New York: Vintage Books. Originally published by Random House in 1946.

Arnstein, Sherry. 1972. "Maximum Feasible Manipulation." Public Administration Review 32 (Sept.): 377–492.

Christenson, James A. 1989. "Themes of Community Development." In James A. Christenson and Jerry W. Robinson, Jr. (eds.), Community Development in Perspective. Ames: Iowa State University Press.

Davis, Donald. 1991. Contested Ground: Collective Action and the Urban Neighborhood. Ithaca, NY: Cornell University Press.

Davis, Donald, and John Gaventa. No date. "Altered States: Grassroots Movements and the Formation of Rural Policy." Working manuscript, to be published in The State, Rural Policy, and Rural Disadvantage in the Late Twentieth Century, ed. Rural Sociological Society Task Force on Rural Poverty, The State and Rural Policy Working Group, Fred Buttel, Cornell University, Chair.

Eisenger, Peter K. 1988. The Rise of the Entrepreneurial State: State and Local Economic Development Policy in the United States. Madison: University of Wisconsin Press.

Flora, Jan L., and Cornelia Flora. 1991. "Local Economic Development Projects: Key Factors." Pp. 141–156 in Norman Walzer (ed.), Rural Community Development in the Midwest. New York: Praeger.

Green, Gary P., Jan L. Flora, Cornelia Flora, and Frederick E. Schmidt. 1990. "Local Self-Development Strategies: National Survey Results." Journal of the Community Development Society 21 (2): 55–73.

Lapping, Mark B., Thomas L. Daniels, and John W. Keller. 1989. *Rural Planning and Development in the United States.* New York: Guilford.

Littrell, Donald W., and Darryl Hobbs. 1989. "The Self-Help Approach." In James A. Christenson and Jerry W. Robinson, Jr. (eds.), *Community Development in Perspective.* Ames: Iowa State University Press.

Logan, John R., and H. L. Molotch. 1987. *Urban Fortunes: The Political Economy of Place.* Berkeley: University of California Press.

Rosenfeld, Stuart A., Edward M. Bergmar, and Sara Rubin. 1985. *After the Factories.* Research Triangle Park, NC: Southern Growth Policies Board.

Russell, Daniel M. 1990. *Political Organizing in Grassroots Politics.* Lantham, MD: University Press of America.

"The Social Action Process: Selling Ideas and Programs." April 1987. Manhattan: Kansas State University Cooperative Extension Service.

Tilley, C. 1973. "Do Communities Act?" *Sociological Inquiry* 43(3–4): 209–240.

About the Book and Authors

Rural America is a complex mixture of peoples and cultures struggling for survival. It ranges in character from workers in manufacturing plants in Georgia to Laotian immigrants who have relocated in Kansas; from farmers committed to sustainable agriculture to entrepreneurs planning a world-class ski resort in California's Sierra Nevada; from laid-off miners in West Virginia to Native Americans in the Southwest searching for an economy consistent with their cultural values. These are all parts of rural America, seldom heard of in the mass media but deeply reflective of the legacies left by those who settled the land.

This book bridges the gap between social theory and community change by focusing on the problems that face rural America and offering students a framework for applying sociological concepts. The authors explore such issues as the diversity among rural communities; the interactions between communities and the economy; the governmental, economic, and social resources available in rural communities; and how communities organize for action. Although the authors explore community change within a rural context, their findings are applicable to urban neighborhoods as well. The notion of empowerment—that the understanding and analysis provided through the social sciences can result in community action—is unique to this book.

This book can be used as a text for introductory courses in rural sociology, social problems, and community studies or by community groups to explore their own responses to a variety of problems. The book is also the companion text to a PBS college-level telecourse and television series premiering in Spring 1993. The telecourse consists of thirteen one-hour videotapes, portraying the experiences of fifteen rural communities from across the United States. The complete telecourse consists of the videotapes, this text, a study guide, and a faculty manual.

For information about purchasing videocassettes, taping off-air, or licensing the telecourse, call 1-800-LEARNER.

Cornelia Butler Flora is professor and head of the Department of Sociology at the Virginia Polytechnic Institute and State University, where **Jan L. Flora** is professor of agricultural economics and sociology. **Jacqueline D. Spears** is codirector of the Rural Clearinghouse for Lifelong Education and Development at Kansas State University. **Louis E. Swanson** is professor of sociology at the University of Kentucky. **Mark B. Lapping** is dean of the Faculty of Planning at Rutgers University. **Mark L. Weinberg** is professor of political science and director of the Institute for Local Government Administration and Rural Development at Ohio University.

Index

325